Dedication

*This book is affectionately dedicated to my wife, René,
whose longtime support of my outdoor interests
has led to books such as this one.*

101
HIKES
in
Southern
California

Exploring Mountains, Seashore and Desert

Jerry Schad

WILDERNESS PRESS
BERKELEY

FIRST EDITION July 1996

Copyright © 1996 by Jerry Schad

Cover design by Larry Van Dyke
Photos and maps by the author
Cover photos by the author

Library of Congress Card Catalog Number 96-25593
International Standard Book Number 0-89997-193-8

Manufactured in the United States of America

Published by   Wilderness Press
               2440 Bancroft Way
               Berkeley, CA 94704
               (800) 443-7227
               FAX (510) 548-1355

        Write, call or fax us for a free catalog

Cover photos: **Moonrise over Kitchen Creek Falls, Laguna Mountains** *(background)*
                Torrey Pines State Reserve *(top inset)*
                Lower Noble Canyon, Laguna Mountains *(bottom inset)*
Frontispiece: **Vincent Gulch, San Gabriel Mountains**

Library of Congress Cataloging-in-Publication Data

Schad, Jerry.
    101 hikes in Southern California : exploring mountains, seashore, and desert / Jerry
Schad. — 1st ed.
        p.   cm.
    Includes bibliographical references and index.
    ISBN 0-89997-193-8
    1. Hiking—California, Southern—Guidebooks. 2. Trails—California, Southern—Guidebooks.
3. California, Southern—Guidebooks. I. Title.
GV199.42.C22S687   1996
917.94'9—dc20   96-25593
                                                        CIP

Preface

Just beyond the limits of Southern California's ever-spreading urban sprawl lies a world apart. In snippets of open space here, and in sprawling wilderness areas there, California's primeval landscape survives more or less untarnished. In hundreds of hidden places just over the urban horizon (and sometimes within the city itself), you can still find Nature's radiant beauty unfettered—or at least not too seriously compromised—by human intervention.

My purpose in writing this book is to entice you to explore some of these hidden places. In the pages ahead you will find updated versions of trips previously published in my *Afoot and Afield* series guidebooks on Los Angeles, Orange, and San Diego counties, plus additional trips from western San Bernardino and Riverside counties—a total of 101 hikes described in meticulous detail. The 101 Hikes Key Map on page *x* reveals how the majority of hikes chosen for this book cluster around the major urban areas of Los Angeles, Orange County, and San Diego. As a result, no matter where you live within Southern California, it is likely that more than 50 of these hikes are accessible to you in less than a two-hour drive.

Users of the *Afoot and Afield* books will already be familiar with the format and layout of this book. Each hike description includes a capsulized summary with icons allowing you to determine at a glance the nature and difficulty of the trip. Each trip is plotted on an easy-to-read sketch map, and most trips include one or more photos.

All hikes described in this book were hiked at least once by me at one time or another, and every effort has been made to ensure that the information contained herein is up-to-date. Roads, trailheads, and trails can and do change every year, however. You can keep me apprised of recent developments and/or changes by writing me in care of Wilderness Press. Your comments will be appreciated.

Jerry Schad
El Cajon, California
June 1996

Books by Jerry Schad

50 Southern California Bicycle Trips
Backcountry Roads and Trails, San Diego County
Back Roads and Hiking Trails, The Santa Cruz Mountains
Adventure Running
* Afoot and Afield in San Diego County
Cycling San Diego
California Deserts
* Afoot and Afield in Orange County
Cycling Orange County
* Afoot and Afield in Los Angeles County
Physical Science: A Unified Approach
* 101 Hikes in Southern California

* *Published by Wilderness Press*

Contents

101 Hikes—Key Map Showing Locations of Trips

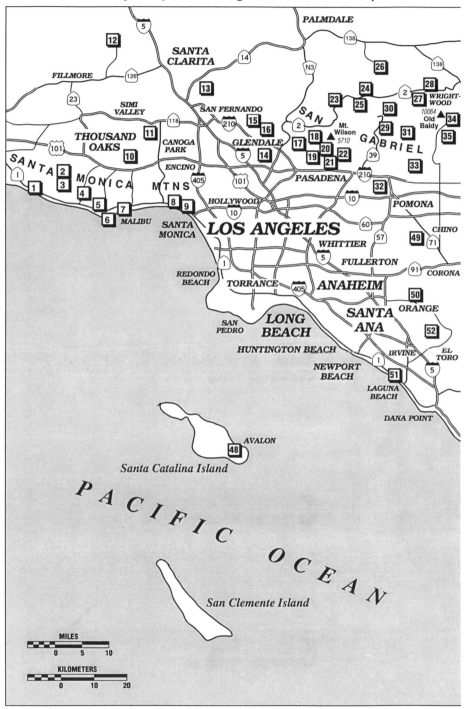

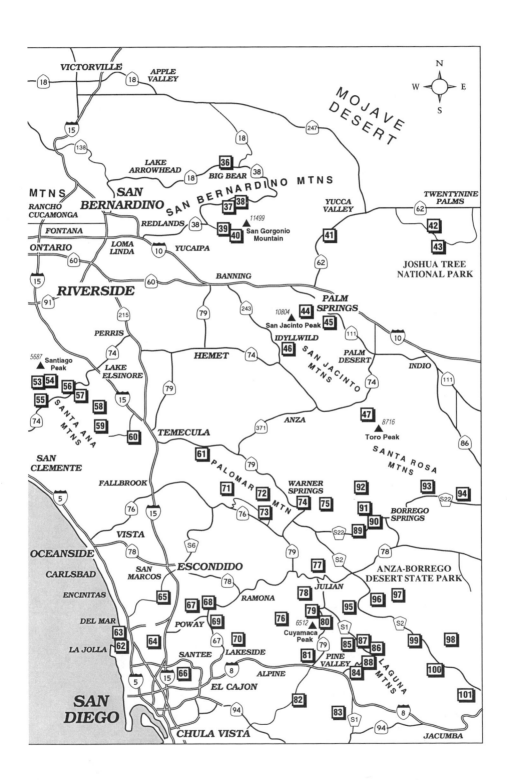

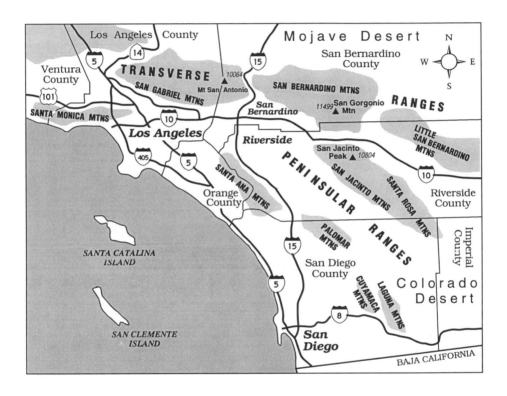

Southern California's Wilderness Rim

Southern California sits astride one of the earth's most significant structural features—the San Andreas Fault. For more than 10 million years, earth movements along the San Andreas and neighboring faults have shaped the dramatic topography evident throughout the region today. The very complexity of the shape of the land has in turn spawned a variety of localized climates. In turn, the varied climates, along with the diverse topography and geology, have resulted in a remarkably plentiful and diverse array of plant and animal life.

Living on the "active" edge of a continent, as we Southern Californians do, has advantages and disadvantages that cannot be untangled. Like the proverbial silver lining in a dark cloud, the rumpled beauty of our youthful, ever-changing coastline, mountains, and desert helps offset the ever-present threat of earthquakes, fires, and floods. It is precisely because Southern California is physically rugged that not all of it has succumbed to the bulldozer or the plow. When you've had the pleasure of hiking beside a crystal-clear mountain stream minutes from downtown L.A., or cooling off in the spray of a cottonwood-fringed waterfall just beyond suburban San Diego, you'll realize that not many regions in the world offer so great a variety of natural pleasures to a population of many millions.

Let us, in the next couple of pages, briefly explore the principal wild and semi-wild natural areas bordering Southern California's coastal plain. When linked together, these natural areas form a broad, curving crescent around Southern California's urban population—now some 20 million strong. About 90 percent of the hikes found in this book fall into this unpopulated or sparsely populated crescent.

The Santa Monica Mountains

We start with the Santa Monica Mountains, which rise abruptly from the Pacific shoreline west of (or "up the coast" from) Los Angeles. They, along with the San Gabriel and San Bernardino Mountains, are part of the Transverse Ranges, so named because they trend east-west and stand crosswise to the usual northwest-southeast grain of nearly every other major mountain range in California. This anomaly, it is thought, is largely due to compression along the San Andreas Fault. There is a kink in the San Andreas Fault north of Los Angeles where the fault, running southeast from the San Francisco Bay Area, jogs east for a while before resuming its course toward the southeast. Compression against this kink has caused the land south of it to crumple and wrinkle upward. The devastating January 1994 Northridge earthquake was just one small episode in the slow but fitful uplift of the Transverse Ranges.

Compared to other Southern California ranges, the Santa Monicas are modest in size—barely more than 3000 feet high—but their rise from the sea is dramatic. They are a shaggy looking range, clothed in tough, drought-resistant vegetation that falls into two principal categories: coastal sage scrub and chaparral. The *coastal sage scrub* plant "community" lies mostly below 2000 feet elevation, on primarily south-facing slopes in the Santa Monica Mountains and elsewhere in the coastal ranges of Southern California. Characterized by various aromatic sages (California sagebrush, black sage, white sage) along with buckwheat, laurel sumac, and lemonade berry shrubs and prickly pear cactus, sage scrub is fast disappearing in the Santa Monicas and elsewhere as urbanization encroaches on it. Much of the sage-scrub vegetation is dormant and dead-looking during the warmer half of the year, but green and aromatic during the cool, wet half.

The *chaparral* plant community is commonly found between 1000 and 5000 feet elevation—almost anywhere there's a slope that hasn't burned recently. Chaparral needs more moisture than sage scrub, so in the Santa Monicas it's often found on the shadier, north-facing slopes and other spots protected from the full glare of the sun. The dominant chaparral plants include chamise, scrub oak, manzanita, toyon, mountain mahogany, and various forms of ceanothus ("wild lilac"). Yuccas, known for their spectacular candle-shaped blooms, often frequent the chaparral zones. The chaparral plants are tough and intricately branched, evergreen shrubs with deep root systems that help the plants survive during the long, hot summers. Chaparral is sometimes called "elfin forest"—a good description of a mature stand. Without benefit of a trail, travel through mature chaparral, which is often 15 feet high and incredibly dense from the ground up, is almost impossible.

A touch of the *southern oak woodland* and *riparian woodland* communities is present in the Santa Monicas and sparsely distributed nearly everywhere else in coastal Southern California. The Santa Monica Mountains include the southernmost stands of the valley oak, a massive, spreading tree that is as much a symbol of the Golden State as are the redwoods farther north. The southern oak woodland is very "parklike" in appearance, especially in the spring when attended by new growths of grass and wildflowers. Riparian (streamside) vegetation includes trees such as willows, sycamores, and alders that thrive wherever water flows year round—typically along the bottoms of the larger canyons. Strolling through the riot of growth in riparian zones is the nearest thing to a jungle experience you can have in arid Southern California. Both types of habitat have declined all over California as a result of urbanization and agricultural development, and the attendant exploitation of water resources.

Wildfire plays a dominant role in the ecology of the Santa Monica Mountains, and indeed almost everywhere else in coastal Southern California. Sage scrub and chaparral vegetation readily renews itself after fire. Before modern times wildfires would incinerate most hillsides every 5 to 15 years, and thick stands of chaparral seldom developed. Over the past century, however, the active prevention and suppression of fires has led to longer growth cycles

Oak woodland in Serrano Canyon, Santa Monica Mountains

and abnormally large accumulations of dead fuelwood. Once started, today's wildfires in chaparral zones are often difficult or impossible to control.

From Malibu east into L.A.'s west side, the Santa Monicas are steadily filling up with custom houses and subdivisions, all of which are in jeopardy from firestorms during the dry summer and fall seasons. The latest holocaust, the October 1993 Malibu conflagration, is but one of a series of past and future fires that will forever torment those who seek to establish permanent residence here.

Today the Santa Monicas are a patchwork quilt of private lands (many already built upon or slated for future development) and public lands, protected from urban development by inclusion within Santa Monica Mountains National Recreation Area, a unit of the National Park system.

The San Gabriel Mountains

Turning our attention farther north and east, we find the San Gabriel Mountains, another segment of the east-west trending Transverse Ranges. Behind the south ramparts of the San Gabriels, whose chaparraled slopes rise sheer from the Los Angeles Basin and the San Gabriel Valley, stands a series of high peaks, the tallest of which—Old Baldy, or Mount San Antonio— exceeds 10,000 feet in elevation. Yawning gorges slash into the range, in one place offering more than a mile of vertical relief between canyon bottom and adjacent ridge.

Geologists figure that the San Gabriels are being squeezed horizontally about a tenth of an inch each year, and being thrust upward much more rapidly than that. Caught in this tectonic frenzy, the San Gabriel Mountains are surging upward as fast as any mountain range on the planet. They are also disintegrating at a spectacular rate. Although the San Gabriels consist mainly of durable granitic rocks, much like those in the sturdy Sierra Nevada, the San Gabriel rocks have been through a tectonic meat grinder. The tops of the San Gabriels are fairly rounded, but the slopes are often appallingly steep and unstable. An

Sugar pines (yellow pine belt, San Gabriel Mountains)

average of 7 tons of material disappears from each acre of the front face each year, most of it coming to rest behind debris barriers and dams in the L.A. Basin below.

The San Gabriel Mountains themselves are relatively young as upthrust units—only a few million years old. This is not true of the ages of most of the rocks that compose them. Some rocks exposed here are representative of the oldest found on the Pacific coast—over 600 million years of age.

Botanically, parts of the San Gabriel Mountains are extremely attractive, especially in zones above 4000 feet that receive enough precipitation. There the *coniferous forest* thrives. This has two phases in Southern California. The "yellow pine" phase includes conifers such as bigcone Douglas-fir, ponderosa pine, Jeffrey pine, sugar pine, incense-cedar, and white fir, and forms tall, open forest. These species are often intermixed with live oaks, California bay (bay laurel), and scattered chaparral shrubs such as manzanita and mountain mahogany. Higher than about 8000 feet, in the "lodgepole pine" phase, lodgepole pine, white fir, and limber pine are the prevailing trees. These trees, somewhat shorter and more weather-beaten than those below, exist in small, sometimes dense stands, interspersed with such shrubs as chinquapin, snowbrush, and manzanita.

Excluding relatively small parcels of private land, the bulk of the higher San Gabriel Mountains lies within Angeles National Forest. Hundreds of square miles of wilderness or near wilderness in the San Gabriels are available within easy reach of millions of Los Angeles residents.

The San Bernardino Mountains

Farther east, across the low gap of Cajon Pass, the Transverse Ranges soar again as the San Bernardino Mountains. With Lake Arrowhead, Big Bear Lake, and winter ski areas, the mid elevations of the San Bernardinos (5000-8000 feet elevation) draw millions of day trippers and vaca-

tioners yearly. Hikers and backpackers can explore the 10,000-foot-plus peaks of the San Gorgonio Wilderness, including 11,500-foot San Gorgonio Mountain itself—Southern California's high point. There it is possible to ascend through the yellow-pine and lodgepole belts to treeline and above.

As in the San Gabriel Mountains, islands of private land in the San Bernardinos are surrounded by large sections of national forest. San Bernardino National Forest encompasses much of the San Bernardino Mountains, as well as the San Jacinto and Santa Rosa mountains to the south.

The Mojave Desert

North and east of the San Gabriel and San Bernardino mountains lies the vast, arid sweep of the Mojave Desert, a zone only partly included in this book. The Mojave, sometimes known as the "high" desert for its generally high average elevation, becomes far less populated and more diverse in its natural features as we move toward east-

Joshua tree woodland, Mojave Desert

ern California. A few of the trips in this book explore the transitional region between high mountain and high desert. There, at elevations of 3000–5000 feet, thrives the *pinyon-juniper woodland*, largely characterized by the rather stunted looking one-leaved pinyon pine and the California juniper. Large sections of the Mojave, again in the elevation range of about 3000-5000 feet, are dominated by *Joshua tree woodland*. Here the indicator plant is an outsized member of the yucca family—the Joshua tree. Joshua Tree National Park preserves some, but hardly all, of the finest stands of these odd, tree-sized plants.

The San Jacinto Mountains

Moving south from the San Bernardino Mountains and Joshua Tree National Park, we find the northwest-southeast trending San Jacinto Mountains and their southerly extension, the Santa Rosa Mountains. These lofty ranges comprise the northern ramparts of what geologists call the Peninsular Ranges—so named because they extend, more or less continuously, south across the Mexican border and comprise the spine of the long, thin peninsula of Baja California.

As the highest peak in the entire Peninsular Ranges province, 10,800-foot San Jacinto Peak would outrank all other Southern California peaks were it not for the slightly higher San Gorgonio massif looming just 20 miles north. For sheer dramatic impact, however, San Jacinto wins hands down. Viewed from Interstate 10 outside Palm Springs, the north and east escarpments of San Jacinto appear to rise nearly straight up from the desert floor—10,000 feet in 10 miles or less. Every plant community we have mentioned so far except Joshua tree woodland thrives at one level or another on the mountain.

San Jacinto's pine clad western slopes shelter several resort communities (such as Idyllwild); otherwise nearly all of the mountain's upper elevations lie within national-forest wilderness or state wilderness areas.

The Colorado Desert

East of the northernmost Peninsular Ranges lie Palm Springs, the Coachella Valley, and the Salton Trough (Salton Sea). They are within the domain known as the Colorado Desert—California's "low" desert—so called because it stretches west from the lower Colorado River which divides California from Arizona. A 1000-square-mile chunk of the Colorado Desert lies within Anza-Borrego Desert State Park, by far the largest state park in California. Especially close and convenient for San Diegans, Anza-Borrego's vast acreage ranges from intricately dissected, desiccated terrain known as "badlands" to the pinyon-juniper and yellow-pine forests of the Peninsular Ranges.

The Laguna, Cuyamaca, Palomar, and Santa Ana Mountains

East and north of San Diego the Peninsular Ranges consist of a number of parallel ranges—primarily the Laguna, Cuyamaca, and Palomar ranges—each attaining heights of just over 6000 feet. Chaparral blankets the slopes of these mountains, while the higher elevations are dominated by the typical yellow-pine assemblage of oak, pine, cedar, and fir. Farther north and east, bordering the rapidly expanding urban zones of southwestern Riverside and southern Orange County, lie the Santa Ana Mountains. They are the northernmost coastal expressions of the Peninsular Ranges.

Suburban sprawl has crept into the foothills of these far-southern ranges, and in some cases threatens to degrade the higher elevations as well. Fortunately, large parts of this mountainous region lie within the jurisdiction of Cleveland National Forest and various state parks.

The crescent-shaped arc of mountain ranges and wild areas we have just described is an invaluable resource for hikers, backpackers, bird- and wildlife-watchers, and

anyone else interested in the outdoors. By
perusing the 101 hike descriptions in this
book, and trying out some of the trips for
yourself, you will easily be convinced of that.

Jeffrey-pine forest, Laguna Mountains

Health, Safety and Courtesy

Good preparation is always important for any kind of recreational pursuit. Hiking the Southern California backcountry is no exception. Although most of the Southland's natural environments are seldom hostile or dangerous to life and limb, there are some pitfalls to be aware of.

Preparation and Equipment

An obvious safety requirement is being in good health. Some degree of physical conditioning is always desirable, even for the trips in this book designated as easy or moderate (rated ★ and ★★ in difficulty). The more challenging trips (rated ★★★, ★★★★ or ★★★★★) require increasing amounts of stamina and technical expertise. Running, bicycling, swimming, aerobic dancing, or any similar exercise that develops both the leg muscles and the aerobic capacity of the whole body are recommended as preparatory exercise.

For the longest hikes in this book, there is no really adequate way to prepare other than hiking itself. Start with easy- or moderate-length trips, then work gradually toward extending both distance and time.

Several of the hiking trips in this book reach elevations of 7000 feet or more—altitudes at which sea-level folks may notice a big difference in their rate of breathing and their energy. A few hours or a day spent at

altitude before exercising will help almost anyone acclimate, but that's often impractical for short day trips. Still, you might consider spending a night or two at a campground with some altitude before tackling the likes of 11,500-foot San Gorgonio Mountain. Altitude sickness strikes some victims at elevations as low as 8000 feet. If you become dizzy or nauseous, or suffer from congested lungs or a severe headache, the antidote may be as simple as descending one or two thousand feet.

Your choice of equipment and supplies on the longer hikes in this book can be critically important. The essentials you should carry with you at all times in the backcountry are the things that would allow you to survive, in a reasonably comfortable manner, one or two unscheduled nights out. It's important to note that no one ever plans these nights! No one plans to get lost, injured, stuck, or pinned down by the weather. Always do a "what if" analysis for a worst-case scenario, and plan

Winter at 6000 feet in Laguna Meadow

accordingly. These essential items are your
safety net; keep them with you on day
hikes, and take them with you in a small day
pack if you leave your backpack and camping equipment behind at a campsite.

Chief among the essential items is *warm
clothing*. Inland Southern California is characterized by wide swings in day and night
temperatures. In mountain valleys susceptible to cold-air drainage, for example,
a midday temperature in the 70s or 80s is
often followed by a subfreezing night.
Carry light, inner layers of clothing consisting
of polypropylene or wool (best for cool or
cold weather), or cotton (adequate for
warm or hot weather, but very poor for cold
and damp weather). Include a thicker insu-
lating layer of "pile" (polyester fiberpile),
wool, or down to put on whenever needed,
especially when you are not moving around
and generating heat. Add to this a cap,
gloves, and a waterproof or water-resistant
shell (a large trash bag will do in a pinch)—
and you'll be quite prepared for all but
the most severe weather.

In hot, sunny weather, sun-shielding
clothing may be another "essential." This
would normally include a sun hat and a
light-colored, long-sleeve top.

Water and *food* are next in importance.
Most streams and even some springs in the
mountains have been shown to contain
unacceptably high levels of bacteria or
other contaminants. Even though most of
the remote watersheds are probably pristine, it's wise to treat by filtering or chemical methods any water obtained outside of
developed camp or picnic sites. Unless the
day is very warm or your trip is a long one,
it's usually easiest to carry (preferably in sturdy plastic bottles) all the water you'll need.
Don't underestimate your water needs:
during a full day's hike in 80° temperatures
you may require as much as a gallon of
water. Know, too, that many springs and
watercourses—even some shown as being
"permanent" on topographic maps—may
run dry at some point during the summer. Food is necessary to stave off the feeling of hunger and keep energy stores up, but

it is not nearly as critical as water is in
emergency situations in which water is
needed to prevent dehydration.

Down the list further, but still "essential,"
are a *map* and *compass*, *flashlight*, *fire-start-
ing devices* (examples: waterproof matches
or lighter, and candle), and *first-aid* kit.

Items not always essential, but potentially
very useful and convenient, are sunglasses, pocket knife, whistle (or other signaling
device), sunscreen, and toilet paper. (Note:
sunglasses are an essential item for travel
over snow.)

The essential items mentioned above
should be carried by every member of a hiking party, because individuals or splinter
groups may end up separating from the
party for one reason or another. If you
plan to hike solo in the backcountry, being
well-equipped is very important. If you
hike alone, be sure to check in with a park
ranger or leave your itinerary with a responsible person. In that way, if you do get
stuck, help will probably come to the right
place—eventually.

Special Hazards

Other than getting lost or pinned down
by a rare sudden storm, the most common hazards found in the Southland are
steep, unstable terrain; icy terrain; spiny
plants; rattlesnakes; ticks; and poison oak.

Exploring some trails—especially those
of the San Gabriel Mountains—may involve
traveling over structurally weak rock on
steep slopes. The erosive effects of flowing
water, of wedging by roots and by ice,
and of brush fires tend to pulverize such rock

even further. Slips on such terrain usually lead to sliding down a hillside some distance. If you explore cross-country, always be on the lookout for dangerous run-outs, such as cliffs, below you. The sidewalls of many canyons in the San Gabriels may look like nice places to practice rock-climbing moves, but this misconception has contributed to many deaths over the years.

Statistically, mishaps associated with snow and ice have caused the greatest number of fatalities in the San Gabriel and San Bernardino mountain ranges. This is not because our local mountains are inherently more dangerous than the Sierra Nevada, the Cascades, or other ranges. Rather, it is because inexperienced lowlanders, never picturing their backyard mountains as true wilderness areas, are attracted here by the novelty of snow and the easy access by way of snow-plowed highways. Icy chutes and slopes capable of avalanching can easily trap such visitors unaware. Winter travel in the more gentle areas of the high country can be accomplished on snowshoes or skis; but the steeper slopes require technical skills and equipment such as ice ax and crampons, just as in other snow-covered mountain ranges.

Most desert hikers will sooner or later suffer punctures by thorns or spines. This is most likely to happen during close encounters with the cholla ("jumping") cactus, whose spine clusters readily break off and attach firmly to your skin, clothes or boots. A comb can be used to gently pull away the spine clusters, and tweezers or lightweight pliers can be used to remove any individual embedded spines. Another problematic spiny plant is the agave, or century plant. It consists of a rosette of fleshy leaves, each tipped with a rigid thorn containing a mild toxin. A headlong fall into either an agave or one of the more vicious kinds of cacti could easily make you swear off desert travel permanently. It's best to give these devilish plants as wide a berth as possible.

Rattlesnakes are common everywhere in Southern California below an elevation of

Diamondback rattlesnake

about 7000 feet. Seldom seen in either cold or very hot weather, they favor temperatures in the 75-90° range—spring and fall in the desert and coastal areas, and summer in the mountains. Most rattlesnakes are as interested in avoiding contact with you as you are with them. Watch carefully where you put your feet, and especially your hands, during the warmer months. In brushy or rocky areas where sight distance is short, try to make your presence known from afar. Tread with heavy footfalls, or use a stick to bang against rocks or bushes. Rattlesnakes will pick up the vibrations through their skin and will usually buzz (unmistakably) before you get too close for comfort. Most bad encounters between rattlesnakes and hikers occur in April and May, when snakes are irritable and hungry after a long hibernation period.

Ticks can sometimes be the scourge of overgrown trails in the coastal foothills and lower mountain slopes, particularly during the first warm spells of the year, when they climb to the tips of shrub branches and lie in wait for warm-blooded hosts. If you can't avoid brushing against vegetation along the trail, be sure to check yourself for ticks frequently. Upon finding a host, a tick will usually crawl upward in search of a protected spot, where it will try to attach itself. If you can be aware of the slightest irritation on your body, you'll usually intercept ticks long before they attempt to bite. Ticks would be of relatively minor concern here, except that tick-borne Lyme disease, which can have serious health effects, has been reported within Southern California.

Poison oak grows profusely along many of the coastal and mountain canyons below 5000 feet elevation. It is often found on the banks of streamcourses in the form of a bush or vine, where it prefers semi-shady habitats. Quite often, it's seen beside or encroaching on well-used trails. Learn to recognize its distinctive three-leafed structure, and avoid touching it with skin or cloth-

Poison-oak leaves

ing. Since poison oak loses its leaves during the winter months (and sometimes during summer and fall drought), but still retains some of the toxic oil in its stems, it can be extra hazardous at that time because it is harder to identify and avoid. Mid-weight pants, like blue jeans, and a long-sleeve shirt will serve as a fair barrier against the toxic oil of the poison oak plant. Do, of course, remove these clothes as soon as the hike is over, and make sure they are washed carefully afterward.

Here are a couple more safety tips:

Deer-hunting season in Southern California usually runs through the middle part of the autumn. Although conflicts between hunters and hikers are rare, you may want to confine your autumn explorations to state and county parks, and wilderness areas where hunting is not permitted.

There is always some risk in leaving a vehicle unattended at a trailhead. It may be worthwhile to disable your car's ignition or attach an anti-theft device to your steering wheel. Never leave valuable property in an automobile, so as to be an invitation for a break-in. Report all theft and vandalism of personal or public property to the county sheriff or the appropriate park or forest agency.

Camping and Permits

If you are planning an overnight trip of some type into the Southern California backcountry, be aware that camping in roadside campgrounds is not always a restful experience. Off-season camping (late fall through early spring) offers relief from crowds, but not from chilly night-time weather. Campgrounds in Angeles, San Bernardino, and Cleveland national forests are less well supervised than those in most state and county parks, and therefore sometimes attract a noisy crowd. In my experience, facilities with a "campground host" promise a better clientele, and a better night's sleep.

The nice advantage of a developed campground is that you can always have a campfire there—unless the facility itself is closed. On trails where backpacking is allowed, fire regulations vary. Most jurisdictions prohibit campfires all or part of the year. Others permit fires, as long as you have the necessary free permit.

Some of the national forest areas allow "remote," primitive-style camping: you are not always restricted to staying at a developed campground or designated trail camp. For sanitation reasons, you are required to locate your camp well away from the nearest source of water. And, of course, you must observe the fire regulations stated earlier. Always check with the Forest Service to confirm these rules if you intend to do any remote camping.

Most federally managed wilderness areas around the state require special wilderness permits for entry. Many in Southern California have self-registering permits at trailheads; other require permits only for overnight visits. The San Gorgonio and San Jacinto wilderness areas are so popular that trailhead quotas have had to be established.

Trail Courtesy

Whenever you travel the backcountry, you take on a burden of responsibility—keeping the wilderness as you found it. Aside from common-sense prohibitions against littering, vandalism, and inappropriate campfires, there are some less obvious guidelines every hiker should be aware of. We'll mention a few:

Never cut trail switchbacks. This practice breaks down the trail tread and hastens erosion. Try to improve designated trails by removing branches, rocks, or other debris. Springtime growth can quite rapidly obscure pathways in the chaparral country, and funding for trail maintenance is often scarce—so try to do your part by joining a volunteer trail crew or by performing your own small maintenance tasks while walking the trails. Report any damage to trails or other facilities to the appropriate ranger office.

When backpacking, be a "no trace" camper. Leave your campsite as you found it—or leave it in an even more natural condition.

Collecting specimens of minerals, plants, animals, and historical objects without special permit is prohibited in state and county parks. This means common things, too, such as pine cones, wildflowers, and lizards. These should be left for all visitors to enjoy. Some limited collecting of items like pine cones may be allowed on the national forest lands—check first.

We've covered most of the general regulations associated with Southern California's public lands. But you, as a visitor, are responsible for knowing any additional rules as well. The capsulized summary for each hike described in this book includes a reference to the agency responsible for the area you'll be visiting. Phone numbers for those agencies appear in the back of this book.

Using This Book

There are three principal ways to find hiking trips in this book suitable for you. First, you can check the key map for all 101 hikes in this book, pages x and xi, and restrict your search to a specific geographic area. Second, you can leaf through the book, browsing trip summaries, descriptions, and photos. Third, you can scan the "Summary of Hikes" matrix in the back of this book.

Please take the time to carefully read, below, about the meaning of the special symbols and other bits of capsulized information which appear before each trip description in this book.

Sketch maps are provided for each trip in this book, in most cases one trip per map, but in some cases two trips per map. A legend for these maps appears on page 14 . The boxed numbers on each map refer to the start/end points of out-and-back and loop trips. All point-to-point trips have two boxed numbers, indicating separate start and end points. For nearly all hikes described in this book, the sketch map we provide is adequate for basic navigation. For a few hikes, a detailed topographic map is recommended in the capsulized summary.

The following is an explanation of the small symbols and capsulized information appearing at the beginning of each trip description. If you're simply browsing through this book, these summaries alone can be used as a tool to eliminate from consideration hikes that are either too difficult, or perhaps too trivial, for your abilities.

Symbols

 Easy Terrain. Roads, trails and easy cross-country hiking

 Moderate Terrain. Cross-country boulder hopping and easy scrambling

 Difficult Terrain. Nontechnical climbing required (WARNING: THESE TRIPS SHOULD BE ATTEMPTED ONLY BY SUITABLY EQUIPPED, EXPERIENCED HIKERS ADEPT AT TRAVELING OVER STEEP OR ROCKY TERRAIN REQUIRING THE USE OF THE HANDS AS WELL AS THE FEET.)

Only *one* of these three symbols appears for a given trip, indicating the general character of the terrain encountered. A trip almost entirely on roads and trails, but including a short section of boulder-hopping, for example, will be rated as easy terrain, and the difficulties will be duly noted in the text. As the symbols suggest, light footwear (running shoes) is appropriate for easy terrain, while sturdy hiking boots are recommended for more difficult terrain.

Nontechnical climbing includes everything up to and including Class 3 on the rock-climber's scale. While ropes and climbing hardware are not normally required, a hiker should have a good sense of balance, and enough experience to recognize dangerous moves and situations.

Bushwhacking.

Cross-country travel through dense brush. This symbol is included for trips requiring a substantial amount of off-trail "bushwhacking." Wear long pants and be especially alert for ticks and rattlesnakes.

Only *one* of these two symbols appears:

 Marked Trails/Obvious Routes

 Navigation by Map and Compass Required. (WARNING: THESE TRIPS SHOULD BE ATTEMPTED ONLY BY HIKERS SKILLED IN NAVIGATION TECHNIQUES.)

Unambiguous cross-country routes—up a canyon, for example—are included in the first category. The hiker, of course, should never be without a map, even if there are marked trails or the route seems obvious.

 Point-to-Point Route

 Out-and-Back Route

 Loop Route

Only *one* of these three symbols appears, reflecting the trip as described. There is some flexibility, of course, in the way in which a hiker can actually follow the trip.

 Suitable for Backpacking

Many of the trips in this book are not. Some parks and trails are closed at night, others allow night hiking but prohibit camping. Sometimes, overnight camping is permitted at some spot off the route but nearby.

 Best for Kids

These trips are especially recommended for inquisitive children. They were chosen on the basis of their safety and ease of travel (at the time they were researched by the author), and their potential for entertaining the whole family.

Capsulized Summaries

Location. The general location of the trip is stated: a well-known park, mountain range, or nearby city or town.

Highlights. One or two engaging features of the hike are mentioned.

Distance. An estimate of total distance is given. Out-and-back trips show the sum of the distances of the out and back segments.

Total Elevation Gain/Loss. These are estimates of the sum of all the vertical gain segments and the sum of all the vertical loss segments along the total length of the route (both ways for out-and-back trips). This is often considerably more than the net difference in elevation between the high and low points of the hike.

Hiking Time. This figure is for the average hiker, and includes only the time spent in motion. It *does not* include time spent for rest stops, lunch, etc. Fast walkers can complete the routes in perhaps 30% less time, and slower hikers may take 50% longer. We assume the hiker is traveling with a light day pack. (IMPORTANT NOTE: Do realize that "hiking time" stated in this book is for *time-in-motion* only. Also, hikers carrying heavy packs could easily take nearly twice as long, especially if they are traveling under adverse weather conditions. Remember, too, that the progress made by a group as a whole is limited by pace of the slowest member or members.)

Optional/Recommended Map(s). The topographic maps listed are nearly all U.S. Geological Survey 7.5-minute series topographic maps. Usually, these are the most complete and accurate maps of the physical features (if not always the cultural features) of the area you'll be traveling in. These maps are typically stocked by backpacking, outdoor sports, and map shops around the Southland.

Best Times. Because of the extreme heat, the longer desert trips in this book should generally be avoided during any period except the one recommended here. Trips elsewhere in Southern California are usually safe enough at other than "best" times, but usually less rewarding.

Agency. These code letters refer to the agency, or office, that has jurisdiction or management over the area being hiked (for example, ANF/ASD means Angeles National Forest, Arroyo Seco District). You can contact the agency for more information. Full names, phone numbers, and some addresses (of larger agencies) are listed in the back of this book.

Difficulty. The author's subjective, overall rating takes into account the length of the trip and the nature of the terrain. The following are general definitions of the five categories:

★ *Easy.* Suitable for every member of the family.

★★ *Moderate.* Suitable for all physically fit people.

★★★ *Moderately Strenuous.* Long length, substantial elevation gain, and/or difficult terrain. Recommended for experienced hikers only.

★★★★ *Strenuous.* Full day's hike (or a backpack trip) over a long and/or challenging route. Suitable only for experienced hikers in excellent physical condition.

★★★★★ *Very Strenuous.* Long and rugged route in extremely remote area. Suitable only for experienced hikers/climbers in top physical condition. (Only one hike in this book, number 45, gets this rating.)

Each higher level represents more or less a doubling of the difficulty. On average, ★★ trips are twice as hard as ★ trips, ★★★ trips are twice as hard as ★★ trips, and so on.

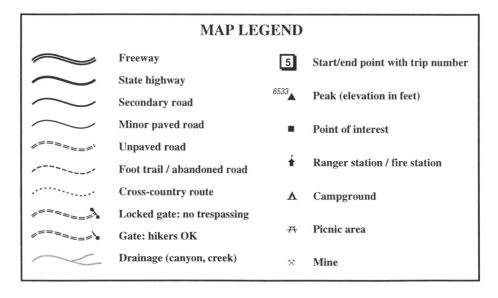

MAP LEGEND

Freeway	**5** Start/end point with trip number
State highway	
Secondary road	6533▲ Peak (elevation in feet)
Minor paved road	■ Point of interest
Unpaved road	
Foot trail / abandoned road	↑ Ranger station / fire station
Cross-country route	Λ Campground
Locked gate: no trespassing	
Gate: hikers OK	⊼ Picnic area
Drainage (canyon, creek)	✗ Mine

TRIP 1
La Jolla Valley-Mugu Peak

Location	Point Mugu State Park, Santa Monica Mountains
Highlights	Spectacular ocean views; rare native vegetation
Distance	10.8 miles
Total Elevation Gain/Loss	1950'/1950'
Hiking Time	5½ hours
Optional Map	USGS 7.5-min *Point Mugu*
Best Times	October through June
Agency	PMSP
Difficulty	★★★

Lazily curving up the rumpled slopes of the western Santa Monica Mountains, the Ray Miller Trail (formerly the La Jolla Ridge Trail) takes in sweeping views of the Point Mugu coastline and the distant Channel Islands. This is the westernmost link in the not-quite-finished Backbone Trail, which will skim along the crest of the Santa Monicas for some 65 miles. The Ray Miller Trail offers a well-graded and scenic approach to the rounded ridge that divides the two largest canyons in Point Mugu State Park: La Jolla and Big Sycamore canyons.

The La Jolla Ridge Trail is just the start of the big loop we're suggesting here: a comprehensive trek through the western quadrant of Point Mugu State Park. If this is too big a chunk to bite off for a single day, there are short cuts, as our map suggests. You could also extend your trip by staying overnight at La Jolla Valley (walk-in) Camp. For that, you must register with a park ranger first.

Point Mugu State Park lies some 32 miles west of Santa Monica via Pacific Coast Highway. Park at the Ray Miller Trailhead, off the coast highway, at the mouth of La Jolla Canyon. Two trails diverge from the parking lot. The wide one going up along the dry canyon bottom ahead is the La Jolla Canyon Trail—your return route. To begin, take the narrower Ray Miller Trail to your right. It starts by curl-

ing up along the toe of a ridge, where it meets a short spur trail going down to an equestrian staging area. It then doggedly climbs 2.4 miles to a junction with the Overlook Trail, a wide fire road. Northward on the Overlook Trail, wend your way around several bumps on the undulating ridge, and arrive at a saddle (4.5 miles from the start), from where roads descend east into Wood Canyon and west into La Jolla Valley. Go left (west) and descend moderately toward the green- or flaxen-colored (depending on the season) floor of the valley.

The valley is managed by the state park as a natural preserve to protect the native bunchgrasses that flourish there. Because so much of California's coast ranges have been biologically perturbed by grazing for more than a century, opportunistic, non-native grasses have taken over just about everywhere. The authentic California "tallgrass prairie" in parts of La Jolla Valley is a notable exception.

La Jolla Valley Camp (5.0 miles by way of our circuitous route) has piped water, restrooms, and oak-shaded picnic tables. Just south of there, beside a trail leading directly back to the Ray Miller Trailhead, you'll find a tule-fringed cattle pond, seasonally dry in some years. Look for chocolate lilies on the slopes around it.

From La Jolla Valley Camp, continue west in the direction of a military radar instal-

Mugu Peak summit, looking east

lation on Laguna Peak (off-limits to hikers). Ignore trails going left, right, and left; you'll want to gradually circle to the southwest and south, heading for a saddle on the right (northwest) shoulder of rounded Mugu Peak. Attaining that saddle at 6.8 miles, you'll have a great view of the Pacific Ocean. The popping noises you may hear below are from a military shooting range, near Pacific Coast Highway. Up the coast lies the Point Mugu Naval Air Station.

From the saddle, the trail contours south and then east around the south flank of Mugu Peak. You arrive (7.7 miles) at another saddle just east of Mugu's 1266-foot summit. Five minutes of climbing on a steep path put you on the barren top, where hikers have fashioned a large rock cairn and planted pine saplings. You can look down upon The Great Sand Dune (coastal dunes) and Pacific Coast Highway where it barely squeezes past some coastal bluffs. On warm days there's a desertlike feel to this rocky and sparsely vegetated mountain, oddly juxtaposed with the sights and sounds of the surf below.

Return to the saddle east of the peak and continue descending to a junction (9.0 miles) in a wooded recess of La Jolla Canyon. Turn right, proceed east along a hillside, and then hook up with the La Jolla Canyon Trail, where you turn right again.

There's an exciting stretch down through a rock-walled section of La Jolla Canyon,

where you'll see magnificent springtime displays of giant coreopsis. This plant is quite common in the Channel Islands, but found only in scattered coastal locales from far western Los Angeles County to San Luis Obispo County. Some coreopsis plants have forked stems towering as high as 10 feet, head and shoulders above the surrounding scrub. The massed, yellow, daisylike flowers are an unforgettable sight in March and April.

Nearing the canyon's mouth, you'll pass a little grove of native walnut trees and a small, seasonal waterfall. You descend to join a dirt road built to haul stone out of the area for the construction of the coast highway, and arrive about 15 minutes later at the Ray Miller Trailhead.

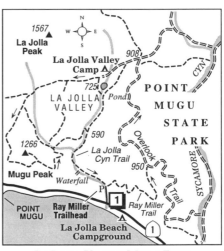

La Jolla Valley-Mugu Peak

TRIP 2
Sandstone Peak

Location	Circle X Ranch (Santa Monica Mountains National Recreation Area)
Highlights	Most inclusive view in the Santa Monicas; volcanic rock formations
Distance	5.8 miles
Total Elevation Gain/Loss	1400'/1400'
Hiking Time	3½ hours
Optional Maps	USGS 7.5-min *Triunfo Pass, Newbury Park*
Best Times	October through June
Agency	SMMNRA
Difficulty	★★★

Sandstone Peak, *the* destination for peak baggers in the Santa Monicas, can be reached in as little as 1½ miles by way of the short, very steep Boney Ridge Trail. Much more rewarding and relaxing is the looping route outlined below. Take a picnic lunch and plan to make a half day of it. You should come on a crystalline day in late fall or winter to take best advantage of the skyline views. Throughout spring, wildflowers put on a good show (despite the ravages of the fall 1993 wildfires which incinerated much of the Santa Monica Mountains; abundant rainfall since has spurred a rapid regrowth of vegetation). In addition to blue-flowering stands of ceanothus, the early-to-mid-spring bloom includes monkey flower, nightshade, Chinese houses, wild peony, wild hyacinth, morning glory, and phacelia. Delicate, orangish Humboldt lilies unfold by June.

Sandstone Peak lies within Circle X Ranch—formerly owned by the Boy Scouts of America, and now a unit of the Santa Monica Mountains National Recreation Area. Backpacking, as well as hiking, is allowed here and is rewarding in just about any season. In the heat of summer, you can travel during the cooler late afternoon and early morning hours, with a layover at the backcountry trail camp about halfway along the route. Reservations are required—call (818) 597-9192 for details.

You'll start hiking at the large parking lot on the north side of Yerba Buena Road, 1 mile east of the Circle X park office. This same point is 6.4 miles north of Pacific Coast Highway and 4.5 miles west of Mulholland Highway. (Either way you face a white-knuckle drive on the paved, but very narrow and curvy, Yerba Buena Road.)

Proceed on foot past a gate and up a fire road 0.3 mile to where the marked Mishe Mokwa Trail branches right. On it, right away you plunge into tough, scratchy chaparral vegetation. The hand-tooled route is delightfully primitive, but requires frequent maintenance so as to keep the chaparral from knitting together across the path. Both your hands and your feet will come into play over the next 40 or 50 minutes as you're forced to scramble a bit over rough-textured outcrops of volcanic rock. You'll make intimate acquaintance with mosses and ferns and several of the more attractive chaparral shrubs: toyon, holly-leaf cherry, manzanita, and red shanks (a.k.a. ribbonwood), which is identified by its wispy foliage and perpetually peeling, rust-colored bark. You'll also pass several small bay trees. After about a half hour on the Mishe Mokwa Trail, keep an eye out for an amazing balanced rock that rests precariously on the opposite wall of the canyon that lies just below you.

By 1.7 miles from the start you will have worked you way around to the north flank of Sandstone Peak, where you suddenly come upon a couple of picnic tables and "Split Rock," a fractured volcanic boulder with a gap wide enough to walk through (please do so to maintain the Scouts' tradition). From then on, you continue on an old dirt road that crosses the aforementioned canyon and turns west (upstream). You pass beneath some hefty volcanic outcrops and at 2.5 miles come to a junction with a trail on the right which goes over a summit and down into Point Mugu State Park. Continue on the road and circle south to the trail campground (2.8 miles) on the left, nestled in a little draw.

A side trail leads west from the campground and then north to the bouldery summit of Tri Peaks, one of several high points that make up the skeletal ridge aptly named Boney Mountain. The half-hour climb is worth it if you have the time and energy. Most of Point Mugu State Park, to the north and west, is visible from the top.

Our route continues south, then east on the main trail, still a dirt road. About 200 yards beyond the junction of a spur road leading past some water tanks, look for an obscure side path going right. This takes you about 50 yards to the top of an outcrop—Inspiration Point. The direction-finder there indicates local features as well as very distant points such as Mount San Antonio, Santa Catalina Island, and San Clemente Island.

Press on and pass the junction of the Boney Ridge Trail, but don't miss the junction of the Sandstone Peak summit trail, just

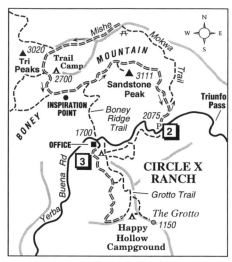

SANDSTONE PEAK & THE GROTTO

past two closely spaced hairpin turns in the road. Make your way up the slippery path to the windswept top. The plaque on the summit block honors W. Herbert Allen, a long-time benefactor of the Scouts and Circle X Ranch. To the Scouts this mountain is "Mt. Allen," although that name has not, so far, been accepted by cartographers. In any event, the peak's real name is misleading. It, along with Boney Mountain and most of the western crest of the Santa Monicas, consists of beige- and rust-colored volcanic rock, not unlike sandstone when seen from a distance.

On a clear day the view is truly panoramic from here, with distant mountain ranges, the hazy Los Angeles Basin, and the island-dimpled surface of the ocean occupying all 360° of the horizon. Before you leave the summit, don't forget to sign the register, housed in a little cubbyhole. To return, go back down to the dirt road and resume your travel eastward. One and a half miles of twisting descent will take you back to the trailhead.

Atop Sandstone Peak

TRIP 3
The Grotto

Location	Circle X Ranch (Santa Monica Mountains National Recreation Area)
Highlights	Spooky rock formations; live oak groves
Distance	2.6 miles round trip
Total Elevation Gain/Loss	650' / 650'
Hiking Time	1½ hours (round trip)
Optional Map	USGS 7.5-min *Triunfo Pass*
Best Times	All year
Agency	SMMNRA
Difficulty	★★

The 1655-acre Circle X Ranch, formerly run by the Boy Scouts of America but now administered by the National Park Service, is positively riddled with Tom Sawyer-esque hiking paths. Some have succumbed to encroaching brush and a devastating wildfire in Fall 1993, but one that remains in good shape—the Grotto Trail—is perfect for young (or young-in-thought) adventurers.

You may start hiking at the Circle X park office, on Yerba Buena Road 5.4 miles north of Pacific Coast Highway, or 5.5 miles west of Mulholland Highway. Leave your car either in the upper parking area just off Yerba Buena Road, or 0.1 mile below in the lot next to the office.

Start by following the dirt road leading downhill toward Happy Hollow Campground. At a point about 100 yards down, veer left at the entrance to a group campground. Walk through or skirt the campsites, and pick up a trail heading south down along a shady, seasonal creek.

Live-oak woodland above The Grotto

Keep heading downhill as you pass, in quick succession, two trails coming in from the left. Very shortly afterward, you cross the creek at a point immediately above a 30-foot ledge which becomes a trickling waterfall in winter and spring. You then go uphill, gaining about 50 feet of elevation, and cross an open meadow offering fine views of both Boney Mountain above and a deep-cut gorge (the west fork of Arroyo Sequit) below. Pass a short trail angling over to the Happy Hollow road on the right, and keep descending, more sharply now, toward the bottom of the gorge.

When you come upon an old road at the bottom, bear left, cross the creek, and continue downstream on a narrowing trail along the shaded east bank. Pass some campsites (part of Happy Hollow Campground) and then curve left when you reach a grove of fantastically twisted live oaks at the confluence of two stream forks. On the edge of this grove, an overflow

pipe coming out of a tank discharges tepid spring water. Continue another 200 yards down the now-lively brook to The Grotto, a narrow, spooky constriction flanked by sheer volcanic-rock walls. If your sense of balance is good, you can clamber over gray-colored rock ledges and massive boulders fallen from the canyon walls—just as thousands of Boy Scouts have done before you. At one spot you can peer cautiously into a gloomy cavern, where the subterranean stream is more easily heard than seen. Water marks on the boulders above are evidence that this part of the gorge probably supports a two-tier stream in times of flood.

When you've had your fill of adventuring, return by the same route, uphill almost the whole way. As an option you could hike west through the campground and then follow the dirt road up. This alternative is longer, more gradual, and less scenic than the trail.

The Grotto

TRIP 4
Charmlee Natural Area

Location	Santa Monica Mountains
Highlights	Spring wildflowers; ocean views
Distance	2.8 miles
Total Elevation Gain/Loss	500′/500′
Hiking Time	1½ hours
Optional Map	USGS 7.5-min *Triunfo Pass*
Best Times	All year
Agency	CNA
Difficulty	★

Charmlee Natural Area, 460 acres of meadow, oak woodland, sage scrub, and chaparral, was first opened to the public in 1981. Never designed to accommodate a large number of visitors, its parking lot is often full on the weekends. Charmlee is a great place to take family and friends wildflower hunting in the spring, or ocean watching on a cool, clear winter day.

To reach Charmlee Natural Area from Santa Monica, drive 25 miles west on Pacific Coast Highway (Highway 1), turn north on Encinal Canyon Road, and proceed north 4 miles to the park's well-marked entrance. Gates are open 8 a.m. to sunset daily.

From the parking lot, walk on pavement to the nature center (inside, pick up a guide for the Fire Ecology Trail and other interpretive materials). Bear right on a paved road, soon dirt, that bends north up a slope. Make an acute left turn at the top, follow a ridge road past a hilltop water tank (detour and walk around the tank for a good overview of the park and the ocean), and then curve down to a T-intersection. Jog right, then go left on the Fire Ecology Trail. After a few minutes you will be passing under some fire-singed coast live oaks, which are well known for their ability to survive fast-moving wildfires.

At post 10 on the Fire Ecology Trail, go right on a road that winds along the west edge of Charmlee's large, central meadow. Continue all the way to a dry ridge topped by some old eucalyptus trees and a concrete-

lined cistern, both relics of cattle-ranching days. From there descend south (stay right at the next junction) to the "Ocean Vista," which really delivers in a big way what its name suggests, especially on clear days.

Circle north from Ocean Vista around the hill with the cistern and then along the east side of the meadow. When you come to the northeast part of the meadow and the dirt road curves west, pick up the hard-to-spot Botany Trail on the right. It winds through mostly chaparral vegetation and takes you to the picnic area just above your starting point.

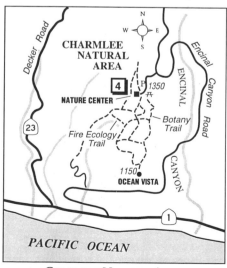

CHARMLEE NATURAL AREA

TRIP 5
Zuma Canyon

Location	Santa Monica Mountains
Highlights	Spectacular, wild canyon trek; ocean views on the return
Distance	8.0 miles
Total Elevation Gain/Loss	1700′/1700′
Hiking Time	6 hours
Optional Map	USGS 7.5-min *Point Dume*
Best Times	October through June
Agency	SMMNRA
Difficulty	★★★★

Although it slices only 6 miles inland from the Pacific shoreline, Zuma Canyon harbors one of the deepest gorges in the Santa Monica Mountains. Easily on a par with nearby Malibu and Topanga canyons in scenic wealth but much less known, Zuma Canyon holds a further distinction of never having suffered the invasion of a major road. Under cover of junglelike growths of willow, sycamore, oak and bay, the canyon's small stream cascades over sculpted sandstone boulders and gathers in limpid pools adorned with ferns. These natural treasures yield their secrets begrudgingly, as they should, only to those willing to scramble over boulders, plow through sucking mud and cattails, and thrash through scratchy undergrowth.

On this challenging trek, you'll proceed straight up the canyon's scenic midsection, climb out of the canyon depths via a powerline service road, and loop back to your starting point on the ridge-running Zuma Ridge Trail (a fire road). The roads are shadeless, yet they offer great vistas of the canyon, the ocean, and the seemingly interminable east-west sweep of the Santa Monica Mountains.

Hiking the canyon bottom is least problematical in the fall season before the heavy rains set in. The stream may have shrunk to isolated pools by then, and you'll step mostly on dry rocks with good traction.

Winter flooding can render the canyon impassable, but such episodes are rare and short-lived. During spring, the stream flows heartily and there's plenty of greenery and wildflowers; at the same time there's an increased threat of exposure to poison oak (which is found in fair abundance along the banks) and you're likely to surprise a rattlesnake. Summer days are usually too oppressively warm and humid for such a difficult hike. Whatever the season, take along plenty of water; the water in the canyon is not potable.

A good starting place is the north end of Busch Drive, one mile from Pacific Coast Highway at the far western margins of the community of Malibu. The fire road on your left, the Zuma Ridge Trail, is your return route. Take the path across the hillside to your right (east). You lose about 300 feet of elevation as you zigzag down to the wide flood plain issuing from the mouth of Zuma Canyon. (The small network of trails hereabouts is worth exploring should you choose not to—for whatever reason—tackle the narrow, rough section of canyon ahead.)

Descend to Zuma Canyon's creekbed, cross it, and turn left on the path going upstream along the winter-wet, summer-dry creek. You'll pass statuesque sycamores, tall laurel sumac bushes, and scattered wildflowers in season. This is a promising

The wilds of Zuma Canyon

area for spotting wildlife anytime—squirrels, rabbits, and coyotes are commonly seen, deer and bobcats less so.

After about a mile's walk along the creek, the canyon walls close in tighter, oaks appear in greater numbers, and you'll notice a small grove of eucalyptus trees on a little terrace. A short while later, the path abruptly ends at a pile of sandstone boulders. During the dry months, surface water may get only this far down the canyon. Usually, however, the water trickles or tumbles past here, disappearing at some point downstream into the porous substrate of the canyon floor. Now you begin a nearly 2-mile stretch of boulder-hopping (and possibly wading), 2 or 3 hours worth depending on the conditions. Other than a few rusting pieces of pipeline from an old dam and irrigation system, you may find that the canyon is completely litter-free; please keep it that way.

The great variety of rocks that have been washed down the stream or have fallen from the canyon walls says a lot about the geologic complexity of the Santa Monicas. You'll scramble over fine-grained siltstones and sandstones, conglomerates that look like poorly mixed aggregate concrete, and volcanic rocks of the sort that make up

Saddle Rock (a local landmark near the head of Zuma Canyon) and the Goat Buttes of nearby Malibu Creek State Park. Some of the larger boulders attain the dimensions of mid-sized trucks, presenting an obstacle course that must be negotiated by moderate hand-and-foot climbing.

About 0.5 mile shy of the dirt road crossing, you'll pass directly under a set of high-voltage transmission lines—so high they're hard to spot. These lines, plus the graded road built to give access to the towers, represent the major incursion of civilization into Zuma Canyon. If you can ignore them, however, it's easy to imagine what all the large canyons in the Santa Monicas were like only a century ago.

When you finally reach the service road, turn left and follow it to the top of the west ridge. From there, turn left on the Zuma Ridge Trail and follow its lazily curving, downhill course back to the starting point. This and other dirt roads in the Santa Monicas that are closed to motorized vehicles have become popular mountain-biking routes.

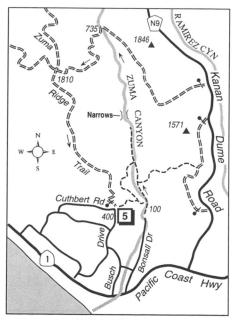

ZUMA CANYON

TRIP 6
Point Dume to Paradise Cove

Location	Malibu coast
Highlights	Panoramic ocean vistas; superb intertidal exploration
Distance	2.1 miles one way
Total Elevation Gain/Loss	(Nearly flat)
Hiking Time	1½ hours
Optional Map	USGS 7.5-min *Point Dume*
Best Times	All year (passable during low tides)
Agency	SMMNRA
Difficulty	★★

Like the armored bow of an ice-breaker, flat-topped Point Dume juts into the Pacific about 20 miles west of Santa Monica. Just east of the point itself, an unbroken cliff wall shelters a secluded beach from the sights and sounds of the civilized world. Below the sometimes-narrow stretch of sand east of Point Dume, a strip of rocky coastline harbors tidal pools and a mind-boggling array of plant and animal life.

A pleasant walk anytime the tide is low, this trip is doubly rewarding when the tide dips as low as –2 feet. Here are some of the creatures we spotted one warm October afternoon during a –1.5 foot tide: limpets, periwinkles, chitons, tube snails, sandcastle worms, sculpins, mussels, shore and hermit crabs, green and aggregate anemones, three kinds of barnacles, and two kinds of sea stars. Extreme low tides occur during the afternoon two or three times each month from October through March. During the summer, negative tides are rarer, and you'll have to get up early to catch them. Consult tide tables to find out exactly when.

Starting out at Westward Beach (open daylight hours—parking fee charged) on the west side of Point Dume, you have a choice between two routes: The shorter, much easier route (and the only practical alternative during all but extremely low tides) is the trail slanting left up the cliff. On top you'll come

to an area very popular for sighting gray whales during their southward migration in winter. You'll also discover a state historic monument. Point Dume, you'll learn, was christened by the British naval commander George Vancouver, who sailed by in 1793.

As you stand on Point Dume's apex, note the marked contrast between the lighter sed-

Dume Cove at low tide

imentary rock exposed on the cliff faces both east and west, and the darker volcanic rock just below. This unusually tough mass of volcanic rock has thus far resisted the onslaught of the ocean swells. After you descend from the apex, some metal stairs will take you down to crescent-shaped Dume Cove.

The alternate route is for expert climbers only. During the very lowest tides, you round the point itself, making your way by hand-and-toe climbing in a couple of spots over huge, angular shards of volcanic rock along the base of the cliffs. The tidepools here and to the east along Dume Cove's shoreline have some of the best displays of intertidal marine life in Southern California. This visual feast will remain for others to enjoy if you refrain from taking or disturbing in any way the organisms that live there. (WARNING: Exploring the lower intertidal zones can be hazardous. Be very cautious when traveling over slippery rocks, and always be aware of the incoming swells. Don't let a rogue wave catch you by surprise.)

The going is easy once you're on Dume Cove's ribbon of sand. Signs posted here warn against nude bathing and sunning. This was once a popular nude beach, much to the chagrin of some of those living in the cliffside mansions overlooking the area.

When you reach the northeast end of Dume Cove, swing left around a lesser point and continue another mile over a somewhat wider beach to Paradise Cove, site of an elegant beach-side restaurant, private pier, and parking lot (public welcome, fee charged). If you've parked a second car here, then your hike ends here. Otherwise you can return the way you came or wend your way along the residential streets of Point Dume to return to Westward Beach.

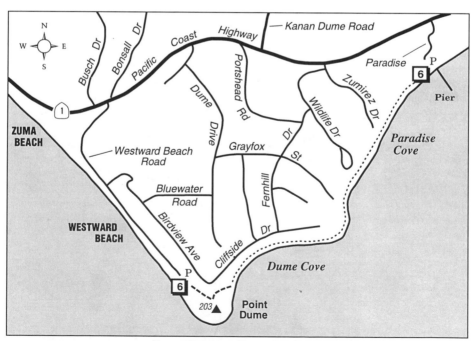

POINT DUME TO PARADISE COVE

TRIP 7
Solstice Canyon

Location	Santa Monica Mountains (Malibu)
Highlights	Superb oak woodland; lessons in fire ecology
Distance	2.6 miles round trip (to Tropical Terrace)
Total Elevation Gain/Loss	400'/400'
Hiking Time	1½ hours (round trip)
Optional Maps	USGS 7.5-min *Malibu Beach, Point Dume*
Best Times	All year
Agency	SCP
Difficulty	★

Solstice Canyon Park, one of the newest and most attractive additions to the Santa Monica Mountains National Recreation Area, invites your attention. Since its unveiling in 1988, workers have been busy transforming these 556 acres into a hiker's showplace. Old buildings have been restored, junk has been hauled away, weedy plants have been replaced by native ones, new trails have been cut, and old roads have been either revegetated or incorporated into the trail system. Except for the ruins of the architecturally noted "Tropical Terrace" home built by the previous owners of the property (the Roberts family), not much remains of the devastation wrought by a devastating 1982 fire which burned large sections of Malibu.

It would be hard to find a better-maintained public park or preserve anywhere in Los Angeles County—perhaps because the Santa Monica Mountains Conservancy (a state-funded operation charged with acquiring land for public use) maintains its headquarters here.

Tropical Terrace

For all of its virtues, Solstice Canyon Park is not well advertised. Its simple gateway is found along Corral Canyon Road, 0.2 mile north of Pacific Coast Highway in Malibu. There's parking space here for about 6 cars. More space to park is available in a larger lot near the park office. Park hours are 8 a.m. to 5 p.m., and a parking fee is charged.

Drop by the office, housed in a beautifully restored 1940s cottage. There you can obtain a map and lots of printed (or oral) information about the area. Across from the office, the Dry Creek Trail goes northeast up an oak-shaded ravine for about 0.6 mile before entering unposted private property. An outrageously cantilevered "Darth Vader" house overlooks the ravine as well as a 100-foot-high precipice that on rare occasions becomes a spectacular waterfall.

The TRW Trail, heading north from the office, loops up to the hillside headquarters of the Santa Monica Mountains Conservancy, housed in a silo-shaped building formerly used by TRW, Inc. as a test facility for satellite instrumentation.

On our way to Tropical Terrace, however, we ignore these side trips and follow the paved road (or a parallel trail through a creekside picnic area) up-canyon through a fantastic woodland of sycamore, bay, and live oaks—the latter with trunks up to 18 feet in circumference.

After 15 minutes or so, you pass a circa 1865 stone cottage on the right—thought to be the oldest house in Malibu—undergoing restoration. Just beyond is another picnic area nestled alongside the melodious creek. At 1.5 miles, you arrive at the remains of Tropical Terrace. In a setting of palms and giant birds-of-paradise, curved flagstone steps sweep toward the roofless remains of what was for 26 years one of Malibu's grand homes. Beyond the house, crumbling stone steps and pathways lead to what used to be elaborately decorated rock grottoes, and a waterfall on Solstice Canyon's creek. Large chunks of sandstone have cleaved from the canyon walls, adding to the rubble. For all its perfectly natural setting, Tropical Terrace's destiny was that of a temporary paradise, defenseless against both fire and flood.

The easiest way back is simply to retrace your steps. Alternately, you can try the steep, rugged Sostomo or Rising Sun trails, which ascend the canyon walls and offer coastline views stretching from the Palos Verdes peninsula to Point Dume.

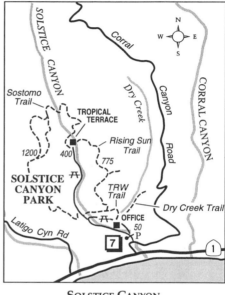

SOLSTICE CANYON

TRIP 8
Temescal Canyon

Location	Santa Monica Mountains (Pacific Palisades)
Highlights	Pseudo-aerial coastline views; shady riparian/oak woodland
Distance	2.8 miles
Total Elevation Gain/Loss	850'/850'
Hiking Time	1½ hours
Optional Map	USGS 7.5-min *Topanga*
Best Times	All year
Agency	SMMNRA
Difficulty	★★

Spring lingers long on the coastal slopes of the Santa Monica Mountains, which are frequently bathed from May till July in the sopping-wet breath of the marine layer. This is quintessential coastal sage-scrub and chaparral country, a particular habitat that is fast succumbing to urban development all over Southern California. All through spring and early summer, you can enjoy the scents of sage and wildflowers on the trails of Temescal Canyon, part of the Santa Monica Mountains National Recreation Area. With an early start on a foggy morn, you may find yourself punching right through the mist as you ascend into the bright, sunny world above.

Park at the entrance to the Presbyterian Conference Grounds just north of Sunset

Oak woodland in Solstice Canyon

Boulevard on Temescal Canyon Road. Since part of the route ahead passes through church property, you must sign a register at the hiker's booth. Don't forget to *sign out* in the same register upon your return.

I enjoy making the loop clockwise, climbing the scrubby west wall of Temescal Canyon on the way up, and then making a nice, easy descent down through the canyon. To do that, simply take the steep, narrow path going left just beyond the booth. After eight short switchbacks, the path sticks to an open ridge with a 180° view of distant horizons. Pause often so you can admire the coastline curving from Santa Monica Bay to Malibu. One winter afternoon on this ridge, I watched a leaden cumulus cloud drop its load over Temescal Canyon and then move on, leaving a vivid rainbow in its wake.

At 1.3 miles, the path meets the Temescal Ridge Trail, a fire road that follows a viewful but shadeless ridge north toward Mulholland Drive on the crest of the Santa Monicas. At this juncture you have the option of making a side trip north 0.5 mile to a wind-carved, sandstone outcrop known as Skull Rock.

Staying on the loop route, turn right and start down the eroded bed of the former Temescal Fire Road. When you hit the shady canyon bottom (1.7 miles), scramble around the stonework buttresses of a fallen bridge and pick up a better section of the old fire road on the far side of the creek. Above and below this crossing are small, trickling waterfalls and shallow, limpid pools. Poke around the creek a bit for a look at its typical denizens—water striders and newts.

The final stretch follows the canyon bottom, then contours along a slope to the right of the church buildings. Lots of live oak, sycamore, willow, and bay trees, their woodsy scents commingling on the ocean breeze, highlight your return.

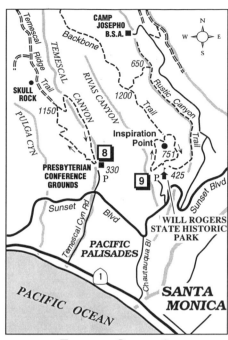

TEMESCAL CANYON &
WILL ROGERS PARK

TRIP 9
Will Rogers Park

Location	Santa Monica Mountains (Pacific Palisades)
Highlights	City, ocean, and mountain views in a single stance
Distance	2.0 miles
Total Elevation Gain/Loss	350'/350'
Hiking Time	1 hour
Optional Map	USGS 7.5-min *Topanga*
Best Times	All year
Agency	WRSHP
Difficulty	★

Drive up a short mile from the speedway known as Sunset Boulevard toward Will Rogers State Historic Park, and you'll instantly leave the rat race behind. Especially on weekdays or early on weekend mornings, this quiet spot is perfect for getting some exercise and taking advantage of multi-million-dollar views of Santa Monica, West L.A. and downtown L.A. The park is open daily, except certain holidays, from 8 a.m. to 5 p.m. A parking fee is charged.

Newspaperman, radio commentator, movie star and pop-philosopher Will Rogers purchased this 182-acre property in 1922 and lived with his family here from 1928 until his death in 1935. Historic only by Southern California standards, his 31-room mansion is nevertheless interesting to tour.

Our main goal, however, is to reach Inspiration Point, a flat-topped bump on a ridge overlooking the entire spread. Follow the main, wide, riding and hiking trail that makes a 2-mile loop, starting at the north end of the big lawn adjoining the Rogers home. Or use any of several shorter, more direct paths. You may want to obtain a copy of the detailed hikers' map, available at the gift shop in a wing of the home. Printed on the map is one of Will's memorable aphorisms, "...if your time is worth anything, travel by air. If not, you might just as well walk."

Relaxing on the benches at the top on a clear day, you can admire true-as-advertised, inspiring vistas stretching east to the front range of the San Gabriel Mountains and southeast to the Santa Ana Mountains. South past the swelling Palos Verdes peninsula you can sometimes spot Santa Catalina Island, rising in ethereal majesty from the shining surface of the sea.

Will Rogers Park serves as the east terminus of the Backbone Trail, which when completed will skim some 65 miles along the crest of the Santa Monica Mountains. A glance at our map reveals other, longer hiking routes you can follow nearby. The Rustic Canyon Trail—itself a bit rustic and rough-hewn—is rewarding if you have the time.

Lower Rustic Canyon

TRIP 10
Cheeseboro Canyon

Location	Simi Hills (east of Thousand Oaks)
Highlights	Classic California green/golden grassland dotted with oaks
Distance	6.5 miles
Total Elevation Gain/Loss	850'/850'
Hiking Time	3 hours
Optional Map	USGS 7.5-min *Calabasas*
Best Times	November through May
Agency	SMMNRA
Difficulty	★★

Instantly a hit when it first opened to the public in the late 1980s, Cheeseboro Canyon Park (a unit of the Santa Monica Mountains National Recreation Area) now draws a mix of hikers, mountain bikers, equestrians, and even wheelchair explorers—tens of thousands of visitors yearly—to its network of old roads and newer trails. Friendly rangers patrol the roads and trails on horseback, eager to tell anyone willing to lend an ear about the park's natural features and wildlife (deer and coyotes, especially).

For a good overview of the entire area, follow the 6.5-mile route described here, which goes up the canyon floor and back along the east ridge. Two optional, worthwhile side trips could add another 5 miles—if you're up to it.

Take the Chesebro (sic) Road exit from the Ventura Freeway, go north about 200

Rangers on patrol, Cheeseboro Canyon

yards, and then turn right on the country road signed CHESEBRO ROAD. Drive 0.7 mile north to the park's entrance and trailhead on the right. From there, the popular Sulfur Springs Trail goes east and then bends north up the wide, nearly flat canyon floor, while the Modello Trail slants left and curves up along the canyon's rounded west wall. Stay on the Sulfur Springs Trail, passing statuesque valley oaks, which are deciduous, and gnarled coast live oaks, which retain their leaves year round. The extension of a major east-west road (Thousand Oaks Boulevard) across this part of Cheeseboro Canyon may one day spoil the serenity, but for now you see and hear almost nothing of the world beyond the canyon rim.

After 2.5 miles, turn right on the steep, narrow Baleen Wall Trail—no mountain bikes allowed—and begin climbing the grass- and sage-covered east canyon wall. (From this junction you could make an out-and-back side trip: By keeping straight on the main trail, you would pass some sulfurous-smelling seeps and later emerge in an open valley dotted with sandstone boulders. An old sheep corral made of wire lies at trail's end in the upper reaches of Cheeseboro Canyon, 2 miles from the Baleen Wall turnoff.)

After some huffing and puffing up the Baleen Wall Trail, you come to a powerline access road roughly following the east ridgeline. (Here begins a second side trip: north along the road 0.5 mile to the lip of the Baleen Wall, a whitish sedimentary outcrop, for an impressive view of the upper canyon.)

To continue on the main route, walk south on the access road past a large water tank and down to a T-intersection. Turn right and continue descending toward the main trail on Cheeseboro Canyon's floor. Then, retrace your steps an easy 1.5 miles back to the trailhead.

Just west of Cheeseboro Canyon, another large parcel of open space known as Palo Comado Canyon was recently added

to the National Recreation Area. These and other newly acquired land parcels, it is hoped, will continue to serve as wildlife corridors between the interior mountain ranges and the coast—even as L.A.'s outer suburbs continue their relentless march over hill and dale.

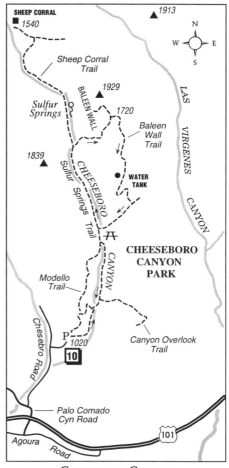

CHEESEBORO CANYON

TRIP 11
Old Stagecoach Road

Location	San Fernando Valley
Highlights	Valley views, historical interest
Distance	2.6 miles round trip
Total Elevation Gain/Loss	650'/650'
Hiking Time	1½ hours (round trip)
Optional Maps	USGS 7.5-min *Oat Mountain, Santa Susana*
Best Times	All year
Agency	CP
Difficulty	★★

Sunrises are as spectacular as they come when viewed on clear winter mornings from the Old Stagecoach Road above Chatsworth. To the east, a hundred thousand valley lights fade while the cirrus-streaked sky cycles through a spectrum of hue and intensity. To the west, boulder-stacked hillsides materialize out of gray gloom to become perfect copies of the golden backdrops seen in so many Western movies and television productions.

Hiking the Stagecoach Road at dawn is inspiring—but not recommended unless you're familiar with the area. Pay a visit in daylight first so you can memorize the route, which is not always well marked nor easy to follow.

At the entrance to Chatsworth Park South (west terminus of Devonshire Street), pick up the path signed OLD STAGECOACH ROAD on the left. After reaching the west end of the park (0.4 mile) you start climbing into the bouldered hills, where a maze of roads and old vehicle tracks complicates route-finding. Head generally southwest and uphill to a low ridge distinguished by a row of bushy olive trees (0.6 mile). From there, turn right (northwest) up the ridge and aim toward a large, white, rectangular plaque embedded in sandstone on the hillside about 0.4 mile away. You're now on a well-preserved section of what used to be

called the Devil's Slide, a key link in the 1860-90 coastal stage road linking Los Angeles and San Francisco. As you walk up the hard sandstone bed, notice the carefully hewn drainage chutes on both sides. With a little detective work you may also find a couple of old cisterns, used to capture rainwater for relay teams of horses that pulled wagons up the formidable grade.

The tiled historical plaque, placed in 1939, remains in good shape. Beyond the plaque, you can follow the stagecoach road bed another 0.3 mile to the Devil's Slide summit (1630'), where a fence marks the L.A.-Ventura county line. Private homes lie to the west, but to the north there's more to explore if you're willing to do some off-trail walking. The next ridge north, for example, offers a view of Santa Susana Pass, threaded by the Simi Valley Freeway and the older Santa Susana Pass Road. About 600 feet below you is the midpoint of the 1.4-mile-long Santa Susana railroad tunnel. The tunnel's east entrance can be seen back near Chatsworth Park South.

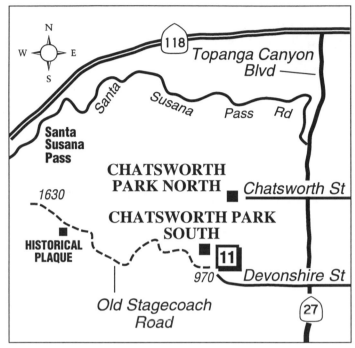

OLD STAGECOACH ROAD

TRIP 12
The Pothole

Location	Los Padres National Forest (Ventura County)
Highlights	Crystalline streams, eroded rock formations
Distance	11.4 miles
Total Elevation Gain/Loss	2900'/2900'
Hiking Time	6 hours
Recommended Map	USGS 7.5-min *Cobblestone Mtn.*
Best Times	November through May
Agency	LPNF/OD
Difficulty	★★★

This trip samples the charms of the vast Sespe Wilderness stretching through interior Ventura County. Just west lies the last stronghold of the California condor, which nearly became extinct in the mid-1980s. In the early 1990s, these giant vulturelike birds were reintroduced into the area after being raised in captive breeding programs at the Los Angeles Zoo and the San Diego Wild Animal Park. It is too early to tell whether the condors will thrive here without further human intervention. Aside from the possible sighting of a condor while on this hike, you'll enjoy erosion-whittled ridges, gentle *potreros* (pastures), and sandstone gorges where pond turtles sun themselves on rocks overlooking emerald pools.

To reach the starting point, exit Interstate 5 at westbound Highway 126 (just north of Santa Clarita). Drive 11 miles west to the town of Piru and follow the signs to Lake Piru. Pass the entrance station for the recreation area at the lake (you do not have to pay if you are camping at Blue Point Campground or using the national-forest trails ahead, but you will need to pick up a wilderness permit, for day or overnight use, here) and continue 6 miles farther on narrow pavement to Blue Point Campground. If Piru Creek isn't flowing heavily, you'll be able to drive over a wide ford just beyond the campground and

reach a parking and picnic area. Otherwise you can park at the campground. After heavy rains, the ford is too dangerous to cross on foot, and you won't be able to complete the loop hike as described here.

Start by walking back along the paved road to a point 1.3 miles south of the campground. There you'll find the signed Pothole Trail. Follow it straight up a ridge where cattle have grazed amid the chaparral, and a few small walnut trees stand like lonely sentinels. Soon there are expansive views of the sandstone outcrops, including Blue Point, on neighboring ridges. Pass a wildlife guzzler on a hilltop (3.4 miles from the campground, 3000') and continue down and then up the ridgeline to a junction (4.0 miles, 3240'), where remnants of an old fire break continue up the ridge. There you veer right, following the circuitous Pothole Trail down along a ridge overlooking a spread of chaparral and grassland to the west—Devils Potrero.

Where the trail hits bottom on the edge of the potrero itself, there's a sharp turn north (5.7 miles). Find the obscure path going 0.2 mile south, through tall chaparral, to The Pothole. This large, flat, perfectly isolated basin—a true topographical depression, is filled with grasses and rimmed by cottonwoods and willows. It's easy to imagine a painter with paintbrush and palette at work here under the big sky. Bring your camera with wide-angle lens, or a sketchpad. Geologically, this strange formation is a "sag pond," owing its existence to the Agua Blanca thrust fault paralleling Agua Blanca Creek to the north.

Return to the Pothole Trail and descend north another mile to Agua Blanca Creek. On the way you'll pass an old abandoned cabin, a fern-draped brook, lots of oak trees, masses of poison oak, and a few big-cone Douglas-firs. When you arrive at the creek, Log Cabin trail camp lies a short distance upstream, while the sheer-walled Devils Gateway lies just below. The trail itself detours around the Gateway by rising some 250 feet up and around the north wall, but as an option you can wade through the 20-foot-wide Gateway itself—in water that's likely to be waist-deep or more during winter and early spring.

Past Devils Gateway, the trail follows a well-graded route, mostly along the steep, shaded south wall of the canyon cut by the creek, or down in the flood plain itself. At several creek crossings, you can admire the extraordinary transparency of the water.

At the mouth of the canyon (10.1 miles) you pass a couple of buildings at Kesters, a small, private inholding in the national forest, and then hook up with a dirt road leading down along Piru Creek to Blue Point Campground.

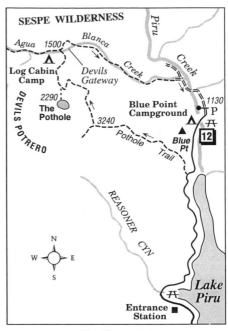

THE POTHOLE

TRIP 13
Placerita Canyon

Location	Santa Clarita
Highlights	Wooded ravines; waterfall; historical interest
Distance	5.0 miles round trip (to waterfall)
Total Elevation Gain/Loss	700'/700'
Hiking Time	2½ hours (round trip)
Optional Maps	USGS 7.5-min *Mint Canyon, San Fernando*
Best Times	All year
Agency	PCNA
Difficulty	★★

Barely 10 minutes drive from northern San Fernando Valley and the sprawling suburban city of Santa Clarita, Placerita Canyon Natural Area nestles comfortably at the foot of one of the more verdant slopes of the San Gabriel Mountains. The park's wild backcountry sector (the subject of this hike, as described) is complemented by a very civilized nature center—the envy of many a national park—housing exhibits on local history, pre-history, geology, plants, and wildlife.

Placerita Canyon's fascinating history is highlighted by the discovery of gold there in 1842. That event, which touched off California's first (and relatively trivial) gold rush, predated by six years John Marshall's famous discovery of gold at Sutter's Mill in Northern California. By the 1950s, Placerita Canyon had become one of the more popular generic Western site locations used by Hollywood's movie makers and early television producers. The canyon was eventually acquired as parkland—first by the state, then by the county.

Take the Placerita Canyon exit from Antelope Valley Freeway (Highway 14) at Newhall, and drive east 1.5 miles to reach the park's main gate, open 9 a.m. to 5 p.m. Nearby lie the nature center and a paved path leading under Placerita Canyon Road to the "Oak of the Golden Dream," the exact site (according to legend) where gold was discovered in 1842 by a herdsman pulling up wild onions for his after-siesta meal.

To start the somewhat ambitious hike described here, head east from the nature center on the Placerita Canyon Trail. The canyon's melodious creek flows decently about half the year (winter and spring), caressing the ears with white noise that echoes from the canyon walls. During the fall, when the creek may be bone-dry, you make your own noise instead by crunching through the crispy leaf litter of sycamore and live oak. Down by the grassy banks are wild blackberry vines, lots of willows, and occasionally cottonwood and alder trees.

Soaring canyon walls ahead tell the story of thousands of years of natural erosion, as well as the destructive effects of hydraulic mining, which involved aiming high-pressure water hoses at hillsides to loosen and wash away ores. Used extensively in Northern California during the big Gold Rush, "hydraulicking" was finally banned in 1884 after catastrophic damages to waterways and farms downstream. At Placerita Canyon, several hundred thousand dollars worth of gold were ultimately recovered, but at considerable cost, effort, and general messiness.

After about 1 mile you reach a split. Go either way; the two paths join later.

After the two paths converge, you reach the scant remains of some early-20th-Century cottages hand-built by settler Frank Walker, his wife, and some of his 12 children. The area is now used as a group campground; drinking water is available.

Our way lies ahead, along the Waterfall Trail, which leads into Los Pinetos Canyon. Don't confuse this trail with the better-traveled Los Pinetos Trail on the right. The Waterfall Trail momentarily slants upward along the canyon's steep west wall, then drops onto the canyon's sunny flood plain. Presently you bear right into a narrow ravine (Los Pinetos Canyon), avoiding a wider tributary bending left (east).

Continue, now on an ill-defined path, past and sometimes over water-polished, meta-morphic rock. Live oaks and bigcone Douglas-firs cling to the slopes above, and a few bigleaf maples grace the canyon bottom. About 0.2 mile after the first fork in the canyon, there's a second fork. Go right and continue 50 yards to a sublime little grotto, cool and dark except when the sun passes almost straight overhead, and a small waterfall. As you listen to water dashing or dribbling down the chute, enjoy the serenity of this private place and contemplate that it lies only 3 miles—but a world away—from the creeping boundary of the L.A. metropolis. Return the way you came.

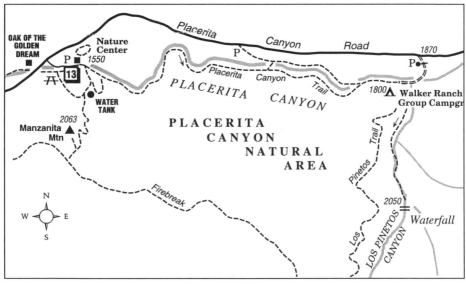

PLACERITA CANYON

TRIP 14

Verdugo Mountains, South End Loop

Location	Glendale
Highlights	Incomparable city and regional views
Distance	5.5 miles
Total Elevation Gain/Loss	1500'/1500'
Hiking Time	3½ hours
Optional Maps	USGS 7.5-min *Pasadena, Burbank*
Best Times	November through May
Difficulty	★★★

The Verdugo Mountains stand as a remarkable island of undeveloped land—a haven for wildlife such as deer and coyotes—completely encircled by an urbanized domain. Public access to the network of trails and fire roads on the mountain is by foot, horse, or mountain bike—great news if you're looking for a quick escape from the ubiquitous automobile and the pressures of city life.

Along the south crest of the Verdugos, your gaze takes in the San Gabriel Mountains, much of the L.A. megalopolis, and even the ocean on occasion. Do this trip late in the day if you want to enjoy both a spectacular sunset and a blaze of lights after twilight fades. At best, try this on any cloud-free, smog-free day that falls within two weeks on either side of the winter solstice (December 21). During that period, the sun sets on the flat ocean horizon behind Santa Monica Bay. At other times of year, the sun's sinking path is likely to intersect the coastal mountains. The seemingly strange fact of the sun setting over land most of the year is a consequence of the east-west orientation of California's coastline in the first miles "up-coast" from Los Angeles.

You'll find the starting point for this hike on Beaudry Boulevard, 0.4 mile west of Country Club Drive in the city of Glendale (not to be confused with Country Club Drive in nearby Burbank). Park on the street, walk up a paved segment of fire road, bypass a vehicle gate, and continue on dirt past a debris basin to where the fire road splits (0.3 mile). Choose for your way the shadier but less viewful right branch, Beaudry North Fire Road. You'll return to this junction by way of the left branch, the Beaudry South Fire Road. About halfway up the north road you'll come to a trickling spring and a water tank nestled in a shady ravine, a good place for a breather.

When you reach the summit ridge (2.3 miles), turn sharply left on Verdugo Fire Road and continue climbing another 0.4 mile toward a cluster of brightly painted radio towers atop a 2656-foot bump—the highest point along this hike. From the towers, continue south along the ridge 0.6 mile to a road junction at 2420 feet. The right branch descends to Sunshine Drive in Glendale; you take the left branch and return along an east ridge to the split just above the debris basin.

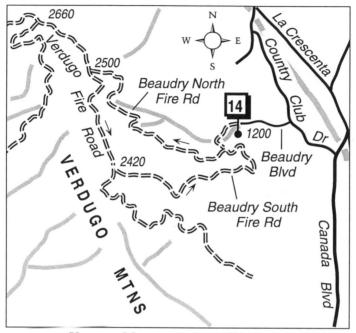

VERDUGO MOUNTAINS, SOUTH END LOOP

TRIP 15
Trail Canyon Falls

Location	San Gabriel Mountains, near Sunland
Highlights	Lively stream and waterfall (in the wet season)
Distance	3.0 miles round trip
Total Elevation Gain/Loss	700'/700'
Hiking Time	1½ hours (round trip)
Optional Map	USGS 7.5-min *Sunland*
Best Times	December through May
Agency	ANF/TD
Difficulty	★★

Rising starkly behind the San Fernando and La Crescenta valley communities of Sylmar, San Fernando, Sunland and Tujunga, the western ridges of the San Gabriel Mountains have a lean and hungry look. Yet there is a gentler, mostly hidden side, to these mountains, too. That's what you'll discover along Trail Canyon, where riparian glens and pocket forests of oak squeeze between canyon walls punctuated by eroding, angular rock outcrops and blanketed by tough chaparral.

When soaking rains come, Trail Canyon's normally indolent flow becomes a lively torrent. After tumbling through miles of rockbound constrictions and sliding across many gently inclined declivities, the water comes to the lip of a real precipice. There the bubbly mixture momentarily attains weightlessness during a free-fall of about 30 feet. If you can manage to ignore the vastly smaller scale of this spectacle, you might easily imagine yourself in Yosemite Valley during spring runoff.

The falls in Trail Canyon are easy to approach, except during the most intense flooding, when the several fords you must cross on the way may be dangerously deep. Sturdy footwear (which is not needed during the drier summer months) may be helpful at some of the deeper crossings in high water.

To reach the trailhead, drive 5 miles up Big Tujunga Canyon Road from Sunland to a dirt road on the left, indicated by a sign reading TRAIL CANYON TRAIL. Drive 0.2 mile uphill on this road to a fork, go right, and

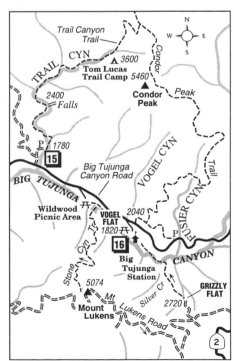

TRAIL CANYON FALLS & MOUNT LUKENS-
GRIZZLY FLAT LOOP

descend 0.2 mile to an oak-shaded parking area on the right, just above Trail Canyon's melodious creek. Continue up the same road on foot, passing a few cabins and fording the creek for the first time. The now-very-deteriorated road goes on to follow an east tributary for a while, doubles back, contours around a ridge, and drops into Trail Canyon again (0.6 mile). The road ends there, and you continue up-canyon on a footpath. The path clings to the banks for 0.5 mile, crossing the stream several times, and then climbs the west wall to avoid a narrow, alder-choked section of the canyon. The falls come into view as you round a sharp bend about 1.5 miles from the parking area.

Although many people have obviously done so, it's difficult and dangerous to slide down from the trail to the base of the falls. The falls can also be reached by bushwhacking up the canyon from the point where the trail begins its ascent of the west wall; this is fun scrambling during low water, hazardous during high water.

Past the falls, Trail Canyon Trail continues upstream to cozy Tom Lucas Trail Camp (4 miles from the start) and onward to a junction with the Condor Peak Trail. Ambitious hikers and backpackers can set their sights on a significant high point, Condor Peak, straightforwardly reached by means of a short, steep scramble from the Condor Peak Trail. One or more of the Channel Islands, floating above the coastal haze or smog, are frequently seen from Condor Peak's windswept summit.

Trail Canyon Falls

Mount Lukens-Grizzly Flat Loop

Location	San Gabriel Mountains, near Sunland
Highlights	Urban, mountain, and ocean vistas
Distance	12.2 miles
Total Elevation Gain/Loss	3400'/3400'
Hiking Time	8 hours
Recommended Map	USGS 7.5-min *Condor Peak*
Best Times	October through May
Agency	ANF/TD
Difficulty	★★★★

This all-day adventure lets you explore the massive flanks and the top of Mount Lukens, the highest elevation in the city limits of Los Angeles. After a grueling climb up the Stone Canyon Trail, you circle back by way of a long, gradually descending route that passes through secluded Grizzly Flat. The hike feels best on a cool day, but beware of periods following heavy rain: the trip begins and ends with crossings of Big Tujunga creek, which can be hazardous in high water. If you're in doubt, call the Forest Service to check on flood conditions.

From Sunland, drive up Big Tujunga Canyon Road 7 miles to the Vogel Flat Picnic Area/Big Tujunga Station turnoff on the right (south side of road). Drive to the bottom of the hill, turn right, and park at the Vogel Flat parking lot, open from 8 a.m. to 10 p.m.

On foot, head west down a narrow, paved road (private, but with public easement) through the cabin community of Stonyvale. When the pavement ends after 0.7 mile, continue on dirt for another ¼ mile or so. Choose a safe place to ford Big Tujunga creek, wade across, and find the Stone Canyon Trail on the far bank. From afar you can spot this trail going straight up the sloping terrace just left (east) of Stone Canyon's wide, boulder-filled mouth. Once on the terrace, settle into a pace that will allow you to persevere over the next 3 miles and 3200 feet of vertical ascent.

From the vantage point of the first switchback, you can look down on the thousands of storm-tossed granitic boulders filling Stone Canyon from wall to wall. Although the boulders are frozen in place, you can almost sense their movement over geologic time. Indeed, floods continue to reshape this canyon and many others in the San Gabriels during every major deluge.

Ahead, you twist and turn along precipitous slopes covered by a thick blanket of chaparral. At or near ground level, a profusion of ferns, mosses, and herbaceous plants forms its own pygmy understory.

The dizzying view encompasses a long, obviously linear stretch of Big Tujunga Canyon. This segment of the canyon is underlain by the San Gabriel Fault and its offshoot, the Sierra Madre Fault. The latter fault splits from the former near Vogel Flat and continues southeast past Grizzly Flat, following a course roughly coincident with the final leg of our loop hike. According to current understanding, the San Gabriel Fault is presently inactive and not likely to be the cause of major movement or earthquakes in the foreseeable future. The impressive depth of Big Tujunga Canyon and the steepness of its walls are due primarily to stream cutting following uplift of the whole mountain range.

Between 1.8 and 2.6 miles (from the start), the trail hovers above an unnamed canyon to the east, nearly equal in drainage to Stone Canyon, but very steep and narrow. Down below you can often hear, and barely glimpse, an inaccessible waterfall. Long and short switchback segments take you rapidly higher to a steep, bulldozed track leading to the bald summit ridge of Mt. Lukens. Go 0.5 mile farther (connecting with Mt. Lukens Road along the way) to reach the highest point on the ridge (4.2 miles), which is occupied by several antenna structures. Technically the summit lies within the city limit of Los Angeles, and is the highest point in any incorporated city in the county. Glendale almost claims this honor, as its corporate limit reaches within 300 yards of the summit. Both cities encompass parts of the Angeles National Forest. The views of the city below and the ocean in the distance can be fabulous—but only when strong winds evict the nearly ever-present smog from the L.A. basin and valleys below.

The remaining two-thirds of the hike is almost entirely downhill—a little monotonous at times, but not too jarring on the knees. Follow Mt. Lukens Road southeast down the main ridge, keeping left at the next two road junctions. At 7.2 miles you begin descending toward a saddle. At the four-way junction there (9.0 miles), choose the road to the far left and continue on a zigzag course past beautiful oaks and bay laurels to Grizzly Flat (10.0 miles), where planted pines fill most of a terrace sloping down to a ravine called Vasquez Creek. The leftmost of several diverging roads on the flat leads to a water tank. Behind that you'll find a remnant of the old Dark Canyon Trail from Angeles Crest Highway to Big Tujunga Canyon—roughly the escape route used by the infamous outlaw Tibercio Vasquez and his unsuccessful pursuers during a hot chase over a century ago.

From the water tank, follow the maintained trail down to a creek bedecked with woodwardia fern and wild strawberry. You then descend moderately through oak forest, descend sharply down a ridge overlooking the pitlike gorge of Silver Creek, and finally reach a wildflower-dotted bench along Big Tujunga creek. Wild fruit trees and eucalyptus there silently speak of former homesteads. Head downstream, wading or stepping across the creek five times in the next mile, to reach Stonyvale Picnic Area, a scant 1/4 mile from your car at Vogel Flat.

TRIP 17
Down the Arroyo Seco

Location	San Gabriel Mountains, above Pasadena
Highlights	Sylvan glens and a sparkling stream
Distance	10.0 miles
Total Elevation Gain/Loss	700'/2850'
Hiking Time	5 hours
Optional Maps	USGS 7.5-min *Condor Peak, Pasadena*
Best Times	October through June
Agency	ANF/ASD
Difficulty	★★★

The Spanish colonists who christened Arroyo Seco ("dry creek") evidently observed only its lower end—a hot, boulder-strewn wash emptying into the Los Angeles River. Upstream, inside the confines of the San Gabriels, Arroyo Seco is a scenic treasure—all the more astounding when you consider that its exquisite sylvan glens and sparkling brook lie just 12-15 miles from L.A.'s city center. If you haven't yet been freed from the notion that Los Angeles is nothing but a seething megalopolis, walk down the canyon of the Arroyo Seco. You'll be convinced otherwise.

A botanist's and wildflower seeker's dream, the canyon features generous growths of canyon live oak, western sycamore, California bay, white alder, bigleaf maple, bigcone Douglas-fir, and arroyo willow. A quick census one spring day (in a dry year, no less) yielded for me the following blooming plants: golden yarrow, prickly phlox, western wallflower, Indian pink, live-forever, wild pea, deerweed, bush lupine, Spanish broom, baby-blue-eyes, yerba santa, phacelia, chia, black sage, bush poppy, California buckwheat, shooting star, western clematis, Indian paintbrush, sticky monkey flower, scarlet bugler, and purple nightshade.

You'll be traveling the westernmost leg of the Gabrielino Trail, one of four routes in Angeles National Forest specially designated as "National Recreation Trails." The Arroyo Seco stretch of the Gabrielino Trail receives considerable use—and also a lot of much-needed maintenance—by mountain-bike club members. The upper and middle portions, which are in places narrow with steep drops to one side, are challenging even for expert riders, although not at all hard for hikers. The lower end consists of remnants of an old road built as far up the canyon as the Oak Wilde resort (now Oakwilde Picnic Area) in the 1920s.

Several rest stops and picnic sites line the trail's lower half, making this a great route for a leisurely saunter. Most of these stops are located on the sites of early tourist camps or cabins erected in the early 1900s. Virtually all the structures were either destroyed by flooding in 1938 or removed through condemnation proceedings (based on water and flood-control needs) in the '20s, '30s, and '40s. Carry along whatever drinking water you'll need for the duration of the trip; there may be piped water at Paul Little Picnic Area, but don't count on it.

You'll start your hike from a parking lot on Angeles Crest Highway (mile 34.2; 10 miles from I-210 at La Canada). You'll finish, 10 miles later, at the corner of Windsor Avenue and Ventura Street, a mile north of Interstate 210, opposite the sprawling California Institute of Technology/Jet Propulsion Laboratory. Some kind of car-shuttle or drop-off-and-pick-up transportation arrangement is obviously required for this long one-way trip.

From Angeles Crest Highway, descend on narrow pavement for 0.4 mile to the site of Switzer Picnic Area, a once-popular site recently closed to public use as a budget-cutting measure. Bearing right (west), pick up the signed Gabrielino Trail and make your way down along the alder-shaded stream. Soon nothing but the clear-flowing stream and rustling leaves disturb the silence. Remnants of an old paved road are occasionally underfoot. In a couple of spots you ford the stream by boulder-hopping—no problem except after heavy rain.

One mile down the canyon you come upon the foundation remnants of Switzer's Camp—now occupied by a trail campground. Established in 1884, the camp became the San Gabriels' premier wilderness resort in the early 1900s, patronized by Hollywood celebrities as well as anyone who had the gumption to hike or ride a burro up the tortuous Arroyo Seco trail from Pasadena. After the construction of Angeles Crest Highway in the early '30s and a severe flood in the 1938, the resort lost its appeal. It was finally razed in the late '50s.

Walk down to a fork in the trail 0.2 mile beyond the trail camp. You will probably hear, if not clearly see, the 50-foot cascade known as Switzer Falls, to the west. Our way continues on the right fork (Gabrielino Trail), which now begins a mile-long traverse through chaparral. This less-than-perfectly-scenic stretch avoids a narrow, twisting trench called Royal Gorge, through which the Arroyo Seco stream tumbles and sometimes abruptly drops.

At 2.7 miles (from the start) the trail joins a shady tributary of Long Canyon, and later Long Canyon itself, replete with a trickling stream. Alongside the trail you'll discover at least five kinds of ferns, plus mosses, poison oak, and Humboldt lilies (in bloom during early summer).

At 3.8 miles, the waters of Long Canyon swish down through a sculpted grotto to join Arroyo Seco. The trail descends to Arroyo Seco canyon's narrow floor and stays there, crossing and recrossing many times over the next few miles. The stretch from Long Canyon to Oakwilde Picnic Area (4.9 miles) is perhaps the most gorgeous of all, flanked by soaring walls and dappled with shade cast by the ever-present alders. Bigleaf maples put on a great show here in November, their bright yellow leaves boldly contrasting with the earthy greens, grays, and browns of the canyon's dimly lit bottom.

Beyond Oakwilde Picnic Area (4.9 miles) the canyon widens a bit and the trail assumes a more gentle gradient. There's a sharp climb at 5.7 miles—to bypass the large Brown Canyon Debris Dam—then a long trek out to the mouth of the canyon with no further significant climbing. Toward the end, the trail becomes a dirt road, and finally a paved service road, complete with bridged crossings of the Arroyo Seco (purists can follow a narrow, equestrian trail alongside). During the last couple of miles you're likely to run into lots of cyclists, joggers, parents pushing strollers, and even skateboarders.

Gabrielino Trail in Arroyo Seco

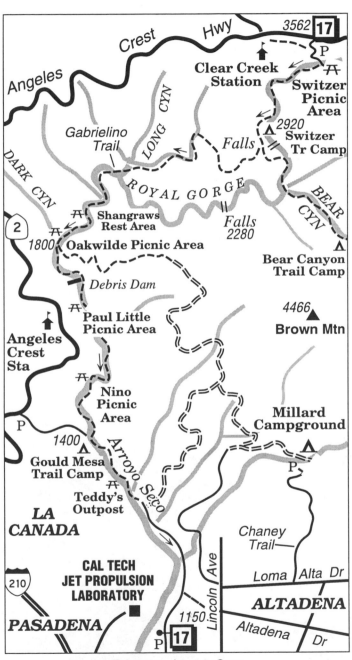

DOWN THE ARROYO SECO

TRIP 18

Mount Lowe

Location	San Gabriel Mountains, above Pasadena
Highlights	Mountain, city, and ocean views
Distance	3.2 miles round trip
Total Elevation Gain/Loss	500'/500'
Hiking Time	1½ hours (round trip)
Optional Map	USGS 7.5-min *Mount Wilson*
Best Times	All year
Agency	ANF/ASD
Difficulty	★★

Late in the year, when the smog lightens, but temperatures still hover within a moderate register, come up to Mt. Lowe to toast the setting sun. You can sit on an old bench, pour the champagne, and watch Old Sol sink into Santa Monica Bay.

To reach the starting point from I-210 at La Canada, drive up Angeles Crest Highway for 14 miles to Red Box Divide and turn right on Mt. Wilson Road. Proceed 2.4 miles to a large roadside parking area at unmarked

Eaton Saddle. Walk past the gate on the west side and proceed up the dirt road (Mt. Lowe fire road) that carves its way under the precipitous south face of San Gabriel Peak.

As you approach a short tunnel (0.3 mile) dating from 1942, look for the remnants of a former cliff-hanging trail to the left of the tunnel's east entrance. At Markham Saddle (0.5 mile) the fire road starts to descend slightly. Don't continue on the

San Gabriel Valley at dawn from Mt. Lowe

road. Instead, find the unmarked Mt. Lowe Trail on the left (south). On it, you contour southwest above the fire road for about 0.6 mile, and then start climbing across the east flank of Mt. Lowe without much change of direction.

At 1.3 miles, make a sharp right turn. Proceed 0.2 mile uphill, then go left on a short spur trail to Mt. Lowe's barren summit. Mt. Lowe was the proposed upper terminus for Professor Thaddeus Lowe's famed scenic railway (see Trip 20). Funding ran out, however, and tracks were never laid

higher than Ye Alpine Tavern, 1200 feet below. During the railway's heyday in the early 1900s, thousands disembarked at the tavern and tramped Mt. Lowe's east- and west-side trails for world-class views of the basin and the surrounding mountains. Some reminders of that era remain on the summit of Mt. Lowe and along some of the trails: volunteers have repainted, relettered, and returned to their proper places some the many sighting tubes that helped the early tourists familiarize themselves with the surrounding geography.

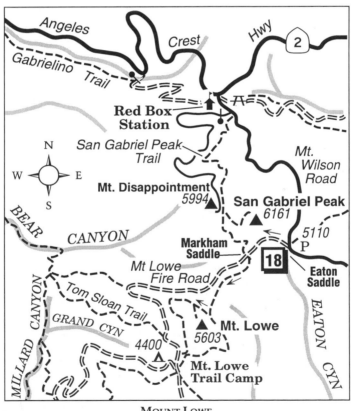

MOUNT LOWE

TRIP 19
Millard Canyon

Location	San Gabriel Mountains, above Pasadena
Highlights	Beautiful canyon stream; historical interest
Distance	6.0 miles
Total Elevation Gain/Loss	1600'/1600'
Hiking Time	3½ hours
Optional Map	USGS 7.5-min *Pasadena*
Best Times	October through June
Agency	ANF/ASD
Difficulty	★★★

Millard Canyon's happily splashing stream, presided over by oaks, alders, maples, and bigcone Douglas-firs, is the main attraction on this hike. But you can also do a little snooping around the site of the Dawn Mine, one of the more promising gold prospects in the San Gabriels, worked intermittently from 1895 until the early '50s.

An early start is emphatically recommended. That way you'll take advantage of shade during the climbing phase of the hike, and you'll be assured of finding a place to park your car at the trailhead (which is as popular with mountain bikers as with hikers).

From Loma Alta Drive in Altadena, drive up the Chaney Trail (past a locked gate that swings open at 6 a.m.) to the top of Sunset Ridge, where there's parking by the roadside. Walk east on the gated, paved Sunset Ridge fire road. After about 100 yards, you pass a foot trail on the left leading down to Millard Campground. Continue another 300 yards to a second foot trail on the left (Sunset Ridge Trail). Take it. On it you contour north and east along Millard Canyon's south wall, passing above a sometimes-vociferous 50-foot waterfall. You begin climbing in earnest at about 0.9 mile and soon reach a trail fork. The left branch (your return route) goes down 100 yards past a private cabin to the canyon bot-

tom. You go right, uphill. Switchbacks long and short take you farther up along the pleasantly shaded canyon wall to an intersection with Sunset Ridge fire road (2.4 miles), just below a rocky knob called Cape of Good Hope.

Turn left on the fire road, and walk past Cape of Good Hope. The trail to Echo Mountain, intersecting on the right, and the fire road ahead are both part of the original Mt. Lowe Railway bed (see Trip 20)—now a self-guiding historical trail. Continue your ascent on the fire road/railway bed to post #4 on the left (2.9 miles). There you'll find a trail descending to Dawn Mine in Millard Canyon. This is a recently reworked but primitive version of the mule path once used to haul ore from the mine to the railway above. On the way down you may encounter a dicey passage or two across loose talus.

After reaching the gloomy canyon bottom (3.6 miles), the trail goes upstream along the east bank for about 100 yards to the long-abandoned Dawn Mine, perched on the west-side slope. The gaping entrance to the lower shaft may seem inviting to explore, but it is unwise to enter it.

From the mine, head down-canyon past crystalline mini-pools, the flotsam and jetsam of the mining days, and storm-tossed boulders. Much of the original trail in the canyon has been washed away, but a new generation of hikers has beaten down a pretty good semblance of a path. About ½ mile below the mine a wider area of the canyon, with a high and dry terrace on the right, could be used as a wilderness campsite for backpackers.

After you swing around an abrupt bend to the right, the canyon becomes dark and gloomy once again. After another 0.5 mile you come to your outbound trail climbing up to the left. Stay right and hook up with the Sunset Ridge Trail, which will take you back to the Sunset Ridge fire road and your car.

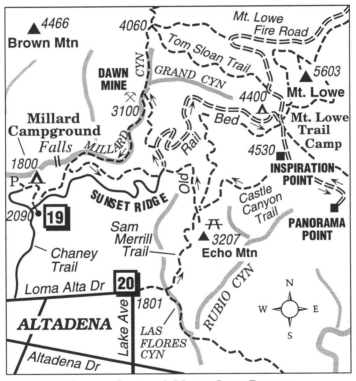

MILLARD CANYON & MOUNT LOWE RAILWAY

TRIP 20
Mount Lowe Railway

Location	San Gabriel Mountains, above Pasadena
Highlights	Grand vistas; historical interest
Distance	11.2 miles
Total Elevation Gain/Loss	2800'/2800'
Hiking Time	6 hours
Optional Maps	USGS 7.5-min *Mount Wilson, Pasadena*
Best Times	October through May
Agency	ANF/ASD
Difficulty	★★★

An engineering marvel when built in the 1890s, the Mt. Lowe Railway has lived a checkered past full of both glory and destruction. Before its final abandonment in the mid-'30s, the line carried over 3 million passengers—virtually all of them tourists. Unheard of by millions of Southland newcomers today, the railway was for many years the most popular outdoor attraction in Southern California.

Today hikers are taking a new interest in the old road bed; the Rails-to-Trails Conservancy (which promotes the conversion of abandoned rail corridors into recreation trails) ranked the Mt. Lowe Railway as one of the nation's 12 most scenic and historically significant recycled rail lines.

The line consisted of three stages, of which almost nothing remains today. Passengers rode a trolley from Altadena into lower Rubio Canyon, then boarded a steeply inclined cable railway which took them 1300 feet higher to Echo Mountain, where two hotels, a number of small tourist attractions, and an observatory stood. At Echo Mountain, non-acrophobic passengers hopped onto the third phase, a mountain trolley that climbed another 1200 vertical feet along airy slopes to the end of the line—Ye Alpine Tavern (later Mt. Lowe Tavern, on whose ruins stands today's Mt. Lowe Trail Camp).

The Forest Service and volunteers have put together a self-guiding trail, featuring ten markers fashioned from railroad rails, along the route of the mountain trolley. The middle portion of the old railway bed can be reached by hiking either the paved road or the trail coming up from the Chaney Trail above Millard Canyon. The more direct, easier, and more exciting way to reach Station 1 at Echo Mountain, however, is to go by way of the Sam Merrill Trail from Altadena.

The Sam Merrill trailhead lies on the grounds of the long-demolished Cobb Estate, at the north end of Lake Avenue in Altadena. Walk east past the stone pillars at the entrance and continue 150 yards on a narrow, blacktop driveway. The driveway bends left, but you keep walking straight (east). Soon you come to a water fountain on the rim of Las Flores Canyon and a sign indicating the start of the Sam Merrill Trail. This trail goes left over the top of a small debris dam and begins a switchback ascent of Las Flores Canyon's precipitous east wall, while another trail (the Altadena Crest equestrian trail) veers to the right, down the canyon.

Inspired by the fabulous views (assuming you're doing this early on one of L.A.'s clear winter days), the 2.5 miles of steady ascent on the Sam Merrill Trail may seem to go rather quickly. Turn right at the top of the trail and walk south over to Echo Mountain, which is more like the shoulder of a ridge. There you'll find a historical plaque and some picnic tables near a grove of incense cedars and bigleaf maples. Poke around and you'll find many foundation ruins and piles of concrete rubble. An old "bullwheel" and cables for the incline railway were thoughtfully left behind after the Forest Service cleared away what remained of the buildings here in the '50s and '60s. After visiting Echo Mountain, you'll go north on the signed Echo Mountain Trail, where you'll walk over railroad ties still imbedded in the ground.

Since the self-guiding brochure for the rail bed ahead is not always available from the Forest Service, I'll briefly summarize the stops. Numbers in parentheses refer to hiking mileage starting from Echo Mountain.

Station 1 (0.0) Echo Mountain. This was known as the White City during its brief heyday in the late 1890s, but most of its tourist facilities were destroyed by fire or windstorms in the first decade of the 1900s. The mountain remained a transfer point for passengers until the mid-'30s.

Station 2 (0.5) View of Circular Bridge. You can't see it from here, but passengers at this point first noticed the 400'-diameter circular bridge (Station 6) jutting from the slope above. As you walk on ahead, you'll notice the many concrete footings that supported trestles bridging the side ravines of Las Flores Canyon.

Station 3 (0.8) Cape of Good Hope. You're now at the junction of the Echo Mountain Trail and Sunset Ridge fire road. The tracks swung in a 200° arc around the rocky promontory just west—Cape of Good Hope. (Walk around the Cape, if you like, to get a feel for the experience.) North of this dizzying passage, riders were treated to the longest stretch of straight track—only 225 feet long. The entire original line from Echo Mountain to Ye Alpine Tavern had 127 curves and 114 straight sections.

Station 4 (1.0) Dawn Station/Devil's Slide. Dawn Mine lies below in Millard Canyon. Gold-bearing ore, packed up by mules from the canyon bottom, was loaded onto the train here. Ahead lay a treacherous stretch of crumbling granite, the Devil's Slide, which was eventually bridged by a trestle.

Los Angeles on a clear day from the Sam Merrill Trail

(The current fire road has been shored up with much new concrete, and cement-lined spillways seem to do a good job of carrying away flood debris.)

Station 5 (1.2) Horseshoe Curve. Just beyond this station, Horseshoe Curve enabled the railway to gain elevation above Millard Canyon. The grade just beyond Horseshoe Curve was 7 percent—steepest on the mountain segment of the line.

Station 6 (1.6) Circular Bridge. An engineering accomplishment of worldwide fame, the Circular Bridge carried startled passengers into midair over the upper walls of Las Flores Canyon. Look for the concrete supports of this bridge down along the chaparral-covered slopes to the right.

Station 7 (2.0) Horseshoe Curve Overview. Passengers here looked down on Horseshoe Curve, and could also see all three levels of steep, twisting track climbing the east wall of Millard Canyon.

Station 8 (2.4) Granite Gate. A narrow slot carefully blasted out of solid granite on a sheer north-facing slope, Granite Gate took 8 months to cut. Look for the electric wire support dangling from the rock above.

Station 9 (3.4) Ye Alpine Tavern. The tavern, which later became a fancy hotel, was located at Crystal Springs, the source that still provides water (which now requires purification) for backpackers staying overnight at today's Mt. Lowe Trail Camp. The rails never got farther than here, although it was hoped they would one day reach the summit of Mt. Lowe, 1200 feet higher.

Station 10 (3.9) Inspiration Point. From Ye Alpine Tavern, tourists could saunter over to Inspiration Point along part of the never-finished rail extension to Mt. Lowe. Sighting tubes (still in place there) helped visitors locate places of interest below.

Inspiration Point is the last station on the self-guiding trail. The fastest and easiest way to return is by way of the Castle Canyon Trail, which descends directly below Inspiration Point. After 2 miles you'll arrive back on the old railway grade just north of Echo Mountain. Retrace your steps on the Sam Merrill Trail.

TRIP 21

Eaton Canyon

Location	Altadena
Highlights	Lessons in fire ecology; waterfall
Distance	3.4 miles round trip (to waterfall)
Total Elevation Gain/Loss	400'/400'
Hiking Time	1½ hours (round trip)
Optional Map	USGS 7.5-min *Mount Wilson*
Best Times	All year
Agency	ECCP
Difficulty	★★

On October 27, 1993, the floor of Eaton Canyon (along with 118 homes in surrounding neighborhoods) was reduced to white ash and black cinders by a devastating wildfire. By the following spring, which came on the heels of a wetter-than-average rainy season, visitors to the 184-acre Eaton Canyon County Park could only gasp in wonder as they beheld millions of wildflowers, swaying in the breeze, on the canyon floor. It is a California truism that from what seems the worst possible disaster, new life—and hope—can emerge triumphantly.

The brash, fire-following wildflowers will diminish in number with every passing season. The oaks and chaparral shrubbery that characterized the canyon rim before the fire will eventually regenerate—at least until the next fire, which will surely come, perhaps within a few years, or perhaps within a few decades.

Upstream and just outside the park, where the waters of Eaton Canyon have carved a raw groove in the San Gabriel Mountains, you'll discover Eaton Canyon Falls. Impressive only during the wetter half of the year, the falls possesses, as John Muir once put it, "a low sweet voice, singing like a bird." Unfortunately, this all-too-easily-reached grotto has suffered from years of vandalism. The graffiti sprayed on the rock walls is hard to ignore.

But the falls are worth visiting, especially in the aftermath of a larger winter storm, if only to witness the power of large volumes of falling water.

Park in the lot beyond the nature center at Eaton Canyon County Park, whose entrance is on Altadena Drive just north of New York Drive in Altadena. Follow the Eaton Canyon Trail across the cobbled

Eaton Canyon Falls

flood plain, or stream. Beyond, the trail sticks to an elevated stream terrace for a mile, passing some live-oak woods. At 0.5 mile you pass a horse trail going up a draw to the right, and at 1.1 miles you rise to meet the Mt. Wilson Toll Road bridge over Eaton Canyon. Cross to the west end of the bridge, descend on the upstream side, and then make your way up the trailless canyon (don't do this if the stream is too lively and dangerous to ford). You'll skip across rocks in the stream several times, or resort to wading. Except for a line of alders along part of the stream and some live oaks on benches just above the reach of floods, the canyon bottom and the precipitous walls are desolate and desertlike.

After ½ mile of canyon-bottom travel, you come to the falls, where the water slides and then free-falls a total of about 35 vertical feet down a narrow chute in the bedrock.

If you prefer, you can shorten the walk to the falls by starting from the lower gate of Mt. Wilson Toll Road on Pinecrest Drive; or by parking in a dirt lot just east of Altadena Drive across from Roosevelt Avenue, and descending a path leading to Eaton Canyon's floor and the trail on the terrace, 0.5 mile south of the toll-road bridge.

EATON CANYON

TRIP 22
Big Santa Anita Loop

Location	San Gabriel Mountains, above Arcadia
Highlights	Sparkling streams; botanical and historical interest
Distance	9.4 miles
Total Elevation Gain/Loss	2100'/2100'
Hiking Time	5½ hours
Optional Map	USGS 7.5-min *Mount Wilson*
Best Times	October through June
Agency	ANF/ASD
Difficulty	★★★

In the lush, shady recesses of Big Santa Anita Canyon and its tributary, Winter Creek, you can easily lose all sight and sense of the hundreds of square miles of dense metropolis, and the millions of people, that lie just over the ridge to the south. With easy access from the San Gabriel Valley by city street and mountain road, you can be strolling along a fern-lined path less than half an hour after leaving the freeway traffic behind.

Chantry Flat, popular as a drive-up destination as well as the trailhead for Big Santa Anita, perches high above the Los Angeles Basin in the fortresslike folds of the San Gabriel Mountains (follow Santa Anita Avenue north from Arcadia to get there). There you'll find a ranger station, a picnic ground, a mom-and-pop refreshment stand, and an old-fashioned freight business—the last pack station operating year round in California. Most every day, horses, mules and burros carry supplies and building materials from the station down into canyon bottom, where an anachronistic cabin community has survived since the early 1900s.

In this scenic loop trip from Chantry Flat, you'll climb by way of the Gabrielino Trail to historic Sturtevant Camp, and return by way of the Mt. Zion and Upper Winter Creek trails. Do it in a day, or take your time on an overnight backpacking trip, with a stay

at Spruce Grove Trail Camp. The trail camp is a popular one, so plan to get there early to secure a spot on the weekend—or go on a weekday.

From the south edge of the lower parking lot at Chantry Flat, hike the first, paved segment of the Gabrielino Trail down to the confluence of Winter Creek and Big Santa Anita Canyon (0.6 mile). Pavement ends at a metal bridge spanning Winter Creek. Pass the restrooms and continue up alder-lined Big Santa Anita Canyon on a wide road bed following the left bank. Edging alongside a number of small cabins, the deteriorating road soon assumes the proportions of a foot trail.

At 1.4 miles, amidst a beautiful oak woodland, you come to a 4-way junction of trails. The right branch goes up-canyon to the base of 50-foot-high Sturtevant Falls, a worthy side trip during the wet season. The middle and left branches join again about a mile upstream. The left, upper trail is recommended for horses. Take the middle (lower) trail—the more scenic and exciting alternative—unless you fear heights. The lower trail slices across a sheer wall above the falls and continues through a veritable fairyland of miniature cascades and crystalline pools bedecked with giant chain ferns.

A half mile past the reconvergence of the upper and lower trails, you come upon

In the canyon below Spruce Grove

Cascade Picnic Area (2.8 miles—tables and restrooms here), named for a smooth chute in the stream bottom just below. Press on past a hulking crib dam (flood check dam) to reach Spruce Grove Trail Camp, 3.5 miles, named for the bigcone Douglas-fir (bigcone spruce) trees that attain truly inspiring proportions hereabouts.

A little higher, at a fork, the Gabrielino Trail goes right. You go left on the signed Sturtevant Trail. After only 0.1 mile, Sturtevant Camp comes into view. This is both the oldest (1893) and the only remaining resort in the Big Santa Anita drainage. Run by the Methodist Church as a retreat (but available to other groups by reservation), the camp remains accessible only by foot trail. All supplies are packed in from Chantry Flat on the backs of pack animals, not unlike a century ago.

Next, you cross above a crib dam to the opposite side of the creek from the camp, continue another 0.1 mile, and look for stone steps rising on the left—the beginning of the Mt. Zion Trail (3.9 miles). This restored version of the original trail to Sturtevant Camp (reconstructed in the late '70s and early '80s) winds delightfully upward across a ravine and then along timber-shaded, north-facing slopes.

When the trail crests at a notch just northwest of Mt. Zion, take the short side path up through manzanita and ceanothus to the summit, where a broad if somewhat

unremarkable view can be had of surrounding ridges and a small slice of the San Gabriel Valley.

Return to the main trail and begin a long, switchback descent (1000 feet of elevation loss in about 1.5 miles) down the dry, north canyon wall of Winter Creek—a sweaty affair if the day is sunny and warm. At the foot of this stretch you reach the cool canyon bottom and a T-intersection with the Winter Creek Trail (6.7 miles), lying just above Hoegees Trail Camp. Turn right, going upstream momentarily, follow the trail across the creek, and climb to the next trail junction. Bear left on the Upper Winter Creek Trail and complete the remaining 2.6 miles of easy, mostly level hiking, cool and semi-shaded nearly all the way.

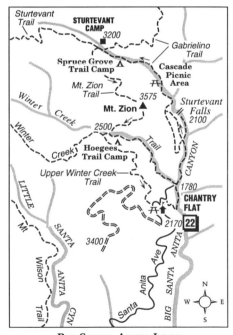

Big Santa Anita Loop

TRIP 23
Vetter Mountain

Location	Central San Gabriel Mountains
Highlight	Mountain vistas from an old fire lookout
Distance	3.3 miles
Total Elevation Gain/Loss	700'/700'
Hiking Time	1½ hours
Optional Map	USGS 7.5-min *Chilao Flat*
Best Times	All year
Agency	ANF/ASD
Difficulty	★★

Vetter Mountain lies within Angeles National Forest's Charlton-Chilao Recreation Area—a gateway of sorts to the high country of the San Gabriel Mountains. Here, Angelenos heading up Angeles Crest Highway from the west first come upon what looks like true forest—stately pines, firs and cedars.

Vetter Mountain's pint-sized fire-lookout building, perched on a rounded summit nearly devoid of vegetation, takes advantage of a 360° view over the midsection of the San Gabriels. But fire watchers no longer spend lonely vigils here in cramped quarters. Smoggy air below and budget-cutting long ago took care of that. Today's ubiquitous cellular phones are yet another reason why fire lookouts are becoming obsolete all over the West.

This loop hike over Vetter's summit includes pleasant passages through Charlton Flats' heterogeneous forest of live oak, Coulter pine, Jeffrey pine, sugar pine, incense cedar, and bigcone Douglas-fir. With binoculars, a bird book, and a wildflower guide, you and your kids can take your sweet time, stopping as you please to admire a soaring hawk or raven, a noisy acorn woodpecker or Steller's jay, or an unfamiliar plant in bloom.

To get to the starting point, drive 24 miles east of I-210 in La Canada to the Charlton Flats Picnic Area (mile 47.5 according to the mileage markers along Highway 2, Angeles Crest Highway). During the off-season, part or all of the picnic area may be closed to auto traffic and you may have to walk in to reach the trailhead. Otherwise, drive in, make an immediate right, and continue ½ mile to the start of the signed Vetter Mountain Trail, on your left.

About 200 yards up the path, the Silver Moccasin Trail swings left—don't take it; this is your return route. Keeping straight, you ascend through mixed forest and then scattered pines, crossing paved service roads twice. A final switchbacking stretch through chaparral leads to the lookout, 1.3 miles from the start. The old lookout building remains, though there is talk of someday moving it to nearby Chilao Visitor Center for use as an interpretive exhibit.

Looking north and east from the lookout perch, you'll spot Pacifico Mountain, Mt. Williamson, Waterman Mountain, Twin Peaks, Old Baldy, and other prominent peaks of the San Gabriel Mountains. The "Front Range" of the San Gabriels, which defines the north rim of the San Gabriel Valley and the L.A. Basin, sprawls west and south, blocking from view most of the city.

When it's time to descend, follow the dirt road downhill instead of the trail. After 0.7 mile you'll meet a paved service road. Continue straight (east) on the pavement for another 0.6 mile and look carefully for the crossing of the Silver Moccasin Trail. Turn left on the trail, cross pavement again in a short while, and complete the final, mostly level stretch across a forested slope.

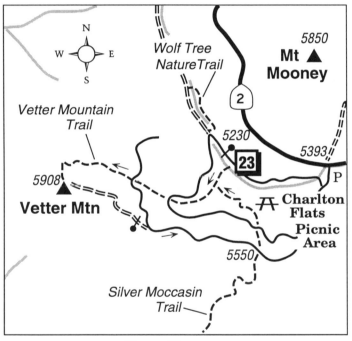

VETTER MOUNTAIN

TRIP 24
Cooper Canyon Falls

Location	Central San Gabriel Mountains
Highlight	Beautiful, hidden waterfall
Distance	3.0 miles round trip
Total Elevation Gain/Loss	800'/800'
Hiking Time	1½ hours (round trip)
Optional Map	USGS 7.5-min *Waterman Mtn.*
Best Times	April through November
Agency	ANF/ASD
Difficulty	★★

Cooper Canyon Falls roars with the melting snows of early spring, then settles down to a quiet whisper by June or July. You can cool off in the spray of the 25-foot cascade, or at least sit on a water-smoothed log and soak your feet in the chilly, alder-shaded pool just below the base of the falls. In the right season (April or May most years) these falls are one of the best unheralded attractions of the San Gabriel Mountains. Very little water can be found around here by the early fall season, but at least you can enjoy outstanding displays of autumn color along the chilly ravines.

The Burkhart Trail takes you quickly to the falls, downhill all the way, and then uphill all the way back. The forest traversed by the trail is dense enough to give plenty of cool shade for most of the unrelenting climb back up.

To get to the start of the Burkhart Trail, drive from I-210 in La Canada on Angeles Crest Highway (Highway 2) to the Buckhorn Campground entrance road, mile 58.3 according to the roadside mileposts. Drive all the way through the campground to the far (northeast) end, where a short stub of dirt road leads to a trailhead parking area.

The trail takes off down the west wall of an unnamed, usually wet canyon garnished by two waterfalls. The first—a little gem of a cascade dropping 10 feet into a rock grotto—is easy to reach by descending

from the trailside. The second, some 30 feet high, is dangerous to approach from above, but is reachable from below by scrambling up the canyon bottom from Cooper Canyon.

At 1.2 miles, the trail bends east to follow Cooper Canyon's south bank. Continue another 0.3 mile, down past the junction of the trail (Pacific Crest Trail) that goes left to follow the north bank upstream. Look or listen for water plunging over the rocky declivity to the left. A rough pathway leads down off the trail to the alder-fringed pool below.

Cooper Canyon Falls

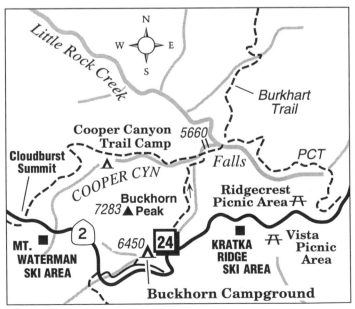

COOPER CANYON FALLS

TRIP 25
Mount Waterman Trail

Location	Central San Gabriel Mountains
Highlights	Vistas of yawning canyons; possible bighorn sheep sightings
Distance	7.7 miles
Total Elevation Gain/Loss	1400'/2250'
Hiking Time	4½ hours
Optional Map	USGS 7.5-min *Waterman Mtn.*
Best Times	May through November
Agency	ANF/ASD
Difficulty	★★★

The Mt. Waterman Trail traverse across the north rim of San Gabriel Wilderness provides almost constant views of statuesque pines, yawning chasms, and distant, hazy ridges. You start near the entrance to Buckhorn Campground and you end up half-circling broad-shouldered Waterman Mountain by the time you arrive at Three Points, 5 miles away by car. Snow can linger on the easternmost mile of the trail until May, but it tends to disappear much earlier on the remaining (mostly south-facing) parts of the trail. This is one of the most popular High Country summer hikes—one that I can heartily recommend for all but the warmest days.

(If you prefer, you can shave some time, distance, and elevation gain from this hike by making use of the Mt. Waterman Ski Lift, which is open on summer weekends to cater to hikers. The lift carries you 900 feet up from Angeles Crest Highway to a point about 3/4 mile north of Waterman Mountain's summit. It helps to have the topographic map listed above if you are going to try to locate the Mt. Waterman Trail from there.)

The Mt. Waterman Trail starts on the south side of Angeles Crest Highway, opposite the Buckhorn trailhead, where you'll find a parking lot and restrooms (mile 58.0 by the highway markers). Three Points trailhead, at the far end of the hike, is located at the intersection of Santa Clara Divide Road, mile 52.8 on Angeles Crest Highway.

From the Buckhorn end, follow the well-graded foot trail—not the old road bed paralleling the trail at first—along a shady slope. After 1.0 mile of easy ascent through gorgeous mixed-conifer forest, you come to a saddle overlooking Bear Creek. The trail turns west, follows a viewful ridge, and then ascends on six long switchbacks to a trail junction, 2.1 miles. A trail to Waterman Mountain's summit goes right; you stay left and contour west about 1/2 mile, then zigzag south down to a second junction, 3.5 miles. Twin Peaks saddle, a spacious spot suitable for camping, lies below to the left. If you're day-hiking this stretch, then stay right (west).

The remaining 4+ miles take you gradually downhill (more steep at the very end) along a generally south-facing slope. You wind in and out of broad ravines, either shaded by huge incense cedars and vanilla-scented Jeffrey pines, or exposed to the warm sunshine on chaparral-covered slopes. The older cedar trees are gnarled veterans of past fires. The rugged topography of San Gabriel Wilderness below conceals the hangouts of herds of Nelson bighorn sheep. This area and another to the east,

Sheep Mountain Wilderness, were set aside in part to preserve the habitat of these magnificent animals.

Near the end of the Mt. Waterman Trail, you hook up briefly with the Pacific Crest Trail. You swing down to cross Angeles Crest Highway, and climb up on the other side to reach the parking lot at Three Points.

An excellent way to extend and embellish this hike is to tackle either or both summits of Twin Peaks. Getting to either involves considerable scrambling, though a decently worn-in use trail exists between Twin Peaks Saddle and the ridge between the two peaks. The east peak is easier to reach. There, on rock outcrops just below the summit, you can get a dizzying view of the canyons below. Quite often you can look out over a low-lying blanket of smog in the L.A. Basin and see Santa Catalina Island floating out at sea beyond the hazy dome of Palos Verdes. The Santa Anas, Palomar Mountain, the Santa Rosas, San Jacinto Peak and Old Baldy arc around the horizon from south to east.

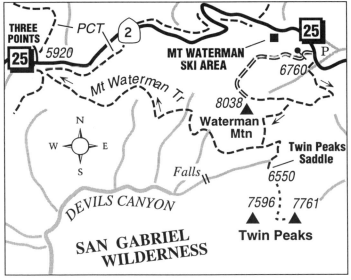

MOUNT WATERMAN TRAIL

TRIP 26
Devil's Punchbowl

Location	San Gabriel Mountains, north slope
Highlight	Spectacular geological formations
Distance	1.0 mile
Total Elevation Gain/Loss	300'/300'
Hiking Time	½ hour
Optional Map	USGS 7.5-min *Valyermo*
Best Times	All year
Agency	DPNA
Difficulty	★

Tens of millions of years in the making, Devil's Punchbowl is without a doubt Los Angeles County's most spectacular geological showplace. Looking down into this 300-foot-deep chasm, you immediately sense the enormity of the forces that produced the tilted and tangled collection of beige sandstone slabs.

The Punchbowl is caught between two active faults—the main San Andreas Fault and an offshoot, the Punchbowl Fault—along which old sedimentary formations have been pushed upward and crumpled downward, as well as transported horizontally. Weathering and erosion have put the final touches on the scene, roughing out the bowl-shaped gorge of Punchbowl Canyon and carving, in a host of unique ways, the rocks exposed at the surface.

Devil's Punchbowl Natural Area lies in the pinyon-juniper transition zone between the Mojave Desert and the richly forested slopes of the higher San Gabriels. The park features a superb nature center, a

Inside the Punchbowl in winter

couple of short nature walks (including the loop trail described here), and the Punchbowl Trail—a part of the High Desert National Recreation Trail. South of the punchbowl are long-distance trails leading through Angeles National Forest to the high country along Angeles Crest Highway.

The park is open 7 days a week from sunrise to sunset, with a fee charged. To get there from most parts of L.A., exit Antelope Valley Freeway (Highway 14) at Pearblossom Highway, and follow it east through the town of Littlerock to Pearblossom. At Pearblossom, turn right (south) on Longview Road (County N6) and follow signs for the park, 7.5 miles ahead.

The 1-mile Loop Trail is a perfect introduction to the Punchbowl area. It begins just behind the nature center, zigzags down off the rim to touch the seasonal creek in Punchbowl Canyon, and then climbs back out of the canyon opposite some of the tallest upright rock formations in the park. Near the start of the trail is a side path—the

0.3-mile Pinon Pathway—a self-guiding nature trail that loops through the pinyon-juniper forest along the Punchbowl rim.

During winter, occasional snowfalls dust the Punchbowl and leave a lingering, thicker mantle of white on the pine-dotted slopes above it. At these times the Loop Trail can become muddy and slippery, and therefore probably not suitable for small children.

Peripatetic walkers may wish to undertake the 6-mile-round-trip trek via the Punchbowl Trail to the Devil's Chair, which perches on the upper rim of the canyon complex that generally encompasses the Punchbowl. At the fenced viewpoint there, you can peer over what looks like frozen chaos—a vast assemblage of sandstone chunks and slabs tipped at odd angles, bent, seemingly pulled apart here, compressed there. There's a reason for this chaos: Devil's Chair sits practically astride the "crush zone" of the Punchbowl Fault.

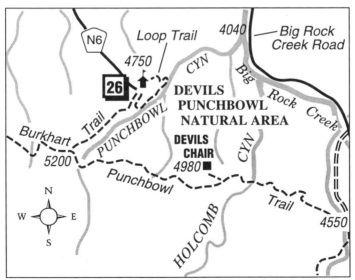

DEVIL'S PUNCHBOWL

TRIP 27
Mount Baden-Powell Traverse

Location	Eastern San Gabriel Mountains
Highlights	Subalpine habitat; panoramic views; possible bighorn sheep sightings
Distance	9.2 miles (includes Throop Peak and Mt. Burnham summits)
Total Elevation Gain/Loss	2400'/3700'
Hiking Time	6 hours
Optional Map	USGS 7.5-min *Crystal Lake*
Best Times	May through November
Agency	ANF/VD
Difficulty	★★★

Massive Mt. Baden-Powell stands head and shoulders above the foggy or smoggy marine layer that often enshrouds the lowlands of the Los Angeles Basin and the Inland Empire. From Baden Powell's flattish top, the brown Mojave Desert floor seems to stretch interminably inland toward some hazy vanishing point. The disembodied summit ridges of mountain ranges as far west as Ventura County and as far south as San Diego County seem to float over opaque blankets of haze. Santa Catalina, and sometimes other islands, are visible on an average early-summer morning.

Named in honor of Lord Baden-Powell, the British Army officer who started the Boy Scout movement in 1907, Baden-Powell soars higher (9399') than any other mountain in the San Gabriel mountain range—except for the Mt. San Antonio (Old Baldy) complex to the east. Many thousands of hikers troop to Baden-Powell's summit yearly, most of them by way of the trail from Vincent Gap on Angeles Crest Highway.

If you want to climb Mt. Baden-Powell without having to retrace your steps, you can try a one-way hike, described here, from Dawson Saddle to Vincent Gap. The effort is only bit more than what's involved in the usual round trip from Vincent Gap, and you'll visit two other peaks as well. All three peaks offer their own unique and

panoramic perspective of rugged Sheep Mountain Wilderness to the south. As the name suggests, this wilderness protects the habitat of the Nelson bighorn sheep, which number about 700 in the San Gabriel Mountains. Early-morning sightings of the bighorn are not unusual on and near Mt. Baden-Powell.

At a moderate pace, including a few short breaks and a stop for lunch, this 9-mile

North slope, Mt. Burnham

hike should take you about 6 hours. Snow accumulations can blanket the area until June. Thereafter, there's little or no water to be found on the route, so carry water. The start and end points of the hike are 5 miles apart by way of Angeles Crest Highway, so you should plan to bring either two cars for a car shuttle, or one car plus a bicycle (to be left near the end point for use in retrieving the car from the start point after the hike is over).

The hike begins where the Dawson Saddle Trail meets Angeles Crest Highway (Highway 2), mile 69.6 (according to the highway mileage markers), just east of Dawson Saddle. There's parking space on the north side of the highway. The trail goes immediately uphill (south), switchbacking up through pines and firs to gain the top of a long, gradually ascending ridge that culminates at Throop Peak. An impressive 3540 hours of volunteer labor by Boy Scouts were required to build this trail, which was completed in 1982. About halfway up the trail, lodgepole pines dominate the forest, but keen eyes will spot a few limber pines, which are relatively rare in Southern California. Look closely at the needles: lodgepole-pine needles come in bundles of two, while limber pines have bundles of five.

After 1.8 miles you join the Pacific Crest Trail. From this junction, the first side-trip takes you southwest on the PCT for 200 yards, then off-trail in the same direction another 300 yards to Throop Peak. You'll find a hiker's register there, as well as on the other two peaks you'll reach later.

Return to the Dawson Saddle Trail junction and continue northeast on the PCT, which follows the main, semi-shaded ridgeline. You descend to a saddle, then ascend to Mt. Burnham's north flank, from where switchbacks take you over to Burnham's east shoulder. That's where you can double back (go west) for the easy side trip to Burnham's summit.

After bagging Burnham, continue east, climbing a breathless 400 feet more, to reach the next trail junction. Just above it is Baden-Powell's summit, and an impressive monument constructed by the Boy Scouts. Weather-beaten lodgepole and limber pines dot the summit area.

Return to the junction and take the main, heavily traveled trail that descends Baden-Powell's northeast ridge. After 40 switchbacks and 3.8 miles of steady descent you'll reach the end—the large Vincent Gap parking area at mile 74.8 on Angeles Crest Highway. About halfway down this trail, from the 25th switchback corner, a side trail leads about 200 yards east to a dribbling pipe at Lamel Spring. This is the only normally dependable source of water along the route.

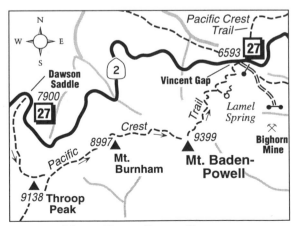

MOUNT BADEN-POWELL TRAVERSE

TRIP 28
Lightning Ridge Nature Trail

Location	Eastern San Gabriel Mountains
Highlight	Botanical features
Distance	0.8 mile
Total Elevation Gain/Loss	250'/250'
Hiking Time	½ hour
Optional Map	USGS 7.5-min *Mount San Antonio*
Best Times	April through November
Agency	ANF/VD
Difficulty	★

On the eastern extremity of the Angeles Crest, far from L.A.'s smoggy blanket of air, lies the Big Pines Recreation Area, an area set aside by the Forest Service specifically for year-round recreation. Blanketed by a heterogeneous mixture of pines, firs, and oaks, and perched high above the desert, Big Pines boasts the clean, dry, evergreen-scented air and crystalline blue skies characteristic of the melding of mountain and desert environments. Winter and spring skiing (sometimes aided by the labors of snow-making machines) is offered at three sites in the Big Pines area. Several trails lace the area including one of the finer interpretive trails around: Lightning Ridge Trail.

From most parts of Los Angeles, the fastest way to get to the Big Pines area is by way of Interstates 10 and 15, then by way of Angeles Crest Highway (Highway 2) through the mountain community of Wrightwood. During winter, this may be the only way to go, as snow blocks other highways, including Angeles Crest Highway west of Big Pines.

The Lightning Ridge Trail (starting opposite Inspiration Point 2 miles west of Big Pines on Angeles Crest Highway) contours through the cool precincts of a wooded northeast-facing slope, then switchbacks upward to meet the Pacific Crest Trail on a windblown crest. You'll see Jeffrey pines, sugar pines, and white firs, and pass right through a beautiful glade of black oaks called Oak Dell—very nice in October when the leaves turn crispy gold and acorns fall. Near the crest are a number of stunted and distorted trees battered by winds and flattened by snow drifts that can pile up 10 feet high.

When you reach the PCT junction, try stepping off the trail and walking a short distance over to the top of the ridgecrest. The view from there is similar to that from Inspiration Point below, only a bit more panoramic. Old Baldy and Mt. Baden-Powell rise like massive sentinels, bracketing the rugged slopes and canyons of Sheep Mountain Wilderness. To the south you look straight down the V-shaped, linear gorge of East Fork San Gabriel River.

The nearby Big Pines visitor center, open year-round Wednesday though Sunday, offers printed leaflets, maps, interpretive brochures for some of the area trails, including Lightning Ridge Trail, and reference materials such as a wildflower identification guide.

Windswept pines on Lightning Ridge

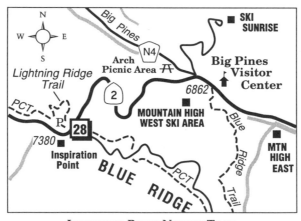

LIGHTNING RIDGE NATURE TRAIL

TRIP 29
Lewis Falls

Location	San Gabriel Mountains, above Azusa
Highlight	Beautiful stream and cascades
Distance	0.8 mile round trip
Total Elevation Gain/Loss	300'/300'
Hiking Time	½ hour (round trip)
Optional Map	USGS 7.5-min *Crystal Lake*
Best Times	All year
Agency	ANF/MBD
Difficulty	★

On the precipice called Lewis Falls, Soldier Creek shoots (or cascades, or merely dribbles) some 50 feet down a two-tiered rock face. The volume of water splattering on rocks and sand below is seldom dramatic; but the cool spray and the sounds of falling water are refreshing. The hike to the base of the falls is short—only about 15 minutes, a manageable adventure (with some assistance) for small children.

Lewis Falls is located off Highway 39—the road from Azusa into San Gabriel Canyon and Crystal Lake Recreation Area. Weekend and holiday visitors to the canyon (Crystal Lake excepted) must purchase a daily pass ($3 per car per day) for roadside parking, which applies for this trip. The parking fee is payable at the San Gabriel Information Station (open 8 a.m. to 5 p.m.) on Highway 39 just north of Azusa, and at certain 24-hour businesses in the Azusa area. Call (818) 335-1251 or (818) 969-1012 for more information.

To reach the starting point drive 2.3 miles north of Coldbrook Campground on Highway 39 to reach a small, shaded turnout on the right (mile 34.8), where Soldier Creek tumbles through a culvert under the highway. Park and make your way up a well-beaten trail on the east side of the creek, under shade-giving oaks, laurels, and bigcone Douglas-firs. Near the last cabin upstream, the trail virtually dis-

appears in the flood-scoured bed of Soldier Creek. A final, 200-yard scramble along the stream takes you to the base of the falls.

Most of the year Soldier Creek is a tame brook, easily jumped by the average adult. But a major storm, or a rapid thaw in the snowpack above, could produce runoff deep and swift enough to be hazardous—at least for kids.

Just above Lewis Falls, but not accessible by the way we've just described, is a beautiful stretch of Soldier Creek featuring half a dozen small cascades. This secret hideaway is also a short walk away from Highway 39. To go that way, drive to mile 36.8 on Highway 39, from where a wide, gated dirt road goes east. Park so as not to block the gate, and on foot follow the dirt road 0.5 mile east to its end. Find a narrow trail on the left, contouring through manzanita brush. It leads 300 yards, sometimes precariously, across a steep slope to the cascades.

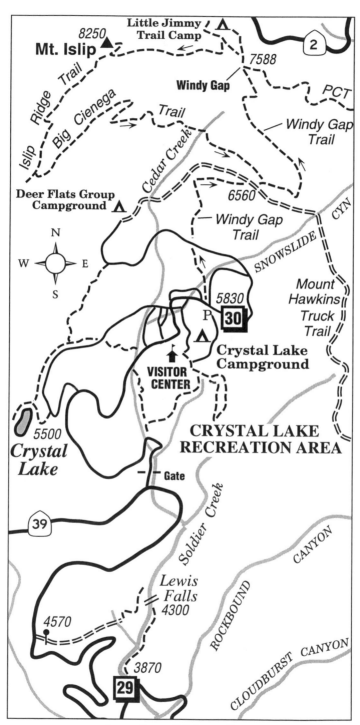

LEWIS FALLS & MOUNT ISLIP

TRIP 30
Mount Islip

Location	San Gabriel Mountains, above Azusa
Highlight	Ocean to desert views
Distance	7.7 miles
Total Elevation Gain/Loss	2400′/2400′
Hiking Time	4 hours
Optional Map	USGS 7.5-min *Crystal Lake*
Best Times	May through November
Agency	ANF/MBD
Difficulty	★★★

The south approach of Mt. Islip, one of the significant high points in the San Gabriel Mountains, feels a bit like real mountain climbing, despite the rather straightforward ascent by way of marked trails. You begin amid spreading oaks and tall conifers in Crystal Lake basin, rise through progressively smaller and sparser timber, and finally reach the nearly bald and often windblown summit. There, a comprehensive view both north over the Mojave Desert and south over the metropolis is offered on clear days. For the slight effort of an extra ½ mile on the way up or down, you can spend the night at Little Jimmy Campground, one of the nicest trail camps in the San Gabriels.

The trailhead lies within Crystal Lake Recreation Area, 25 miles north of Azusa by way of Highway 39. Due to budget-cutting of late, the recreation area may be closed for camping and picnicking on weekdays, or during the winter season. Call (818) 335-1251 or (818) 969-1012 for more information. During such closures, it is possible to park below the locked gate on the road to the recreation area and hoof it an extra mile or two to reach trails going in the direction you want.

Ideally, you start on the marked Windy Gap Trail, which begins at the main hikers' parking lot, 0.5 mile beyond the Crystal Lake Recreation Area visitor center. On the way to Windy Gap (2.5 miles), you cross the Mt. Hawkins Truck Trail twice (on the first crossing the road is paved, on the second it's dirt) and then tackle the steep, upper slopes of the cirquelike rim overlooking Crystal Lake basin. Windy Gap is the lowest spot on the north side of that rim.

At Windy Gap you meet the Pacific Crest Trail, which joins from the right (east). Continue briefly north on the PCT to the next junction. Going left takes you more directly to the summit of Mt. Islip, while going right would lead you to Little Jimmy Campground and a more roundabout ascent of the mountain. In either case, you'll end up on the trail that follows the sunny east ridge of Mt. Islip to its summit. (Note: Hard snow or ice can linger on the steep, north-facing slopes north of Windy Gap until sometime in May. You can avoid that stretch if need be by going straight up the east shoulder of Mt. Islip from Windy Gap; that route becomes snow-free earlier in the season.)

On the summit (3.5 miles) you'll see footings of a fire lookout tower that stood there from 1927 until it was removed to South Mt. Hawkins in 1937. The shell of a stone cabin stands just east of the summit.

On your return, you can take the newer Islip Ridge and Big Cienega trails, the latter completed in 1990. Two switchbacks below the summit of Mt. Islip, turn right on the Islip Ridge Trail, which goes down Mt. Islip's south ridge. A future extension of that trail will go south and east all the way to Crystal Lake. For now, you travel 1.0 mile down Islip Ridge Trail and then turn east on Big Cienega Trail. After another 2.0 miles of gradual descent along wooded south-facing slopes, you join the Windy Gap Trail just north of the upper crossing of Mount Hawkins Truck Trail. Turn right and return to the hikers' parking lot.

Crystal Lake

TRIP 31
Down the East Fork

Location	San Gabriel River, San Gabriel Mountains
Highlights	An epic trek along a cascading stream; nearly a vertical mile of descent
Distance	14.5 miles
Total Elevation Gain/Loss	200'/4800'
Hiking Time	9 hours
Recommended Maps	USGS 7.5-min *Crystal Lake, Mount San Antonio, Glendora*
Best Times	April through November
Agency	ANF/MBD
Difficulty	★★★★

Born from snow-fed rivulets, the many tributaries of the East Fork San Gabriel River gather together to form one of the liveliest and most remote streams in the San Gabriels. At The Narrows of the East Fork, the water squeezes through the deepest gorge in Southern California. From the bottom of The Narrows, the east wall soars about 5200 feet to Iron Mountain, and the west wall rises about 4000 feet to the South Mt. Hawkins divide.

On this grand journey down the upper East Fork, you'll descend nearly a mile in elevation, travel from high-country pines and firs to sun-scorched chaparral, and cross three important geologic faults—the Punchbowl, Vincent Thrust, and San Gabriel faults. During the course of a single day you could experience a temperature increase of as much as 60°F.

You can do this trip in one long day with an early start, or you can camp overnight on one of the shaded streamside terraces near the mid-point of the trek. The better camping sites include former trail camps at Fish and Iron forks, and the lower part of The Narrows. Because the route passes through Sheep Mountain Wilderness, you'll need a wilderness permit from the Forest Service.

Navigation on the trip is easy throughout—you simply head down-canyon the whole way. Consult a detailed map often

if you want to confirm exactly where you are. Heavy runoff after a storm or major snowmelt can create hazardous stream crossings, so check with the rangers first.

It's best to have someone drop you off at the starting point on Angeles Crest Highway (Highway 2) at Vincent Gap, and later pick you up at East Fork Station, an 85-mile drive around by way of Interstate 15, Interstate 10, Highway 39, and East Fork Road leading to the station. After its usual winter closure, Angeles Crest Highway usually opens to traffic from the east (Wrightwood) side sometime in April.

From the parking area on the south side of Vincent Gap, walk down the gated road to the southeast. After only about 200 yards, a footpath veers left, into Sheep Mountain Wilderness. Take it; the road itself continues toward the posted, privately owned Bighorn Mine, an inholding in the wilderness.

Intermittently shaded by bigcone Douglas-firs, white firs, Jeffrey pines, and live oaks, the path descends along the south slope of Vincent Gulch. The gulch itself follows the Punchbowl Fault, a splinter of the San Andreas. At 0.7 mile, on a flat ridge spur, look for an indistinct path intersecting on the right. This leads about 100 yards to an old cabin believed to have been the home of Charles Vincent. Vincent led the life of a hermit, prospector, and big-game hunter in the Baden-Powell/Old Baldy area from 1870 until his death in 1926.

After a few switchbacks, the trail crosses Vincent Gulch (usually dry at this point, wet a short distance below) at 1.6 miles. Thereafter it stays on or above the east bank as far as the confluence of Prairie Fork, 3.8 miles. At Prairie Fork a sign on the left points the way east to Cabin Flat. You veer right (west) down a gravelly wash, good for setting up a camp. Shortly after, at the Mine Gulch confluence, you bend left (south) into the wide bed of the upper East Fork. For several miles to come, there's no well-defined trail.

Proceed down the rock-strewn flood plain, crossing the creek (and battling alder thickets) several times over the next mile. The canyon becomes narrow for a while starting at about 5.0 miles, and you must wade or hop from one slippery rock to another. Fish Fork, on the left at 7.3 miles, is the first large stream below Prairie Fork.

If you have the time for an intriguing side trip, Fish Fork canyon is well worth explor-

Lower falls in Fish Fork

ing. Chock full of alder and bay, narrow with soaring walls, its clear stream tumbling over boulders, the canyon boasts one of the wildest and most beautiful settings in the San Gabriels. About 1.6 miles upstream lies a formidable impasse: There, the waters of Fish Fork drop 12 feet into an emerald-green pool set amid sheer rock walls. A bigger waterfall, inaccessible by means of this approach, lies farther upstream.

Well below Fish Fork, you enter The Narrows. A rough trail, worn in by hikers, traverses this one-mile-plus section of fast-moving water. You'll pass swimmable (if very chilly) pools cupped in the granite and schist bedrock, and cross the stream when necessary. Listen and watch for water ouzels (dippers) by the edges of the pools. Old mining trails once threaded the canyon walls here and to the north (they're still shown on the *Mount San Antonio* topo map), but all are virtually obliterated now.

At the lower portals of The Narrows (9.7 miles), you come upon the enigmatically named Bridge to Nowhere. During the 1930s, road-builders managed to push a highway up along the East Fork stream to just this far. The arched, concrete bridge, similar in style to those built along Angeles Crest Highway, was to be a key link in a route that would carry traffic between the San Gabriel Valley and the desert near Wrightwood. Fate intervened. A great flood in 1938 thoroughly demolished most of the road, leaving the bridge stranded. Another, later attempt to construct a road through the East Fork gorge also resulted in failure. High on the canyon's west rim lies Shoemaker Canyon Road—a "road to nowhere."

Below the bridge, on remnants of the old road washed out in 1938, you'll run into more and more hikers, fishermen, and other travelers out for the day. At 12.0 miles, Swan Rock—an outcrop of metamorphic rock branded with the light-colored imprint of a swan—comes into view on the right. At 14.0 miles you come upon Heaton Flat Campground. From there a final, easy 0.5-mile stroll takes you to the East Fork parking at the end of East Fork Road.

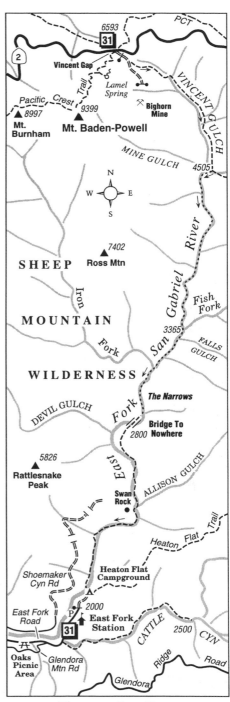

DOWN THE EAST FORK

TRIP 32
Walnut Creek Trail

Location	San Dimas
Highlights	Beautiful riparian and oak woodland habitat
Distance	3.7 miles
Total Elevation Gain/Loss	100'/500'
Hiking Time	1½ hours
Optional Map	USGS 7.5-min *San Dimas*
Best Times	All year
Agency	LADPR
Difficulty	★★

Tucked away in a surprisingly unspoiled canyon just below Bonelli Regional Park and Puddingstone Reservoir is Walnut Creek Park, a ribbon of open space stretching through the cities of San Dimas and Covina. A wide and well-traveled bridle trail goes the length of the park, crossing the stream several times (expect to get your feet soaked in winter and spring!). Plenty of oaks, sycamores, willows, and assorted non-native ornamental trees—but relatively few walnut trees—line the banks.

Steep south canyon walls along most of this stretch of Walnut Creek make it a cool haven on all but the hottest days. Often on winter mornings the canyon bottom is a frosty wonderland, since it acts as a sink for cold, dense night air slinking down the slopes of the nearby San Gabriel Mountains.

Start at the roadside parking area on the west side of San Dimas Avenue, 1 mile north of Via Verde's interchange with Interstate 210. The trail zigzags down the road embankment to the west, and enters the shady canyon. Down along the bottom are several splits in the trail: the first three are merely alternate routes that go along the opposite bank or up onto the steep south slope before returning to the main trail; the fourth is a spur trail that connects with Puente Street.

Past the Puente Street bridge there's not much of a trail at all, and you may well find yourself sloshing through the shallow water. In a while the water enters a cement flood-control channel to be whisked efficiently away. You climb up on the left bank of the flood-control channel. Covina Hills Road lies just ahead—a good place to end this trip provided you've planted a second car there in advance.

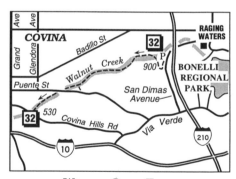

WALNUT CREEK TRAIL

TRIP 33
Marshall Canyon Trail

Location	La Verne
Highlights	Dense oak and riparian woodland; views of San Gabriel Valley
Distance	5.0 miles
Total Elevation Gain/Loss	1100'/1100'
Hiking Time	2½ hours
Optional Map	USGS 7.5-min *Mt. Baldy*
Best Times	October through June
Agency	LADPR
Difficulty	★★★

Although it's been in county ownership for some 30 years, Marshall Canyon Regional Park remains obscure—omitted, even, from some of the popular street maps. This is all the better for hikers and horsemen, who can enjoy these undeveloped 600 acres in peace and quiet.

The park encompasses the upper watersheds of two small canyons—Marshall and Live Oak—which are smothered by a leafy canopy of live oak, sycamore and alder. In some areas luminescent curtains of poison oak and wild grape cling to the trees, while carpets of blackberry vines and vinca (an ornamental ground-cover gone wild) coat the stream banks. Steep, chaparral-covered slopes, dotted here and there with planted pines, eucalyptus and

incense cedar, round out the scene. On the intricate, figure-eight route described here you'll explore parts of both canyons and pay a visit to a shady picnic spot perched high in the foothills of the San Gabriel Mountains.

You begin at the equestrian parking area on Golden Hills Road, 1 mile east of Wheeler Avenue in La Verne. (You can also get there by driving north on Esperanza Drive from Base Line Road.) After only a few steps, you're enveloped in a shade-dappled milieu—Marshall Canyon. Bear left at the first split at 0.1 mile. You'll return to this point later on the fork to the right.

In a little while, you leave Marshall Canyon's shady creek bed and rise to the perimeter of a fenced nursery (0.7 mile), atop the low ridge that divides Marshall and Live

In Live Oak Canyon

Oak canyons. You contour into the latter, where you hook up with a trail coming up along its bottom. Continue upstream to another trail junction (1.2 miles). Stay right and go another 0.1 mile to yet another junction. Take the equestrian trail on the left, ignoring the dirt road that curves right up the hillside. After gaining 400 vertical feet on switchbacks you reach a dirt road atop a ridge-running fire break (1.7 miles, 2220') offering rare, clear-day vistas extending all the way to downtown L.A.'s skyscrapers.

Turn left, continue on the fire break 0.2 mile, and then veer sharply left on a trail that takes you back down into the shady depths of Live Oak Canyon (2.2 miles). Swing right at the bottom (remaining on trail) and continue uphill 0.4 mile to a dirt road. Turn left and follow the road 200 yards down to the picnic area (2.8 miles), which sits in a shady draw at the head of Live Oak Canyon. A restroom and horse trough are here, but there's no potable water.

From the picnic area, keep descending along the dirt road, which at this point follows Live Oak Canyon's mostly sun-exposed north wall. About ¼ mile below, don't miss the pleasant trail that conveniently short-cuts a couple of curves in the road. On the road again you pass well above the point where you turned uphill a mile earlier. Farther ahead, at 3.7 miles, you leave the road and veer left on a path going down a shallow draw. This soon hooks up with the trail through Live Oak Canyon. Retrace your earlier steps for 0.2 mile, then fork left, remaining in Live Oak Canyon. A murmuring stream swishes through here most of the year. At 4.5 miles, the trail abruptly switches back and climbs to an open flat with two large water tanks. Pass to the left of the first, to the right of the second, and pick up the path that descends into Marshall Canyon. You arrive back at the first split you encountered, 0.1 mile east of the parking area.

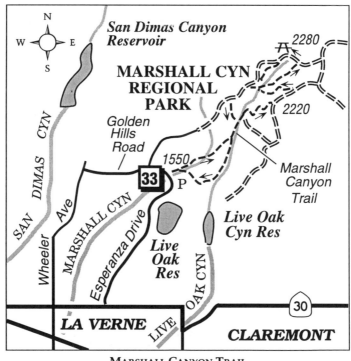

MARSHALL CANYON TRAIL

TRIP 34
Old Baldy

Location	Eastern San Gabriel Mountains
Highlights	Panoramic views along the Devils Backbone and atop L.A. County's highest point
Distance	6.4 miles round trip
Total Elevation Gain/Loss	2300'/2300'
Hiking Time	3½ hours (round trip)
Optional Map	USGS 7.5-min *Mount San Antonio, Telegraph Peak*
Best Times	May through November
Agency	ANF/MBD
Difficulty	★★★

No Southland hiker's repertoire of experiences is complete without at least one ascent of Mt. San Antonio, or "Old Baldy." The east approach is the least taxing of the several routes to the summit, but it's by no means a picnic. You start at 7800 feet, with virtually no altitude acclimatization, and climb expeditiously to over 10,000 feet. Given the easy access, it's beguilingly easy to come unprepared for high winds or bad weather, which although fairly rare may come up suddenly. Ice, if present, can be a serious hazard as well.

By mechanical means (a car) you can get to the upper terminus of Mt. Baldy Road in less than half an hour from the valley flatlands below. Further mechanical means—the Mt. Baldy ski lift—carry you to an elevation of 7800 feet at Mt. Baldy Notch, where you begin hiking. Although the ski lift caters mostly to skiers (7 days a week during the winter season), it remains open during the summer season on weekends (9 a.m. to 4:45 p.m.) for the benefit of sightseers and hikers. If it's a weekday, or you don't like being dangled over an abyss, you can always

Krummholz trees on Old Baldy

walk up the ski-lift-maintenance road starting from Manker Flats. That option adds 3.6 miles and an elevation change of about 1600 feet both on the way up and on the way down. A lodge at the upper terminus of the lift offers food and beverages.

From Mt. Baldy Notch (about 200 yards northeast of the top of the main ski lift), take the maintenance road to the northwest that climbs moderately, then more steeply through groves of Jeffrey pine and incense cedar. After a couple of bends, you come to the road's end (1.3 miles) and the beginning of the trail along the Devils Backbone ridge. Sign in at the register provided near the beginning of the trail. The stretch ahead, once a hair-raiser, lost most of its terror when the Civilian Conservation Corps constructed a wider and safer trail, complete with guard rails, in 1935-36. The guard rails are gone now, but there's plenty of room to maneuver, unless there are problems with strong winds and/or ice. Devils Backbone offers grand vistas of both the Lytle Creek drainage on the north and east and San Antonio Canyon on the south.

The backbone section ends at about 2.0 miles as you start traversing the broad south flank of Mt. Harwood. Scattered lodgepole pines now predominate. At 2.6 miles you arrive at the saddle between Harwood and Old Baldy, where backpackers sometimes set up camp (no water, no facilities here). Continue climbing up the rocky ridge to the west, past stunted, wind-battered conifers barely clinging to survival in the face of yearly onslaughts by cold winter winds. You reach the summit after a total of 3.2 miles.

On the rocky summit, barren of trees, but not of a few inconspicuous alpine plants and lichens, you'll find a rock-walled enclosure and a register book that fills up with the names of hundreds of hikers on a fair-weather weekend. Most days you can easily make out the other two members of the triad of Southern California giants—San Gorgonio Mountain and San Jacinto Peak—about 50 miles east and southeast, respectively. On days of crystalline clarity, the panorama includes 90° of ocean horizon, a 120° slice of the brown desert floor, and far-off ramparts of the southern Sierra Nevada and Panamint ranges, as much as 160 miles away.

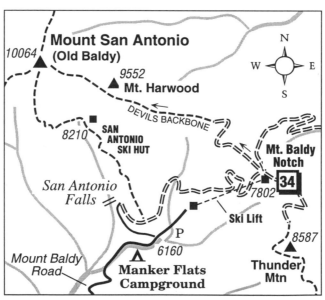

OLD BALDY

TRIP 35
Cucamonga Peak

Location	Eastern San Gabriel Mountains
Highlights	Alder-shaded stream; stupendous valley views during clear weather
Distance	12.0 miles round trip
Total Elevation Gain/Loss	4300'/4300'
Hiking Time	7 hours (round trip)
Optional Maps	USGS 7.5-min *Mt. Baldy, Cucamonga Peak*
Best Times	May through November
Agency	ANF/MBD
Difficulty	★★★★

Cucamonga Peak's south and east slopes feature some of the most dramatic relief in the San Gabriel range. At 8859 feet, the peak stands sentinel-like only 4 miles from the edge of the broad inland valley region known as the Inland Empire. Go all the way to the top for the view, but don't be too disappointed if there's nothing below but haze and smog. So much beautiful high country can be seen along the way that reaching the top is just icing on the cake.

Most of the hike lies within Cucamonga Wilderness, requiring a permit for both day and overnight use. Near Cucamonga's summit you'll tackle a steep, north-facing gully that can retain snow into May. Be sure to discuss with a ranger the possible hazards of snow and ice if it's early or late in the season.

Your trip begins at the Icehouse Canyon parking area, a short way down the spur road signed no outlet, 1.5 miles up San

In Icehouse Canyon

Antonio Canyon from Mt. Baldy village. Walk up the path following the alder-shaded stream. The first couple of miles along the canyon are a fitting introduction to a phase of Southern California scenery not familiar to a lot of visitors and newcomers. Huge bigcone Douglas-fir, incense cedar, and live oak trees cluster on the banks of the stream, which dances over boulder and fallen log. Moisture-loving, flowering plants like columbine sway in the breeze. Some of old cabins along the lower canyon still survive, while others, destroyed by flood or fire, have left evidence in the form of foundations or rock walls.

Old newspaper reports suggest that an ice-packing operation existed in or near Icehouse Canyon during the late 1850s. The ice was packed down San Antonio Canyon on mules to a point accessible to wagons, whereupon it was carted, as quickly as possible, to Los Angeles for use in making ice cream and for chilling beverages. Whether ice was actually quarried in this canyon or in another, Icehouse Canyon's name is apt enough: cold-air drainage pro-

duces refrigeratorlike temperatures on many a summer morning, and deep-freeze temperatures in winter.

Chapman Trail (a longer, alternate route) intersects on the left at 1.0 mile. At Columbine Spring (2.4 miles, last water during the warmer months), the trail starts switchbacking up the north wall. After passing the upper intersection of the Chapman Trail at 2.9 miles, you continue to pine-shaded Icehouse Saddle, 3.5 miles, where trails converge from many directions. The trail to Cucamonga's summit contours southeast, descends moderately, and climbs to a 7654-foot saddle (4.4 miles) between Bighorn and Cucamonga peaks. Thereafter, it switchbacks up a steep slope dotted with lodgepole pines and white firs.

At 5.8 miles, the trail crosses a shady draw 200 feet below and northwest of the summit. A signed but indistinct side path goes straight up to the summit, 6.0 miles from your starting point in Icehouse Canyon. Return the same way, or take the alternate route, the Chapman Trail, if you'd like a longer but more gradual descent from Icehouse Saddle.

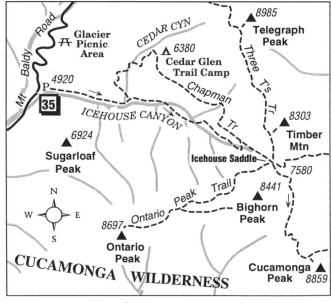

CUCAMONGA PEAK

TRIP 36
Cougar Crest Trail

Location	Big Bear Lake, San Bernardino Mountains
Highlights	Pinyon-juniper forest; lake and mountain views
Distance	6.6 miles round trip (to Bertha Peak)
Total Elevation Gain/Loss	1450'/1450'
Hiking Time	3½ hours (round trip)
Optional Map	USGS 7.5-min *Fawnskin*
Best Times	April through November
Agency	SBNF/BBD
Difficulty	★★

Big Bear Lake, with its popular resorts and ski areas, offers some fine hiking experiences for those willing to stretch their legs a bit. A number of old roads and trails lace the slopes south of Big Bear Lake (the mini-metropolis of that same name on the lake's south shore), but better hiking can be found on the sloping mountain rim that rises above the serene and mostly undeveloped north shore of the lake. It is here that the recently completed Cougar Crest Trail ascends to a junction with the 2600-mile-long Pacific Crest Trail—the world's longest maintained footpath.

The starting point, on Highway 38 some 2 miles east of the village of Fawnskin, and 4 miles west of Big Bear City, is hard to miss. Park in the spacious paved lot at the trailhead, and start heading up the Cougar Crest Trail, formerly an obscure dirt road. Traces of mining activity are evident as you climb upward along a shallow draw filled with a delightful mix of outsized pinyon pines and junipers, and occasional straight and tall Jeffrey pines. The mingling of the sweet and pungent scents exuded by the wood and needles of these trees is intoxicating on a warm day.

After a long mile, the old road becomes a narrow trail and begins to curl and switchback along higher and sunnier slopes. Big Bear Lake comes into view occasionally, its surface azure in the slanting illumination

of a spring or summer morning, or dotted with silvery pinpoints of light on a late fall day.

After about 2 miles, the trail reaches a divide, bends right, and for a short distance traverses a cool (or sometimes cold and icy), north-facing slope. At 2.2 miles, the Cougar Crest Trail joins the Pacific Crest Trail—the latter a path reserved for hikers and horses only (no mountain bikes or other mechanical conveyances are allowed on the entire PCT route between the Mexican

and Canadian borders). You bear right
and start contouring east, high on the
sunny, south-facing slope. Spread before you
now is the lake (technically a shallow reservoir), which half-fills a 10-mile-long trough
in the mountains, and the various resort and
residential communities spread along the
shore and beyond. Behind the lake and
about 12 miles distant, the rounded, often-
snow-mantled ramparts of San Gorgonio
Wilderness gleam.

The southern view does not signifi-
cantly improve as you press on, though the
high point ahead, Bertha Peak, will fur-
nish a better view in other directions. When
the PCT crosses a rock-strewn service road
(2.6 miles from the start), leave the nicely
graded trail and start climbing east on the
road. A sweaty, 0.7-mile ascent takes you
to a small microwave relay station atop
Bertha Peak. Outside the relay station's
perimeter fence you'll find a peak bag-
ger's register, plus fine views over the tree-
tops into Holcomb Valley and the Mojave
Desert to the north.

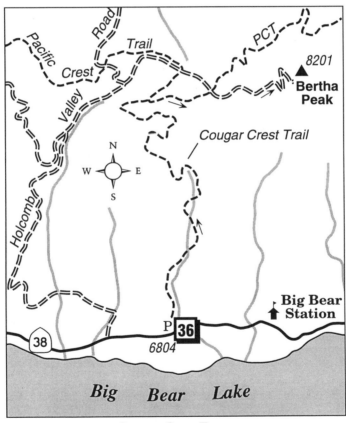

COUGAR CREST TRAIL

TRIP 37
Forsee Creek Trail

Location	San Gorgonio Wilderness, San Bernardino Mountains
Highlight	Peak bagging amid Southern California's highest mountains
Distance	12.6 miles round trip (to Trail Fork Camp)
Total Elevation Gain/Loss	3700'/3700'
Hiking Time	8 hours (round trip)
Recommended Map	Forest Service *San Gorgonio Wilderness* topographic map
Best Times	May through November
Agency	SBNF/SGD
Difficulty	★★★★

Tucked amid the tall, straight trunks of lodgepole pines at nearly 2 miles high, the wind-sheltered and mostly bug-free Trail Fork Camp is a peakbagger's delight. Just above the trail camp lies the lightning-tortured roof of Southern California—San Bernardino Mountain—containing four named highpoints within reach of an easy, half-day stroll. Farther east lies the big daddy of Southern California summits—San Gorgonio Mountain—within reach of an all-day (16-mile round trip) dayhike involving only moderate elevation change.

The trek to Trail Fork Camp and the crest beyond is itself a challenging day-hike. It's somewhat easier if you take one full day to hike in and a partial day to return. The high peaks of San Gorgonio Wilderness tend to create their own local storms in summertime, so be aware of thunderstorm forecasts before embarking on your journey. Raingear and a tent with waterproof fly are musts during such conditions; better yet, consider cancelling or postponing your trip if there is tropical moisture in the area.

To reach the trailhead from Interstate 10 at Redlands, take Highway 38 east through Mentone and up onto the forested highlands of the San Bernardino Mountains. At a point 18 miles beyond Mill Creek Station, turn right on Jenks Lake Road. After 0.3 mile turn right on a rough dirt road signed

FORSEE CREEK TRAIL, and proceed cautiously another 0.6 mile to a large clearing used for parking.

On foot make your way steadily uphill under shade-giving Jeffrey pines, incense-cedars, white firs, and black oaks, and a few sugar pines, quickly passing a side trail to Johns Meadow. Most summers, thin streams of water cascade down two or three gullies traversed by the first 2 miles of trail. After an hour or two of unrelenting labor, you leave the "yellow-pine" vegetation behind and enter a zone dominated by lodgepole pines. Much higher up, the lodgepole pines (with two needles per cluster) are joined by limber pines (having five needles per cluster and rubbery branch tips).

At 4.2 miles, Jackstraw Springs trail camp (prone to mosquitoes in the summer) lies down a side path to the right. At 6.2 miles, the trail bends sharply right and arrives at a junction. Just below, hidden in a clump of bushes, lies Trail Fork Springs—oftentimes the first trickle in the headwaters of Forsee Creek. Retrace your steps about 100 yards on the Forsee Creek Trail to find the steep, narrow side path leading east up to Trail Fork Camp. Several flat sites for camping can be found hereabouts amid the lodgepoles and weathered outcrops of banded metamorphic rock. A bald area on a flat ridge just northeast is the perfect spot to admire a view stretching north toward Big Bear Lake, and to toast the last rays of the setting sun.

If time and energy permit, pay a visit to nearby Shields and Anderson peaks, 0.7 mile and 0.4 mile away, respectively. On the crest between these peaks lie scraggly pines, many battered and stripped of their bark by lightning strikes. North of the crest, in protected pockets, uniformly spaced lodgepole pines grow tall and straight with dark "bathtub rings" around their waists indicating snow accumulations several feet deep.

An optional peak-bagging foray to the west might include both of the San Bernardino peaks, plus the historic Colonel Henry Washington Monument, which commemorates the original San Bernardino baseline and meridian survey point, established in 1852. (The monument lies off-trail; you'll find it by walking 160 yards

straight up the ridge from the southwest-ernmost switchback in the San Bernardino Peak Divide Trail.) For nearly 150 years, all land surveys of Southern California have referred to Colonel Washington's initial baseline. Due west of the monument, start-ing from the foot of the mountain, today's Base Line Road stretches radially outward many miles across the flat, alluvial plain occupied by San Bernardino and several of its satellite cities. As viewed from the mon-ument on clear days, Base Line Road seems to point toward a vanishing point in or beyond the San Gabriel Valley.

It is possible to return to the trailhead via a much longer, looping route via Manzanita Springs to the west (17.5 miles for the entire loop). Be aware that the 2-mile trail segment between Manzanita Springs and Johns Meadow is steep, unmaintained, and sometimes hard to follow.

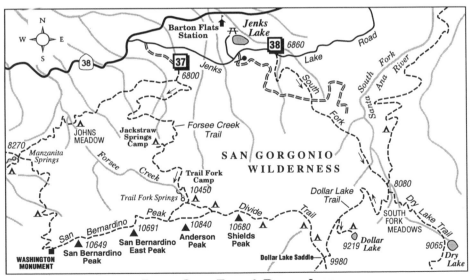

FORSEE CREEK TRAIL & DOLLAR LAKE

TRIP 38
Dollar Lake

Location	San Gorgonio Wilderness, San Bernardino Mountains
Highlight	Sparkling glacial tarn
Distance	12.6 miles round trip
Total Elevation Gain/Loss	2700'/2700'
Hiking Time	7 hours (round trip)
Optional Map	Forest Service *San Gorgonio Wilderness* topographic map
Best Times	May through November
Agency	SBNF/SGD
Difficulty	★★★★

Sparkling and silvery like a freshly minted silver dollar, Dollar Lake lies cupped amid a talus-frosted natural bowl, not far below the great divide of San Bernardino Mountain. Snow lingers late on the steep slopes overlooking the lake, sometimes into August. It's hard to believe this splendid landscape, reminiscent of the High Sierra, exists here in Southern California, only 20 air-miles from the suburban tracts of San Bernardino.

A dayhike to Dollar Lake (via the South Fork Trail) is not only possible but rather straightforwardly easy for any well-conditioned Southern Californian willing to rise early and get to the trailhead by 8 or 9 in the morning. A wilderness permit for day or overnight use of all but the lower part of the trail is required. A limited number of permits are available on a first-come, first-served basis at the Mill Creek Ranger Station, at Mill Creek Road (Highway 38) and Bryant Street, east of the town of Mentone. The station opens at 8 a.m. weekdays and 7 a.m. weekends; some permits may be available by self-registration outside the door before those hours.

To reach the trailhead from Mill Creek Station, drive 18 miles east on Highway 38 to Jenks Lake Road. Turn right and proceed 3 miles to the large South Fork Trailhead parking lot on the left. The trail itself crosses Jenks Lake Road, heading south, and com-

mences a moderate ascent up a shady canyon. Soon, the trail switches back, climbs out of the canyon and climbs southeast toward a bracken-filled clearing—Horse Meadows. Near the meadow's upper edge, you cross a dirt road (1.5 miles). That road, now closed to traffic, leads to a spot known as "Poopout Hill," an earlier trailhead higher on the mountain that used to save hikers about 2 miles of hiking each way as compared to the South Fork route they now must follow.

Continue your ascent through the typical mid-elevation yellow-pine belt, consisting here of mostly of ponderosa pines and white firs. At around 4.0 miles, the trail draws close to the South Fork Santa Ana River. Remain on the right bank of the creek, staying right at the signed junction with the Dry Lake Trail. Off to the left is South Fork Meadows, where many small tributaries combine and funnel into the South Fork. Days or weeks later some of this water will be traveling down the wide Santa Ana River flood-control channel through Anaheim and Santa Ana. Much of the water seeps into gravelly or sandy soils downstream, recharges underground aquifers, and never reaches the ocean. You stay to the right and do not cross the South Fork.

Your ascent continues on the crooked, mostly shaded Dollar Lake Trail. The yellow pine belt fades while stout and straight lodgepole pines appear in greater numbers. At 5.9 miles, just past a large, manzanita-covered patch on the mountainside, you'll come to junction where a side trail starts slanting down toward Dollar Lake, a short half mile away. The San Bernardino Mountains are the only range of mountains within Southern California to show evidence of glaciation (prior to about 10,000 years ago), and the depression occupied by Dollar Lake is suggestive of this.

If your trip involves backpacking, the trail campground at Dollar Lake is a pleasant enough overnight stop. A mile above Dollar Lake (by trail) is Dollar Lake Saddle, and four miles southeast of that is the summit of San Gorgonio Mountain. Prior to the closing of the Poopout Hill trailhead in 1988, northern ascents of Gorgonio via either Dollar Lake or Dry Lake were the easiest, if not quite the shortest. Since then, the easiest and fastest way up the mountain has been by way of Vivian Creek (see Trip 40).

South Fork, Santa Ana River

TRIP 39

Big Falls

Location	San Bernardino Mountains
Highlight	Falls, spectacular when in flood
Distance	0.7 mile round trip
Total Elevation Gain/Loss	200'/200'
Hiking Time	½ hour (round trip)
Optional Map	Forest Service *San Gorgonio Wilderness* topographic map
Best Times	December through June
Agency	SBNF/SGD
Difficulty	★

The day begins bright and clear. The late-winter sun vaults into the sky over drifts of freshly fallen snow on San Bernardino Mountain's sunny side and begins to melt them. Gravity pulls the tiny drips of water across and down through the white, crystalline mazes of ice. Many drips combine into narrow rivulets on the flank of the mountain. Small trickles join forces, and the sum of their flows combines again into a silvery stream rushing headlong toward the south. Gathering strength, the waters of the stream—Falls Creek—rush through a narrow chasm, pitch forward, and transform themselves into a feathery veil of water racing willy nilly over a series of precipices known as Big Falls.

Whether Big Falls is the highest waterfall in all of Southern California is subject to argument, though it is quite fair to call it the tallest of easily accessible cascades. Barely 15 minutes' walk from a paved parking lot gets you to a viewpoint just below the base of the falls. Wait for the right conditions—a warm sunny day in late winter or early spring—and you'll have a real treat during your visit to the falls.

The trailhead lies near the east end (dead end) of Valley of the Falls Boulevard (a.k.a. Forest Home Road), just east of the cabin community of Forest Falls. Valley of the Falls Boulevard intersects Highway 38 at a point 6.2 miles east of the Mill Creek Station and 14 miles east of Redlands.

On the trail you immediately head north across the wide, boulder-tossed bed of Mill Creek. Don't make the crossing (turn back, in other words) if floodwaters are coursing down Mill Creek. Otherwise, boulder-hop or wade across to the far bank of the boulder wash. There you swing left and begin a steep but short climb up the east slope of Falls Canyon leading to an overlook about 200 yards below the cascading water. Stay on the trail. Do not attempt to climb the falls; several people have been killed or injured trying to do just that.

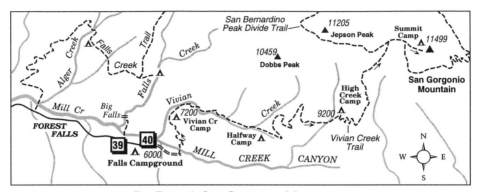

BIG FALLS & SAN GORGONIO MOUNTAIN

TRIP 40
San Gorgonio Mountain

Location	San Gorgonio Wilderness, San Bernardino Mountains
Highlight	Standing atop Southern California's highest spot
Distance	15.6 miles round trip
Total Elevation Gain/Loss	5700'/5700'
Hiking Time	10 hours (round trip)
Optional Map	Forest Service *San Gorgonio Wilderness* topographic map
Best Times	April through November
Agency	SBNF/SGD
Difficulty	★★★★

The barren, talus-strewn summit of San Gorgonio Mountain (or "Greyback," after its steely gray appearance from the valleys below) receives dozens of hikers on most fine-weather weekends. No hiker, however, ever has an easy time of it. Either variation of the popular northern approach (via Dollar Lake or Dry Lake) requires over 20 miles of round-trip hiking. On the southern approach by way of the Vivian Creek Trail, described here, you begin hiking at a point several hundred feet of elevation lower than the northern (South Fork) trailhead, but you save at least 5 miles of distance on the round trip.

The Vivian Creek Trail is the original path to the top of San Gorgonio, built around the turn of the 20th Century. Today, about eight distinct routes (or variations on routes) culminate at the summit. After 1988, when the north-side "Poopout Hill" trailhead closed, the Vivian Creek route once again become the fastest and easiest way up the mountain. The south-facing Vivian Creek route also has the advantage of a longer season; most snow on the upper parts of the trail is gone by May or June, a month or more before the northern routes are similarly clear.

Of those people who approach the summit by way of Vivian Creek, perhaps half do so over a two- or three- day period, hauling their overnight gear to camps such as Halfway or High Creek, and dayhiking from there. Others, in excellent condition and traveling lightly, have taken as little as 7 hours total, with a half-hour spent at the top and some jogging on the way down. At a leisurely pace with plenty of breaks, a day-long summit hike could take a mind- and leg-numbing 14 hours. This is okay in June or July (assuming you start hiking at dawn), but not good during November, when daylight lasts 11 hours or less.

San Gorgonio Mountain lies within the heart of San Gorgonio Wilderness. Whether dayhiking or backpacking, you must secure a wilderness permit from the Mill Creek Ranger Station, at Mill Creek Road (Highway 38) and Bryant Street, east of the town of Mentone. The station opens at 8 a.m. weekdays and 7 a.m. weekends. Some permits may be available by self-registration outside the door before those hours. Others may be available in advance by mail. For this and other hikes in the San Gorgonio Wilderness (Trips 37 and 38 in this book), the new "Guide to the San Gorgonio Wilderness" topographic map, published by the U.S. Forest Service and available for sale at the Mill Creek Station, is a good choice.

The trailhead lies at the east end (dead end) of Valley of the Falls Boulevard (Forest Home Road), just east of the cabin community of Forest Falls. Valley of the Falls Boulevard intersects Highway 38 at a point

6.2 miles east of the Mill Creek Station and 14 miles east of Redlands.

From the paved parking lot at the road-end, walk east (uphill) past a vehicle gate and follow a dirt road for 0.6 mile to its end. Go left across the wide, boulder wash of Mill Creek and find the Vivian Creek Trail going sharply up the oak-clothed canyon wall on the far side. The next half mile is excruciatingly steep; and this pitch is worse on the return, when your weary quadriceps muscles must absorb the punishment of each lurching downhill step.

Mercifully, at the top of the steep section, the trail levels momentarily, then assumes a moderate grade up alongside Vivian Creek. A sylvan Shangri-La unfolds ahead. Pines, firs, and cedars reach for the sky. Bracken fern smothers the banks of the melodious creek, which dances over boulders and fallen trees. After the first October frost, the bracken turns a flaming yellow, made all the more vivid by warm sunlight pouring out of a fierce blue sky.

Near Halfway Camp (2.5 miles) the trail begins climbing timber-dotted slopes covered intermittently by thickets of manzanita. Dobbs Peak, just below timberline, comes into view in the north, though the nearly treeless San Bernardino Mountain divide remains hidden. After several zigs and zags on north-facing slopes, you swing onto a brightly illuminated south-facing slope. Serrated Yucaipa Ridge looms in the south, rising sheer from the depths of Mill Creek Canyon. Soon thereafter, the sound of bubbling water heralds your arrival at High Creek (4.8 miles) and the trail camp of the same name. Be ready for a chilly night if you stay here; cold, nocturnal air often flows down along the bottom of this canyon from the 10,000-foot-plus peaks above.

Past High Creek Camp the trail ascends gently on several long switchback segments through lodgepole pines, and at length attains a saddle on a rocky ridge. The pines thin out and appear more decrepit as you climb crookedly up along this ridge toward timberline. At 7.2 miles, the San

Bernardino Peak Divide Trail intersects from the left. Stay right and keep climbing on a moderate grade across stony slopes dotted with cowering krummholz pines. Soon, nearly all vegetation disappears.

On the right you pass Sky High Trail, which bends around the mountain and descends toward Dry Lake and South Fork Meadows in the north. Don't give up! Keep straight and keep going. A final burst of effort puts you on a boulder pile marking the highest elevation in Southern California (7.8 miles from your starting point). From this vantage, even the soaring north face of Mount San Jacinto to the south appears diminished in stature.

Several campsites surrounded by enclosures of piled-up stones are scattered on the summit plateau. These comprise Summit trail camp, a fine place to stay overnight if the weather is calm and clear (most typically in September and October). At night, planets and stars gleam overhead, but they must compete for attention with the glow of millions of lights below.

Along the Vivian Creek Trail

TRIP 41
Big Morongo Canyon

Location	North of Palm Springs
Highlights	Riparian splendor amidst the desert; excellent birding
Distance	1 to 3 miles
Hiking Time	½ to 2 hours
Optional Map	USGS 7.5-min *Morongo Valley*
Best Times	October through May
Agency	BMCP
Difficulty	★

Nearly 300 species of birds have been spotted along a 6-mile stretch of Big Morongo Canyon, just outside the town of Morongo Valley. Wildlife frequenting the canyon includes bighorn sheep, bobcat, mountain lion, and mule deer. The 4500-acre Big Morongo Canyon Preserve, administered by the federal Bureau of Land Management, encompasses the wettest parts of the canyon. The preserve sits astride a melding of coastal chaparral and desert habitats and is regarded as one of the most important wildlife oases in the California desert. The exotic freshwater marsh found here owes its existence to seepage of water up along a geologic fault associated with a great rift between tectonic plates—the San Andreas Fault Zone—not far to the south.

The uppermost (wet) part of Big Morongo Canyon Preserve lies about 2000 feet above low-lying Palm Springs and the Coachella Valley, so the summer heat is intense but rarely intolerable here. Still, it's best to stick with the cooler months, or else confine your visit to early-morning or late-afternoon hours. The preserve is open daily from 7:30 a.m. to sunset.

From Interstate 10 near Palm Springs, drive 11 miles north on Highway 62 to Morongo Valley. Just past the business district turn right on East Drive, and look for the preserve entrance on the left. For a rewarding 1-mile stroll through contrasting habitats, walk past the visitor information

display and pick up the Desert Wash Trail on the left. It guides you over a sun-blasted terrace dotted with prosaic-looking shrubs such as honey mesquite, desert willow, and yerba santa. The latter exudes an unmistakable sweet-pungent odor. You dip to cross the Big Morongo Wash, and pass a spur trail, the Yucca Ridge Trail, over ½ mile from the start. Continue on the Willow Trail, which will take you through the heart of Big Morongo's riparian oasis and back toward the start. You meander on boardwalks amid a junglelike assemblage of willows, cottonwoods, alders, and fan palms (the latter two apparently introduced, though they lie not far from the edge of their normal range). Watercress and water parsnip have overrun the surface of the shallow waters below your feet.

After a short half-mile on the Willow Trail, you come to a trail intersection. Off to the right a short distance is your parked car. To the left, on the Mesquite and Canyon trails, you can follow the waters of Big Morongo Canyon down as far as you like. About 1 mile down, just as the canyon begins to veer decidedly left (east), look for a short path on the left leading to a small metal dam and artificial waterfall. Downstream a bit farther you can descend to another, shady spot along the stream bank, sit for a while, and watch the silvery water slide by. For casual hiking, this is about as far as it's worth going.

If you're so inclined, and arrange for
transportation on the far end, you can hike
another 5 miles down the canyon all the way
to Indian Avenue, northwest of Desert
Hot Springs. The trail becomes poorer as you
go. At some point, the stream goes underground and your remaining travel is in a dry
wash.

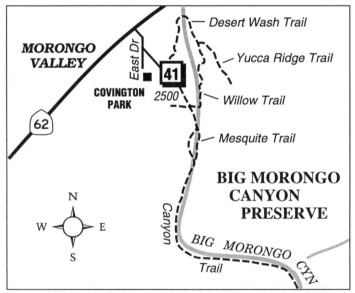

BIG MORONGO CANYON

TRIP 42
Wonderland of Rocks Traverse

Location	Joshua Tree National Park
Highlight	Scrambling amid gigantic boulders
Distance	5.7 miles
Total Elevation Gain/Loss	200'/1200'
Hiking Time	6 hours
Recommended Map	USGS 7.5-min *Indian Cove*
Best Times	October through April
Agency	JTNP
Difficulty	★★★★

More than a hundred million years ago, a molten mass of rock lay several miles underground, cooling and crystallizing by agonizingly slow degrees. As the mass solidified, it contracted slightly, and fractures developed within it. Over geologic time, this mass moved upward while older, overlying layers of rock were eroded away. As the younger rock neared the surface, groundwater seeping into the fractures chemically transformed some of the rock crystals into clay. Large, more-or-less rectangular blocks of rock with rounded corners became isolated from each other in a matrix of loose clay. Once exposed above the surface, the clay quickly washed away, leaving open crevices between the blocks. Also, various mechanical forces and chemical weathering chipped away at boulders and rounded them even further.

The products of all this uplift and shaping are the monzogranite boulders we see today spectacularly exhibited in the Wonderland of Rocks section of Joshua Tree National Park. Everywhere you look, your mind is dazzled by huge, pancake- or loaf-like stacks of rocks (where horizontal fractures predominate), by rocks in columns or spires (where vertical fractures predominate), and by huge domes. Each structure is unique, having been fashioned by a particular set of events occurring over millions of years.

Here we profile a one-way traverse across the Wonderland of Rocks known by some as the "Wonderland Connection." Make no mistake, this is no easy stroll. It's four-star rating is solely on account of the fiercely jumbled landscape you must cross during the latter part of the trip. You should be adept at both boulder hopping and scrambling across tilted rock surfaces. Much of the travel involves meticulously lowering yourself downward over angular boulders—not recommended for the faint of heart. No camping is allowed in the Wonderland area, so this must be a day trip only.

You begin at the Wonderland backcountry board (kiosk) on the north side of Park Boulevard (a.k.a. Quail Springs Road, the main road crossing the national park), 11 miles southeast of the town of Joshua Tree. This is 0.7 mile east of Quail Springs Picnic Area and 2.3 miles northwest of Hidden Valley Campground. You'll end at the Indian Cove camp/picnic area, west and south of the town of Twentynine Palms.

From the Wonderland backcountry board, follow the Boy Scout trail (a dirt road) 1.4 miles north across sandy flats dotted with Joshua trees to the Willow Hole Trail, intersecting on the right. Follow the Willow Hole Trail northeast to where it enters a dry wash, then continue downhill in the wash. The wash soon becomes a canyon bottom flanked by stacks of boulders.

At 3.5 miles you arrive at Willow Hole—large pools flanked by a screen of willows.

Following a beaten-down path, you then work your way through the willows on the right, over a low ridge, and across a gap between two rock piles. Follow the narrow canyon bottom below, which carries water draining from the pools at Willow Hole during the wetter parts of the year. The remaining travel is entirely downhill, but progress is soon impeded as you negotiate a canyon section clogged with boulders.

At 0.7 mile beyond Willow Hole, a north-flowing tributary joins on the right. Stay in the main canyon as it veers north and descends sharply for 0.3 mile to join Rattlesnake Canyon. Exercise care while descending this hazardous stretch. (It was here, during a prearranged rendezvous and car-key exchange between my party and a party traveling in the opposite direction, that one set of keys was dropped into the boulder maze and almost irretrievably lost. The lesson is: always have an extra key in a magnetic box on the car frame or hidden nearby.)

Once you reach Rattlesnake Canyon, only a bit more than a mile of hiking remains. The going is easy for a while as you follow the sandy wash downhill (northeast). Some cottonwood trees brighten the otherwise desolate scene of sand and soaring stone walls. As the canyon bends left for a final descent to the flats of Indian Cove below, you face more episodes of serious scrambling. Keeping to the left-side canyon wall, you work your way around a slotlike canyon worn in the granitic rock. Down in the bottom of the slot are potholes worn by the abrasive action of flash flooding. Only a bit more scrambling and a short walk down the canyon's sandy wash takes you to the end of the hike—the picnic area at Indian Cove.

A good resource for hiking routes and other features in the Wonderland of Rocks area is Patty Furbush's book, *On Foot in Joshua Tree National Park*, available at the park's visitor centers. The book includes a topographic map of the route just described.

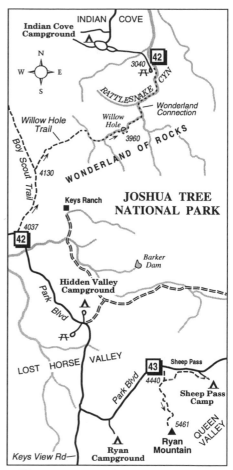

WONDERLAND OF ROCKS TRAVERSE & RYAN MOUNTAIN

TRIP 43
Ryan Mountain

Location	Joshua Tree National Park
Highlights	Panoramic mountain and desert views
Distance	3.0 miles round trip
Total Elevation Gain/Loss	1000′/1000′
Hiking Time	2 hours (round trip)
Optional Maps	USGS 7.5-min *Indian Cove, Key's View*
Best Times	September through May
Agency	JTNP
Difficulty	★★

Elongated Ryan Mountain rises above the boulder-studded plains of Lost Horse and Queen Valleys in Joshua Tree National Park. The view from the top is arguably the best in the national park, encompassing the blocky summits of San Jacinto and San Gorgonio, the intricately dissected Wonderland of Rocks, and a succession of shimmering basins and skeletal mountain ranges stretching east toward the Colorado River and south toward Baja California. The popular trail from the mountain's base to its top is well worn, yet steep and rocky enough to be a hazard for young children (and others) prone to tripping or stumbling.

Your hike begins at the Ryan Mountain parking area, on Park Boulevard one mile west of the entrance to Sheep Pass Group Camp. To reach this point from the national park's headquarters and main visitor center outside Twentynine Palms, drive 16 miles southwest on Utah Trail and Park Boulevard. Alternately, starting from the town of Joshua Tree, drive 17 miles southeast on Park Boulevard.

The trail takes you straightforwardly uphill along the north and west flanks of the mountain, amid scattered juniper and pinyon pine. Very soon, the geologic character of the rock underfoot changes. You cross the boundary between the White Tank monzogranite, the same rock you

see exposed in boulder piles in the valleys below, and the Pinto gneiss, a much older rock into which the monzogranite rock was intruded (many miles underground) some 130 million years ago. The Pinto gneiss, which is foliated with layers of dark minerals, was metamorphosed (changed in form by intense heat and pressure) around 1.5 billion years ago, during an era when life on Earth consisted of nothing more than one-celled organisms.

If you can swing it, try a morning-twilight ascent of Ryan Mountain in the late fall or early winter. As the sun rises, look down and watch the interplay of light and shadow across the Joshua-tree dotted plains and on the monzogranite boulder piles, which rise like battlements out of the alluvium.

TRIP 44
San Jacinto Peak (The Easy Way)

Location	Near Palm Springs
Highlight	Broad view of Southern California from summit
Distance	12.0 miles round trip
Total Elevation Gain/Loss	2600'/2600'
Hiking Time	6 hours (round trip)
Optional Map	USGS 7.5-min *San Jacinto Peak*
Best Times	May through November
Agency	MSJSW
Difficulty	★★★

San Jacinto Peak is a close second after San Gorgonio Mountain on the roster of Southern California high points, but its more sharply defined and imposing bulk makes it instantly identifiable from almost anywhere. Upon witnessing the sunrise from the summit one morning, the famed naturalist John Muir exclaimed, "The view from San Jacinto is the most sublime spectacle to be found anywhere on this earth!"

Despite his propensity for superlatives, Muir may have been right. We may never know. Since his visit over a century ago, 20 million people have come to settle within a 150-mile radius around the mountain. Air pollution dims today's view, even on the clearest days. Still, hundred-mile visibility is not uncommon—out to the Channel Islands in the west, down to the northern sierras of Baja California to the south, and east into Arizona. San Gorgonio and the San Bernardino Mountains rear up in the north, 15 to 20 miles away, blocking vistas of the Mojave Desert.

The north face of San Jacinto, which at one point soars 9000 feet up in four horizontal miles, is one of the most imposing escarpments in the United States. Expert climbers have made the grueling ascent from the north in as little as 9 hours. Fortunately several easier, well-graded trails let you bag the summit from other directions with a lot less effort. Every sum-

mer, thousands of people take advantage of the easiest route of all, the 6-mile trail between the mountain station of the Palm Springs Aerial Tramway (8516 feet) and the top of San Jacinto (10,804 feet). Well-conditioned hikers accustomed to high altitudes will find this a moderate trip. Others, including those with modest or no goals, can still get plenty of pleasure out of shorter trips that don't stray very far from the mountain station. The slopes hereabouts feature some of the most inviting high-country forests and meadows south of the Sierra Nevada.

First, drive up Tramway Road north of Palm Springs to the valley station of the tramway, elevation 2643 feet. After purchasing a ticket (good for the round trip), ride the tram to the mountain station, which features such amenities as a restaurant and a gift shop. A paved pathway leads 0.2 mile down from the station to the Mount San Jacinto State Wilderness ranger hut in Long Valley, where you must obtain a wilderness permit for travel beyond Long Valley.

From the ranger hut, follow the wide trail leading toward Round Valley (about 2 miles) and Wellman Divide (3.3 miles). If you're backpacking, you may stay at designated trail camping areas on the fringe of Round Valley or ½ mile north at Tamarack Valley. The 1-mile section of trail from Round Valley to Wellman Divide is quite

Stone hut below San Jacinto Peak

steep; otherwise you gain elevation gradually almost everywhere else along the route to San Jacinto's summit.

At Wellman Divide you turn north. The leisurely climb ahead takes you through thinning timberlands to a junction just south of the summit. Veer right, follow the path up along the right (east) side of the summit, pass a stone hut, then scramble from boulder to boulder for a couple of minutes to reach the top. Hopefully the weather will allow you to rest a spell in the warm sun, cupped amid the jumbo-sized rocks, and savor the lightheaded sensation of being on top of the world. Make sure that you leave the summit of San Jacinto Peak in time to catch the last downhill tram ride.

Call the Palm Springs Aerial Tramway, (619) 325-1391, for information and operating hours. The tramway closes for a few days in August for maintenance; otherwise, it normally operates 7 days a week year round.

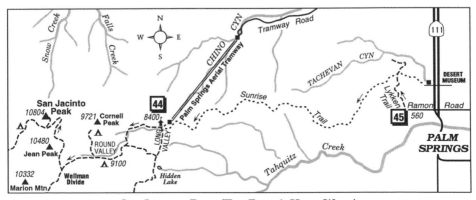

SAN JACINTO PEAK (THE EASY & HARD WAYS)

TRIP 45
San Jacinto Peak (The Hard Way)

Location	Palm Springs
Highlights	Greatest elevation gain of any hike in the Lower 48
Distance	20.0 miles
Total Elevation Gain/Loss	10,600'/2600'
Hiking Time	13 hours or more
Recommended Maps	USGS 7.5-min *Palm Springs, San Jacinto Peak*
Best Times	May through early June; October through early November
Agency	BLM/PS
Difficulty	★★★★★

This hike, known as the Cactus-to-Clouds Hike by Palm Springs hiking enthusiasts, is an absolute hoot—if you survive. For two decades now, ever-increasing numbers of adventurers have set foot in Palm Springs on a former Indian trail hacked into the east slope of Mount San Jacinto. For some, the goal has been San Jacinto Peak, 14 trail-miles away and 10,400 feet higher. Other hikers have settled for Long Valley, where the mountain station of the Palm Springs Aerial Tramway is, a "mere" 8 miles and 8000 feet higher. On Saturday, October 28, 1995, nearly a hundred people from various parts of California made their way up the route like a train of ants. About 25 of this group managed to bag San Jacinto Peak, in times ranging from 7 hours flat to about 10 hours.

You must prepare for this hike with plenty of vigorous physical conditioning. Fortunately there are many good routes on San Jacinto and in the nearby San Bernardino and San Gabriel mountains on which to practice. Conditioning hikes should include 5000 feet or more of elevation gain, plus exposure to elevations of 9000 feet or more.

Because the climate encountered on the full climb ranges from a low-desert type to an arctic-alpine type, you should try this hike only during the most moderate seasons—either late spring or early fall. If you go too early in the spring season, you might encounter treacherous patches of icy snow below Long Valley. In fall, you must wait till typical morning temperatures on the lower trail sink to less than lethally hot levels. The first snows usually arrive in November. For stable weather, it's hard to beat late October most years.

On a cool day during these moderate-season periods, you'll probably consume the better part of a gallon of water before your first dependable fill-up at Long Valley. In warm weather, you'll surely need a full gallon or more. If you go all the way to San Jacinto Peak, remember that you must return to Long Valley and the tram station for a ride back down the mountain. The statistics quoted above in the capsulized summary include the round trip from Long Valley to the peak and back. When you arrive at the mountain station, don't forget to purchase a one-way ticket for the tram ride down. Once you arrive at the bottom of the tram, you can call a taxi to get back to the starting point. Call the Palm Springs Aerial Tramway (619) 325-1391, for information about hours of operation.

A predawn start is mandatory, preferably two hours before sunrise, to beat the worst of the heat and ensure enough daylight on your return. Begin hiking at the west end of Ramon Road in Palm Springs, where pavement ends. Parking space can be found on the nearby residential streets. Follow a dirt road north from the road end, and almost immediately you'll see the Carl Lykken Trail on the left. Climb about 1 mile and 1000 feet up this maintained riding and hiking trail to reach a rocky saddle. A rougher trail comes up from the Palm Springs Desert Museum to this saddle as well. Another trail, also rough, takes off up the ridge to the west, past spray-painted inscriptions on the rocks advising that Long Valley lies 8 miles farther (The actual distance is more like 7 miles from this point, but there's no getting around the fact that there are 7000 vertical feet of ascent ahead.)

The ridge-running trail is variously known as the Chino Canyon Trail, the Sunrise Trail, and the Outlaw Trail. Other than some improvements made by a labor gang in 1933, and light-duty maintenance by contemporary users, the trail remains rugged in places and occasionally hard to follow. The name Outlaw Trail refers to the quasi-disapproval of its use by some rangers. Rescue attempts have been mounted in response to hikers getting into serious trouble, especially those attempting to hike the trail in the downhill direction. *Do not hike the trail downhill from the top.* It is too easy to lose your way and wander down the wrong ridge. Also, because the trail is so steep, the trail is at least as punishing on the leg muscles in the downhill direction as it is in the uphill direction.

Vistas of the Coachella Valley and the vast sweep of the Colorado Desert expand as you trudge uphill, step after step, curling up along one side of the sinuous ridge, then along the other. In a matter of a few hours, you will ascend through low-desert, high desert, and chaparral plant associations into a boreal zone of pines and firs.

At about 5 miles (from Ramon Road), the trail becomes partly overgrown amid the manzanita chaparral and more difficult to follow. *If you lose the trail, back up immediately and try to find it.* You must stay on the route in order to negotiate the steep, rocky, brushy terrain ahead. At about 6 miles (elevation 5800 feet), the trail crosses a shallow ravine, veers left, traverses through some oaks just above the creek, crosses the ravine again, and then climbs out of the ravine toward a ridge. It wanders up this ridge, sparsely dotted with timber to about 7600 feet, where it veers right (northwest) and traverses several steep gullies on a deeply shaded (in the fall, at least) northeast-facing slope. The section ahead is very dangerous if covered by hard-packed snow or ice and you don't have an ice ax and crampons. As you near a sheer rock outcropping, the trail abruptly bends left (southwest) and climbs almost straight up a steep slope to the "lip" of terracelike Long Valley, elevation 8400 feet.

You've come 8 miles and gained 8000 feet. If you choose to bail out at this point, simply head north a few hundred yards to the tram station. Otherwise, pick up a wilderness permit at the Long Valley ranger hut below the tram station and start off on the moderately graded 6-mile ascent by trail to the top of San Jacinto (see Trip 44).

TRIP 46
Tahquitz Peak

Location	Idyllwild
Highlight	Visiting a remote fire lookout
Distance	7.0 miles round trip
Total Elevation Gain/Loss	2000'/2000'
Hiking Time	4 hours (round trip)
Optional Map	USGS 7.5-min *Idyllwild*
Best Times	April through November
Agency	SBNF/SJD
Difficulty	★★★

Tahquitz Peak celebrates a legendary demon who, in the oral tradition of the Cahuilla Indians, used to dine on maidens and create crackling bolts of lightning over the San Jacinto Mountains when displeased. At an elevation of 8828 feet, the forest lookout tower perched atop the peak commands a view westward over haze and smog to the crests of the Santa Ana and San Gabriel Mountains. On rare days of crystalline visibility, the coastline at Santa Monica and Malibu may be glimpsed, as well as the offshore islands of Santa Catalina and San Clemente.

A direct approach to Tahquitz Peak can be mounted by way of the South Ridge Trail out of the mountain hamlet of Idyllwild. First, you'll have to obtain a wilderness permit from the Forest Service station in Idyllwild's town center, off Highway 243. South of the town center, take Saunders Meadow Road to Pine Street, turn north for two blocks, turn right (east) on Tahquitz View Drive, and then right again on South Ridge Road, Forest Road 5S11. If your car is sturdy enough, drive up this potholed road for 1.5 miles to the South Ridge trailhead.

The no-nonsense trail ahead takes you steadily uphill along a viewful ridge, first through Jeffrey pine, live oak, and fir, then past thickets of low-growing chinquapin and stalwart lodgepole pines. Off to the left (north of the trail), you may see or hear some

of the many rock climbers who gingerly make their way up the sheer face of Lily Rock (colloquially known as "Tahquitz"). Finally, after many switchbacks, you reach the fire lookout structure atop Tahquitz Peak. The summit view encompasses the timbered slopes of the southern San Jacinto Mountains and innumerable valleys and ridges spilling west and south toward Southern California's coast.

After taking in the view, descend from the lookout the way you came. The following longer, looping return is possible—perhaps a more suitable way to enjoy the mountain's charms on a two-day backpack: Head northeast, join the Pacific Crest Trail after 0.5 mile, and follow the PCT

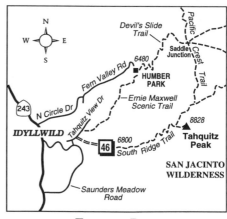

TAHQUITZ PEAK

1.3 miles north to Saddle Junction. (Nearby, to the east, are suitable wilderness campsites in the Tahquitz Valley area.) Descend Devil's Slide Trail 2.5 miles to Humber Park. There, you can arrange to be picked up. Or you can hoof it 2.6 miles down the gently descending Ernie Maxwell Scenic Trail to Tahquitz View Drive, not far away from the dirt road leading to your starting point.

TRIP 47
Toro Peak

Location	Santa Rosa Mountains
Highlight	A forested sky-island overlooking the shimmering desert
Distance	3.0 miles round trip
Total Elevation Gain/Loss	800′/800′
Hiking Time	1½ hours (round trip)
Optional Map	USGS 7.5-min *Toro Peak*
Best Times	May through November
Agency	SBNF/SJD
Difficulty	★★

At 8716 feet Toro Peak crowns the Santa Rosa Mountains, an elongated complex of ridges running for some 35 miles between Palm Springs in Riverside County and Borrego Valley in San Diego County. Perhaps nowhere else in Southern California does the juxtaposition of mountain and desert seem so severe. From the summit, the timbered landscape quickly falls away —to barren slopes, then lower still to the flat Coachella Valley on the east, the saline wasteland of the Salton Sea to the southeast, and the shimmering peaks and valleys of the Anza-Borrego Desert to the south.

Driving up the tortuous road toward Santa Rosa Mountain and Toro Peak is at least half the battle. From a point on Pines to Palms Highway (Highway 74) about 20 miles south of Palm Desert and 5 miles east of the Highway 371 junction above Anza, turn south on the Santa Rosa Mountain Road, Forest Road 7S02. For more than 12 miles you ascend on a progressively more rugged dirt roadway (best suited for 4-wheel-drive vehicles) to a locked gate below Toro Peak. Park so as not to block the gate, and proceed up the road on foot until you reach the peak. This last section of road was cut into the mountain some three decades ago to service a microwave relay station that, unfortunately, sits squarely on the mountain's now-bulldozed top.

Considering the tedious drive in, you might as well make a two-day trip out of an outing to the Santa Rosas. Opportunities for car camping abound along the upper, forest-fringed parts of the road. Winter snows may clog the uppermost 5 miles of the road, down to about Santa Rosa Spring, until sometime in April. If they do, your trek to Toro Peak may be much longer, but rewarding nonetheless as the snow-covered road passes through a gorgeous timberland of Jeffrey pine, sugar pine, and white fir. Within a day or two after a fresh dusting of snow, the gently graded Santa Rosa Mountain Road can be used as a superb cross-country ski route.

Sugar pine cones, Santa Rosa Mountains

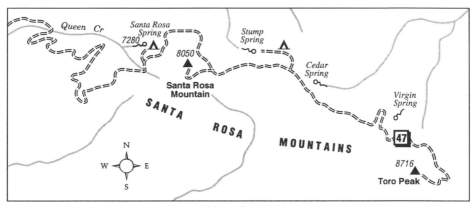

TORO PEAK

TRIP 48
Lone Tree Point on Catalina

Location	Santa Catalina Island
Highlights	Island and sea vistas
Distance	5.5 miles
Total Elevation Gain/Loss	1500'/1500'
Hiking Time	3 hours
Optional Map	USGS 7.5-min *Santa Catalina East*
Best Times	All year
Agency	SCI
Difficulty	★★

Santa Catalina Island, "twenty-six miles across the sea" as the song goes, stretches 21 miles in length and up to 8 miles at maximum width. The town of Avalon snuggles against a cove near the eastern end of the island, protected from prevailing winds that come out of the west and northwest. Avalon experiences the same almost-frost-free climate as the most even-tempered areas of the Southern California coastline, and enjoys possibly the cleanest air of any spot near the Southern California coast. In the hills above Avalon you can find wild mountainsides smothered in Catalina's own unique assemblage of chaparral, spectacular ocean views, and the some of the finest hiking in all of California.

Catalina was for most of this century owned by the Wrigley family (of chewing-gum and Chicago Cubs fame). In 1972 management of most of the island passed into the hands of the Santa Catalina Island Conservancy, whose function is to preserve and protect the island's wild lands. Recreational use of the island today, including camping, hiking, and backpacking, is handled by the Los Angeles County Department of Parks and Recreation.

The languid pace of life on Catalina reflects its aloofness from the increasingly frantic business of living on the Southern California mainland. A weekend visit there is truly relaxing, whether you choose to lodge in Avalon or prefer to rough it at one of the several campgrounds spread around the island's coast and interior.

The hike described here, excellent during the spring wildflower season and on crisp fall or winter days, begins at Hermit Gulch Campground near Avalon and loops over the top of the hills overlooking Avalon and the ocean. (You'll need a free permit for this, available at the Catalina Camping Reservations Office in Avalon.) The highlight of the hike is a side trip over to Lone Tree Point, which commands an unparalleled view of the clifflike Palisades falling sheer to the ocean. You'll encounter a couple of very steep grades on the old fire break leading to Lone Tree Point, so be sure to wear running shoes or boots with a studs or lugs to ensure plenty of traction. Small children will probably need some assistance on that stretch.

Buffalo, boar, deer, and goats—all introduced to the island at one time or another—can be seen on various parts of the island. On this particular trip you're most likely to spot feral goats. The first sighting or two is an engaging experience, but after seeing dozens of these "hoofed locusts," the novelty wears off.

From the campground, start your hike by following the narrow trail up the ravine to the west (Hermit Gulch). Before long, you leave the trickling stream in the canyon bottom and begin a twisting ascent up along a shaggy slope. During the springtime, red monkey flower, shooting star, lupine, and other native wildflowers dot the trailside and adorn small clearings amid the tangles of chaparral. After 1.5 miles and an elevation gain of 1200 feet, you meet Divide Road, the fire road along the eastern spine of the island.

Turn right, walk a few paces, and then climb the steep embankment to the left. Ahead you'll see an old fire break heading southwest, up and over several rounded, barren summits. Continue for 0.7 mile or more, passing over the peaklet designated Lone Tree on most maps. That's where you'll find the best view of the ocean and the shoreline. Sometimes you can gaze south over shore-hugging fog and spy the low dome of San Clemente Island, some 40 miles across the glistening Pacific. During the best visibility you can trace the mainland coast down as far as San Diego, and also spy the long crest of the Peninsular Ranges—the chain of mountains running through Riverside and San Diego counties into Baja California.

After taking in the visual feast, backtrack to Divide Road. From there you loop back to the starting point via a longer but more gradually descending route. Head south down Divide Road for 0.8 mile, then veer left on Memorial Road. Easy walking down this crooked dirt road takes you along a cool, north-facing slope covered by tall and luxuriant (by mainland standards) growths of scrub oak, manzanita, and toyon. At the bottom of the hill you come upon Wrigley Memorial. Below that, you pass through the botanical gardens started by Wrigley's wife in the 1920s. Because of the virtually frost-free climate, an extensive array of California natives and exotics from distant corners of the world are able to thrive here. Once beyond the garden gates, it's but a couple hundred yards back to the campground.

Ferries to Catalina depart terminals at San Pedro, Long Beach, and Newport Beach. Air service is also available from Long Beach. Lodging in Avalon ranges from $60 per night cottages to $100-plus B & Bs. For tourist- and travel-related information, call (800) 428-2566.

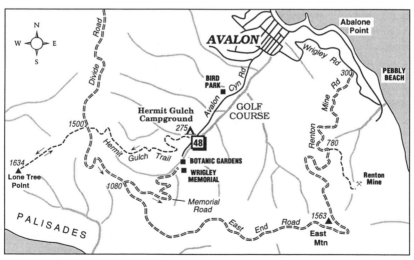

LONE TREE POINT ON CATALINA

TRIP 49
Water Canyon

Location	Chino Hills
Highlight	Secluded woodsy canyon
Distance	4+ miles round trip
Total Elevation Gain/Loss	500'/500'
Hiking Time	2 hours (round trip)
Optional Map	USGS 7.5-min *Prado Dam*
Best Times	November through May
Agency	CHSP
Difficulty	★★

Little known even among local people, who number in the millions, Chino Hills State Park can at least lay claim to being California's most expensive state park. So far the state has spent some $60 million to acquire 13,000 acres of rolling hills midway between the teeming L.A.-Orange County urban plain, and the rapidly urbanizing "Inland Empire" region surrounding Riverside and San Bernardino.

The park is dominated by rolling, grassy hills of a sensuous and classically Californian nature. Down in the moist, hidden hollows, the southern oak woodland plant community thrives. Some of the best remaining stands of California walnut, a tree whose native range is confined to the Los Angeles Basin and surrounding foothills, are found in the park's larger ravines. The park serves as a wildlife refuge as well, hosting mule deer, foxes, rabbits, coyotes, bobcats, badgers, and rattlesnakes. Several rare or endangered species of birds may visit the park, including the southern bald eagle, peregrine falcon, and least Bell's vireo.

If you're searching for the single most intriguing spot in the Chino Hills, you may find it in the upper reaches of Water Canyon. Concealed in the inky depths of this steep-walled ravine, massive sycamores and oaks reach skyward, casting a perennial chill. Except for the occasional buzz of a small aircraft and the rustle of leaves in the

breeze overhead, the silence and stillness are absolute.

Chino Hills State Park has a temporary main entrance that is as obscure as the park itself. From the Riverside Freeway (Highway 91) drive north on Highway 71 seven miles to the Soquel Canyon Parkway exit. From the Pomona Freeway (Highway 60) drive south on Highway 71 five miles south to the same exit. [Note: During 1996 and possibly 1997, construction is underway on Highway 71, widening and upgrading it to a major freeway. Detours may be necessary.] Head west on Soquel Canyon Parkway 1.0 mile to Elinvar Drive. Turn left, left again after 0.2 mile, and then immediately right on the gravel road signed CHINO HILLS STATE PARK. The road ahead is open during park hours, 8 a.m. to sunset. After two miles the road becomes paved and bends sharply right. There's an equestrian staging area on a knoll to the right, and a kiosk on the left, where you can pay day-use or camping fees.

Park at the kiosk or at the equestrian staging area and start walking from there. Head downhill into the campground, and continue south along an old road crossing a flat terrace dotted with graceful, though weedy "trees-of-heaven." Originally from China, these fast-growing ornamental trees have become naturalized throughout California.

About 0.5 mile from the campground, you dip to cross Aliso Canyon's small stream, which can be wet or dry. On the other side, you join another road at a T-intersection. Turn right, go about 100 yards, and go right again on the narrow trail going up Water Canyon. This is one of the few trails in the park reserved exclusively for hikers. Equestrian and bike traffic is prohibited.

Lining Water Canyon is a narrow finger of riparian willow and sycamore growth, flanked by grizzled oaks, well-proportioned walnut trees, and more trees-of-heaven. After a short mile you pass a thicket of prickly pear cacti so dense it forms a trailside wall. The trail, which has received little maintenance of late, deteriorates shortly thereafter and is hard to follow amid the encroaching growth of seasonal grasses. Intrepid hikers can continue another half mile up along the shady canyon bottom, often knee-high in grasses, and finally reach, in the darkest heart of the canyon near its head, a silted-up water tank that once stored water for cattle herds. (Wear long pants and watch for poison oak, stinging nettles, and rattlesnakes if you do this.) The pristine little patch of wilderness in upper Water Canyon is as close—and as far—from modern civilization as you will find anywhere around the L.A. metropolitan area.

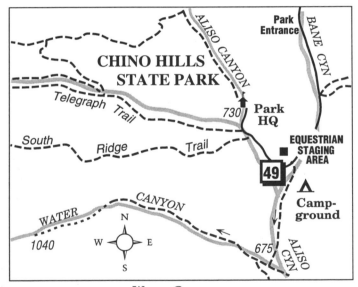

WATER CANYON

TRIP 50
Santiago Oaks Regional Park

Location	City of Orange
Highlights	Oak woodland and trickling stream
Distance	1 to 3 miles
Optional Map	USGS 7.5-min *Orange*
Best Times	All year
Agency	SORP
Difficulty	★

What Santiago Oaks Regional Park lacks in sheer size is more than adequately compensated for by its rare beauty. The core of the park is made up of two former ranch properties acquired in the mid-1970s. A small Valencia orange grove and many acres of ornamental trees planted around 1960 on these properties complement the natural riparian and oak-woodland communities along Santiago Creek.

As you approach the park entrance on Windes Drive (off Santiago Canyon Road),

the outlying subdivisions quickly fade from sight and a lush strip of riparian vegetation—willows and sycamores—presided over by steep, scruffy slopes comes into view on the left. Beyond the entrance (day-use fee collected here) and the parking lot, you can stroll up past some oak-shaded picnic sites to the superb nature center which is housed in a nicely refurbished 60-year-old ranch house.

The park is laced with several miles of trail, the best of which stay close to the

wooded bottomlands of Santiago Creek. You might begin with the self-guiding Windes Nature Trail and its extension—the Pacifica Loop—starting alongside the nature center. Though only about 0.7 mile long, the trail is very steep in places; it meanders up to the northern summit of Rattlesnake Ridge, an isolated, erosion-resistant block of mostly conglomerate rock. A slice of Pacific coastline can be glimpsed from the high point of the trail, and a fenced lookout point nearby offers a view almost straight down on Santiago Creek and the rest of the park.

Back down by the nature center, you can walk upstream along the shaded creek bank to reach a small rock-and-cement dam dating from 1892. This dam replaced an earlier one, built in 1879, that was part of one of Orange County's first irrigation systems. Today, the surviving dam is a historical curiosity, dwarfed by the large Villa Park flood-control dam a short distance upstream, and Santiago Reservoir farther upstream.

West of the nature center, you can ford Santiago Creek and stroll along several paths amid the eucalyptus, pepper, and other exotic trees rooted to the gently sloping bench on the creek's far side. Because of the diversity of its habitats, Santiago Oaks is a delightful birding spot, with species ranging from the tree-dwelling western bluebird and acorn woodpecker to the water-loving great blue heron. On occasion, vultures and ospreys, as well as some common hawks, may be seen soaring overhead.

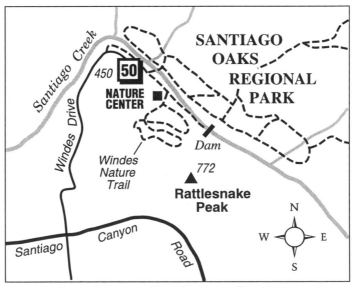

SANTIAGO OAKS REGIONAL PARK

TRIP 51
El Moro Canyon

Location	Laguna Beach
Highlights	Unspoiled coastal hills and canyon
Distance	6.8 miles round trip
Total Elevation Gain/Loss	900'/900'
Hiking Time	3½ hours (round trip)
Optional Map	USGS 7.5-min *Laguna Beach*
Best Times	All year
Agency	CCSP
Difficulty	★★

Crystal Cove State Park preserves one of the last large, undisturbed pieces of open space along the Orange County coast. Besides containing a 3-mile stretch of bluffs and ocean front, the park reaches back into the San Joaquin Hills to encompass the entire watershed of El Moro Canyon—over 4 square miles of natural ravines, ridges, and marine terrace formations. In the backcountry (El Moro Canyon) section of the park alone, visitors can explore 17 miles of dirt roads and paths open to hikers, equestrians, and mountain bicyclists. The entire section was swept by wildfire in October 1993, but several years of good rainfall since then have promoted a vigorous regrowth of the vegetation.

Upper El Moro Canyon is far and away the most beautiful attraction in the park's backcountry. You stroll past thickets of willow, toyon, elderberry, and sycamore, all brightly illuminated by the sun; then you suddenly plunge into cool, dark, cathedral-like recesses overhung by the massive limbs of live oaks. In one such recess, several shallow caves, adorned with ferns at their entrances, pock a sandstone outcrop next to the road. Before the establishment of the California missions, coast-dwelling Indians gathered acorns, seeds, and wild berries in this canyon. These foods, coupled with the abundant marine life nearby, provided a balanced and healthy diet.

To get to El Moro Canyon by the shortest route, start at the park's visitor center, located off Pacific Coast Highway about 2 miles north of Laguna Beach. A fee is charged for parking in the large lot there. Take the trail leading from the parking-lot entrance southwest across a grassy flat and down into shallow El Moro Canyon. There you join a wide trail which goes up the canyon. Turn left and walk uphill on a mostly easy gradient. Other trails intersect left and right; you simply stay in the canyon bottom. At a point about 3 miles up the canyon, the canyon-bottom trail, now called the East Loop, leaves the lushness of the canyon floor and starts climbing very sharply to a ridge above. This is a good spot to turn around and head back the way you came—the easy way. Should you wish to extend your hike, you can loop north and return to your starting point using any of several ridge-running trails.

Coast cholla cactus above El Moro Canyon

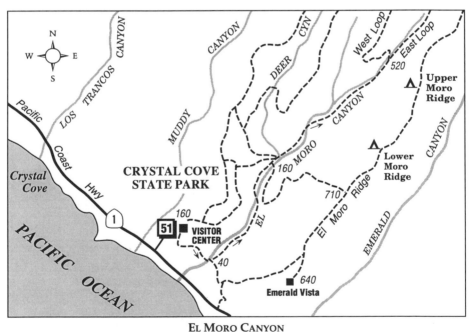

EL MORO CANYON

TRIP 52
Whiting Ranch

Location	Lake Forest/El Toro
Highlight	Orange County's "mini-Grand Canyon"
Distance	4.0 miles round trip
Total Elevation Gain/Loss	500'/500'
Hiking Time	2 hours (round trip)
Optional Map	USGS 7.5-min *El Toro*
Best Times	October through June
Agency	WRWP
Difficulty	★★

In 1991, Orange County opened to the public its newest large open-space preserve—Whiting Ranch Wilderness Park. Currently encompassing some 1500 acres along the rim of the communities of Lake Forest and El Toro, the park is likely to grow dramatically in the next decade or two when thousands of acres of Irvine Company land to the north pass into public ownership in exchange for development rights elsewhere in the county.

Whiting Ranch's rounded hills look a bit nondescript when viewed from the suburbs below, but up close they conceal some pleasant surprises. You can prove this for yourself by trekking 4 miles (out and back) to Red Rock canyon, the site of a spectacular erosional feature—sandstone cliffs banded with layers of ancient sand and mud. Late in the day, the sun's warm glow brings out a reddish tint in the rock.

To reach the park's main entrance from Interstate 5 in southern Orange County, take Lake Forest Drive east and north for 5 miles to Portola Parkway, turn left, and follow Portola for another 1/2 mile. Look for a trailhead parking area on the right, just beyond a shopping center. The lot is open from 7 a.m. to sunset.

Like most trails in the Whiting Ranch Wilderness Park, the wide path ahead is open to mountain biking and horse riding, as well as hiking. You immediately plunge into a densely shaded ravine called Borrego

Canyon, following a trickling stream. For a while, suburbia rims the canyon on both sides, but soon enough it disappears without a trace. The trek up the canyon feels

Whiting Ranch

Tolkienesque as you pass under a crooked-limb canopy of live oaks and sycamores, and sniff the damp odor of the streamside willows. Often in the late fall and winter, frigid air sinks into these shady recesses overnight, and by early morning frost mantles everything below eye-level.

After no more than about 40 minutes of walking, you come to Mustard Road, a fire road that ascends both east and west to ridgetops offering long views of the ocean on clear days. Turn right on Mustard Road, pass a picnic site, and take the second trail to the left, into Red Rock canyon.

Out in the sunshine now, you follow the Red Rock Trail (for travelers on foot only) up the bottom of a sunny canyon that becomes increasingly narrow and steep. Presently, you reach the base of the eroded sandstone cliffs, formed of sediment deposited on a shallow sea bottom about 20 million years ago. This type of rock, which contains the fossilized remains of shellfish and marine mammals, underlies much of Orange County. Rarely is it as well exposed as here.

A brochure and trail map for the entire park is available at the trailhead, and maps or directional signs can be found at several of the trail junctions. After visiting Red Rock canyon, you might decide to return via a more roundabout and lengthy route. If a half day's hike sounds about right, I'd suggest circling east on Mustard Road, then south on Whiting Road down to Serrano Canyon. The woodsy descent through Serrano Canyon takes you back to Portola Parkway, and from there you follow the sidewalk a mile back to your starting point.

In Borrego Canyon

TRIP 53
Santiago Peak

Location	Santa Ana Mountains
Highlight	Best urban/mountain/ocean view in Southern California
Distance	15.0 miles round trip
Total Elevation Gain/Loss	3950'/3950'
Hiking Time	8 hours (round trip)
Optional Map	USGS 7.5-min *Santiago Peak*
Best Times	October through May
Agency	CNF/TD
Difficulty	★★★

To the Indians, it was *Kalawpa* ("a wooded place"), the lofty resting place of the deity Chiningchinish. Early settlers and surveyors named it variously Mount Downey, Trabuco Peak, Temescal Mountain, and Santiago Peak. Finally, mapmakers decided on the name that eventually stuck: Santiago. Today's 'dozer-scraped summit overrun with telecommunications antennae hardly pays just homage to the peak's historic and scenic values. Witness, for example, this record of its first documented ascent in 1853, by a group of lawmen pursuing horse thieves up a canyon from the east:

After an infinite amount of scrambling, danger and hard labor, we stood on the very summit of the Temescal mountain, now by some called Santiago ... where we beheld with pleasure a sublime view, more than worth the journey and ascent ...

In 1861, while making a geologic survey of the Santa Anas, William Brewer and Josiah Whitney reached the same summit on their second try, using a northeast ridge. Their impressions echoed the sentiments of the earlier climbers: "The view more than repaid us for all we had endured."

The view so enthusiastically described by these early climbers is equally spectacular today—given, perhaps, a clearer-than-average winter day. Under good conditions, you can trace the coastline from

Point Loma to Point Dume, spot both Santa Catalina Island and San Clemente Island, and scratch your head trying to identify the plethora of mountain ranges and lesser promontories filling the landscape inland.

Clockwise around the compass from northwest to southeast the major ranges on the horizon are the Santa Monica, San Gabriel, San Bernardino, Little San Bernardino, San Jacinto, Santa Rosa, Palomar, and Cuyamaca mountains. To the south you might see several of the lower ranges along the Mexican border and perhaps glimpse the flat-topped summit of Table Mountain, a few miles inland from the Baja California coast. In the west and northwest, smog permitting, the flat urban tapestry spreads outward, spiked by the glass skyscrapers of downtown Los Angeles.

Don't underestimate the time required to bag Santiago Peak by way of today's most scenic approach, Holy Jim Trail. In winter, you'll need an early start to ensure a daylight return. With summit temperatures roughly 20 degrees cooler than below, you should pack along some extra clothing. Plenty of water is a good idea too: Bear Spring, on the way to the summit, should not be considered a potable source.

The drive up Trabuco Canyon to the trailhead is an adventure itself, not one to be undertaken by low-slung cars. Rocks and potholes are the norm on the unpaved Trabuco Canyon road. This road intersects Live Oak Canyon Road just east of O'Neill Regional Park in southeastern Orange County. Proceed 4.7 miles east up the canyon, taking care not to blunder up someone's dirt driveway, to the Holy Jim parking area on the left. Park here and continue on foot (north) up along the east bank of Holy Jim Canyon's small stream, passing a number of cabins. A century ago this shady hollow was home to settlers who eked out a living by raising bees. One beekeeper—James T. Smith—became so famous for his cursing habit that he was variously nicknamed "Cussin Jim," "Lyin' Smith," "Greasy Jim," and "Salvation Smith." Dignified government cartographers invented a new name, "Holy Jim."

After passing a gate at 0.5 mile, you continue upstream another 0.7 mile, fording the stream seven times. Presently the trail switches back sharply to the left, while a lateral trail continues straight, going another 400 yards up along the stream to Holy Jim Falls. This little gem of a waterfall is worth the side trip if the stream is flowing decently.

Our way zigzags upward through dense chaparral on the west wall of Holy Jim Canyon. Well traveled but minimally cleared of encroaching vegetation, the trail offers intimate glimpses of the immediate surroundings flashing by at eyeball level. There's a sense of motion and accomplishment as you ascend this trail.

Soon a few antenna structures atop Santiago Peak come into view, tantalizingly close, but about 3000 feet higher. At 2.7 miles, the trail crosses the bed of Holy Jim Canyon at elevation 3480 feet, well above the falls. You may be tempted at this point to follow the line of scattered trees that struggle up toward the head of the canyon, or to try another short cut to the summit by way of the scree-covered slopes left or right; however, loose rock and thickets of thorny ceanothus would surely cost you more time, effort, and grief than you ever imagined.

So continue ahead on the trail, where soon you make a delicate traverse over a fresh landslide. After another mile on sunny, south-facing slopes, you contour around a ridge and suddenly enter a dark

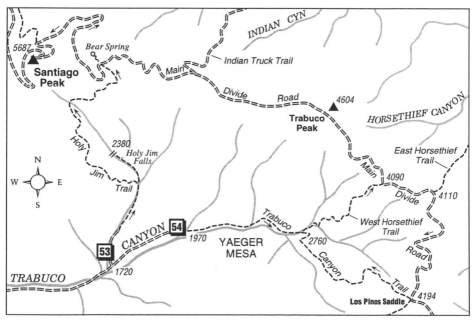

SANTIAGO PEAK & TRABUCO CANYON LOOP

and shady recess filled with oaks, sycamores, bigleaf maples and big-cone Douglas-firs. By 4.5 miles, you come upon Main Divide Road, opposite Bear Spring.

An old, overgrown short-cut trail behind Bear Spring might take you up a little quicker, but it's probably easier and more pleasant to stick to Main Divide Road from now on. Three more miles of steady climbing in sun and in shade bring you to Santiago's summit.

An observation platform, offering the only means of getting a 360° view, is shielded by a formidable fence, so you must walk around the summit area to take in the complete panorama. Modjeska Peak, one mile northwest and about 200 feet lower, isn't high enough to block the view of any far-horizon features.

The fine-grained rock covering both summits of "Old Saddleback" is the prototype of the "Santiago Peak volcanics" exposed on many of the coastal mountain ranges extending south through San Diego County into Baja California. These metamorphosed volcanic-rock formations were originally part of a chain of volcanic islands that collided with our continent some 80 million years ago.

Holy Jim Falls

TRIP 54
Trabuco Canyon Loop

Location	Santa Ana Mountains
Highlights	Spring wildflowers, autumn color, views
Distance	10.0 miles
Total Elevation Gain/Loss	2700'/2700'
Hiking Time	5½ hours
Optional Maps	USGS 7.5-min *Santiago Peak, Alberhill*
Best Times	November through May
Agency	CNF/TD
Difficulty	★★★

Wide-open views atop the Main Divide (Santa Ana Mountains), plus passages through pockets of dense chaparral and timber make this one of the more varied and interesting hikes in this book. Depending on the level of maintenance the trails receive, there may be passages overgrown by brush and poison oak. Wear long pants, or at least have them handy in your pack.

To reach the trailhead, you must navigate up 5.7 miles of poorly maintained dirt road, a job for autos with high clearance and sturdy shock absorbers (see Trip 53 for more details). Beyond the Holy Jim trailhead, drive east another mile up Trabuco Canyon to the road's end, where you can park. A trace of the now-retired road continues up-canyon—for hikers, horses, and mountain bikes only.

On the trail, you stroll past Orange County's biggest alder grove; fine specimens of live oak, bay laurel, and maple; a tiny community of madrones; and a wide variety of spectacular spring wildflowers. In late March and April, look for colorful displays of bush lupine, matilija poppy, paintbrush, wild sweet pea, red and sticky (yellow) monkeyflowers, prickly phlox, Mariposa lily, wild hyacinth, and penstemon along the sunnier spots traversed by the trail. Historically, Trabuco Canyon is significant for its mining activity, and as the site of the killing of California's last wild grizzly bear in 1908.

After 1.0 mile the trail passes close to an old adit, one of several reminders of gold-and-silver-mining activity, which persisted until about 1925. Some scraggly big-cone Douglas-fir trees can be seen on a darkly vegetated slope to the south. Early miner Jake Yaeger built his cabin in the shade of a spreading maple down near the creek.

At 1.8 miles you come to a junction with the West Horsethief Trail branching to the left. Take it. Earlier, you may have spotted switchbacks carving up the treeless slope that now lies ahead. This improved section of the West Horsethief Trail replaces the original, straight-up-the-ridge route used by Indians in prehistoric times and by horse thieves in the Spanish days. Traffic by hikers and mountain bikers in recent years has helped keep today's trail clear of encroaching vegetation. Nonetheless, some sections are very rough and rocky. After following a canyon bottom for a short while, the West Horsethief Trail begins climbing in earnest, zigzagging through dense chaparral. During the coolness of the morning, diligent effort will get you to the top of this tedious stretch fast enough; later in the day this could be a hot, energy-sapping climb.

After 1100 feet of elevation gain the trail straightens, begins to level out atop a ridge, and enters a vegetation zone dominated by manzanita and blue-flowering ceanothus. Cool "mountain" air washes over you, perhaps bearing the scent of the pines that lie ahead. Nearly coincident with the change of vegetation is a change in the rocks and soils underfoot. As you climb higher, light-colored granitic boulders and soil replace the dark-brown, crumbly metasedimentary rocks seen earlier. Although the younger granitic rock does not crop out below, you may remember having seen granitic boulders down in the bed of Trabuco Canyon. These resistant blocks, originally weathered out of the granitic mass above, were swept down during flash floods.

At 3.3 miles from the Trabuco Canyon roadhead, the West Horsethief Trail joins Main Divide Road (a truck trail) in a sparse grove of Coulter pines. Turn right and commence an easygoing, 2.5 mile passage along the "roof line" of Orange County. To the west lies Orange County's urban plain; to the east lies the more sparsely populated yet rapidly urbanizing Riverside County. The linear trough lying below you, north and east, was produced by movements along the Elsinore Fault. On the left you will soon pass the East Horsethief Trail, currently "land-locked" by private property far below. During prehistoric times, the entire Horsethief Trail route was an important trans-mountain route from the coast to the inland valleys.

At 5.8 miles, amid a patch of Coulter pines and incense-cedars, you come to Los Pinos Saddle. At the northwest corner of a large, cleared area in the saddle itself, find and follow the Trabuco Canyon Trail, which angles downward along the uppermost reaches of Trabuco Canyon's main fork. Thick stands of live oak and big-cone Douglas fir keep the upper part of the trail dark and gloomy during the fall and winter months, and delightfully cool at other times. Flowering currant and ceanothus shrubs at the trailside brighten things up in the spring.

One mile below the saddle, the trail veers left, crosses a divide, and begins descending along a tributary of Trabuco

Canyon. You walk by thickets of California bay (bay laurel), which exude an enigmatically pleasant/pungent scent. After crossing the tributary ravine twice, the trail clings to a dry and sunny south-facing slope. Down below, in an almost inaccessible section of the ravine, you may hear water trickling and tumbling over boulders half-hidden under tangles of underbrush and trees. Before long, you arrive back at the junction of the Horsethief Trail in shady Trabuco Canyon, and continue down to the trailhead.

In upper Trabuco Canyon

TRIP 55
Bell Canyon Loop

Location	Caspers Wilderness Park, Santa Ana Mountains foothills
Highlights	Interesting geologic features; wide variety of botanical features.
Distance	3.3 miles
Total Elevation Gain/Loss	400'/400'
Hiking Time	1½ hours
Optional Map	USGS 7.5-min *Canada Gobernadora*
Best Times	October through May
Agency	CWP
Difficulty	★★

Caspers Wilderness Park is the crown jewel of Orange County's regional park system. It is the county's largest park (7600 acres), the least altered by human activities, and the most remote from population centers. ("Remote," of course, is a relative term in Orange County. The county is now about two-thirds urbanized).

Caspers Park is easy to find. From Interstate 5 at San Juan Capistrano, drive east on Ortega Highway (Highway 74) 7.6 miles to the park entrance on the left. You'll need to obtain a wilderness permit at the entrance or in the visitor center as a prerequisite to hiking any of the park's 30-plus miles of old roads and newer trails. Don't miss a stop at the visitor center, which contains a small

Coast live oak in Caspers Park

museum and an open-air loft offering an expansive view of the Santa Ana Mountains.

This hike touches the park's best features, starting with a rather dizzying passage across the top of some curious white sandstone formations, rather like the breaks along the upper Missouri River or the barren cliffs of the South Dakota badlands. You'll loop up and over the main ridge defining the west edge of the park, enjoying views of much of Orange County's remaining rural and wild areas.

Begin hiking at the old windmill (a mile north by paved road from the visitor center) on a path signed nature trail. Follow it across the wide bed of Bell Canyon and into the dense oak woodland on the far side. After 0.3 mile, you'll spot a park bench beneath a gorgeous, spreading oak tree. A little farther on, veer left on the Dick Loskorn Trail. This path meanders up a shallow draw and soon climbs to a sandstone ridgeline that at one point narrows to near-knife-edge width. At one point you step within a foot of a modest but unnerving abyss. The sandstone is part of a marine sedimentary formation, called the Santiago Formation (roughly 45 million years old), which crops out along the coastal strip from here down to mid-San Diego County.

After climbing about 350 feet, you reach a dirt road—the West Ridge Trail. Turn right (north), skirting the fence line of Rancho Mission Viejo, a vast landholding that encompasses much of southern Orange County. Before World War II, it included all of Camp Pendleton as well. To the left you look down on Canada Gobernadora ("Canyon of the Governor's Wife"—though a less literal meaning refers to the invasive chamise, or greasewood, that used to fill the canyon). Canada Gobernadora is now largely given over to agriculture and to the exclusive Coto de Caza housing development.

After 0.7 mile on the West Ridge Trail, turn right on an old road that descends back into Bell Canyon, which is lined with oaks and sycamores. You also look east across the canyon to a large section of the

park that burned over in October 1993. The regrowth of vegetation has been rapid, and within a few years it may be hard to distinguish between the burned and the unburned areas.

Nearing the bottom, veer right on the Oak Trail toward your starting point. On it you meander past California sycamores as well as ancient coast live oaks. In the late autumn, you crunch through the crispy leaf litter beneath the sycamores and watch golden sunbeams dance amid the thousands of fluttering leaves overhead. In early spring, when these leaves are emerging, the sunlight filtering through them bathes the ground shadows in a jungle-green luminance.

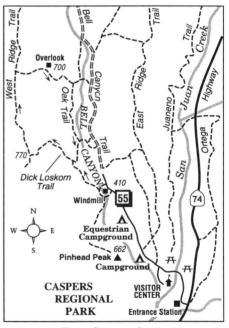

BELL CANYON LOOP

TRIP 56
San Juan Loop Trail

Location	Santa Ana Mountains
Highlights	Trickling stream; small waterfall and pool
Distance	2.1 miles
Total Elevation Gain/Loss	350′/350′
Hiking Time	1 hour
Optional Map	USGS 7.5-min *Sitton Peak*
Best Times	November through June
Agency	CNF/TD
Difficulty	★

From San Juan Capistrano to Lake Elsinore, two-lane Ortega Highway (Highway 74) stretches like a snake over the midriff of the Santa Ana Mountains, giving road warriors a taste of Orange County's wild, unfamiliar side. Even the most casual traveler can get to know the rugged and circumspect beauty of these corrugated mountains better by trying out the San Juan Loop Trail, right off the highway amid one of the most scenic spots in the range.

Drive 19.5 miles east on Ortega Highway from Interstate 5 in San Juan Capistrano to reach the starting point, a parking lot on the left. (On the right is a humble but noted local landmark—the Ortega Oaks Store, or "Candy Store.") From the edge of the lot, a well-worn path takes off north along a slope overlooking the highway. Around a bend to the left, the trail starts threading the side of a narrow gorge that resounds— after the rainy season begins in fall or win-

Reflecting pool in San Juan Creek

ter—with echoes of falling water. A spur trail leads down toward the lip of the falls; from there you can boulder-hop over to the edge of a reflecting pool. A single gnarled juniper clings sentinel-like to a rock face overlooking this pool, very far from its normal, high-desert habitat 50 or more miles north or east. If the mood strikes you, rest your bones amid the smooth contours of the water-polished granite, and settle in for a moment's quiet meditation.

Past the falls, you descend on ramplike switchbacks through dense chaparral and presently reach the oak-dotted floodplain of San Juan Creek. Stay left at the

Chiquito Trail junction to remain on the loop trail. Ahead, you'll plunge into a veritable thicket of centuries-old coast live oak trees. The overarching limbs mute the glare of the sun and sky. In the soft, filtered light, the ground glows with the seasonal greens, browns, and reds of ferns, poison oak, and wild grass.

Touching briefly upon the perimeter of Upper San Juan Campground, the trail veers sharply left to gain an open slope, again parallel to the highway. Continue for another 0.5 mile across this sun-struck slope, dotted with wildflowers in the spring, and arrive back at the parking lot.

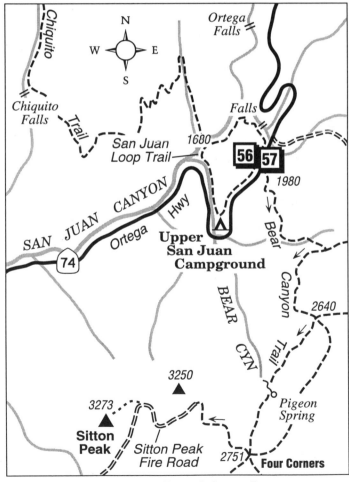

San Juan Loop Trail & Sitton Peak

TRIP 57
Sitton Peak

Location	Santa Ana Mountains
Highlights	Coast and mountain views
Distance	9.5 miles round trip
Total Elevation Gain/Loss	2150′/2150′
Hiking Time	5½ hours (round trip)
Recommended Map	USGS 7.5-min *Sitton Peak*
Best Times	October through May
Agency	CNF/TD
Difficulty	★★★

From below, Sitton Peak looks unimposing—a bump atop the rambling Santa Ana Mountains. On the summit, though, the feeling is decidedly "top of the world." When an east or north wind blows, cleansing the sky of water vapor and air pollution, fifty-mile vistas in every direction are not uncommon.

You begin this hike by taking the Bear Canyon Trail south from the Ortega Oaks Store (see Trip 56 for driving directions). After 1.0 mile of moderate ascent, you come to a trail junction in a patch of oak woodland. Go right (the Morgan Trail forks left) and begin climbing more steeply along a chaparral-clothed slope. At about 2.0 miles, you reach a dirt road, the old Verdugo Truck Trail, which to the right is now part of our Bear Canyon Trail. You can either cross the old road and go straight on a newer footpath, or go right on the road (the old road is a bit more scenic). You are now well inside the boundary of the San Mateo Canyon Wilderness, part of Cleveland National Forest, where trailside camping is permitted (by permit only).

By following the old road south, you soon pass (at 2.7 miles) oak-shaded Pigeon Spring, a seasonal trickle of water at the head of Bear Canyon. An old watering trough is here, with seeps nearby. Enjoy the shade— you won't find much more of it on the road ahead.

Continue south another half-mile to reach a saddle called Four Corners (3.2 miles), where four old roads and the newer footpath join together. Swing right on the road that climbs northwest—a disused section of the Sitton Peak Road. After a steady ascent of about 300 vertical feet, you reach a flat area (4.0 miles) just below a boulder-studded ridge (3250 feet elevation) to the north. Easily climbed, the ridge summit offers a view somewhat similar to the one seen from Sitton Peak. The flat area by the road (just inside the wilderness boundary) makes a good overnight campsite for those who backpack in.

Beyond the flat area the road descends another 0.5 mile to a saddle just below Sitton Peak. From this saddle, you leave the road and follow a steep, informal trail up through scattered manzanita and chamise on the east slope of the peak.

The view from the top is especially impressive to the west. Here the foothills and western canyons of the Santa Anas merge with the creeping suburbs of southern Orange County. Beyond lies the flat, blue ocean punctuated by the profile of Santa Catalina Island. Some 2000 feet below, toy-like cars on the highway make their way down the sinuous course of San Juan Canyon.

TRIP 58
Tenaja Falls

Location	Santa Ana Mountains
Highlight	Beautiful, multilevel waterfall
Distance	1.4 miles round trip
Total Elevation Gain/Loss	300'/300'
Hiking Time	1 hour (round trip)
Optional Map	USGS 7.5-min *Sitton Peak*
Best Times	December through June
Agency	CNF/TD
Difficulty	★

With five tiers and a total drop of about 150 feet, Tenaja Falls is the most interesting natural feature in San Mateo Canyon Wilderness. In late winter and spring, water coursing down the polished rock produces a kind of soothing music not widely heard in this somewhat dry corner of the Santa Ana Mountains.

A new trail, planned for the late 1990s, will skirt the private lands of Potrero de la Cienaga and provide fairly direct hiking access to Tenaja Falls via the Morgan Trail (off Highway 74, Ortega Highway)—a one-way trek of about 6 miles. Meanwhile, the only easy way to reach the falls is to endure (or enjoy, depending on your inclination) a long, bone-shaking drive from Ortega Highway in the north, or from Tenaja Road in the south. From Ortega Highway, follow the paved Killen Trail (formerly South Main Divide Road) south to Wildomar Campground and ORV area. Beyond, the severely rutted Wildomar Road (Forest Road 7S04), for high-clearance vehicles only, continues to a large turnout on the right (16 miles from Ortega Highway) overlooking the tree-covered bottom of San Mateo Canyon. This is the current Tenaja Falls trailhead. From Tenaja Station in the south (see Trip 59), you would drive north 4.6 miles on unpaved (though not so rutty) Old Tenaja Road to reach the same trailhead.

On foot, head down to the creek and cross it on the concrete ford of an old roadbed. If you can't balance on the row of rocks set there, then resign yourself to wading through. Continue north on the steadily rising roadbed and you'll soon be treated to a fairly distant view of the falls. After 0.7 mile the road passes near the upper lip of the falls, where a few large oaks provide welcome shade.

Further exploration of the falls requires rock-climbing skills and extreme caution. The flow of water has worn the granitic rock almost glassy smooth. While scouting the middle tiers and pools, I found that slightly wet bare feet provided much more traction than the soles of my running shoes. Don't be lured into dangerous situations though.

A somewhat safer way of approaching the lower falls is to scramble over the rough-textured rocks well away from the water. You could also backtrack down the road and then scramble down the slope into the brush-choked creekbed down near the base of the falls.

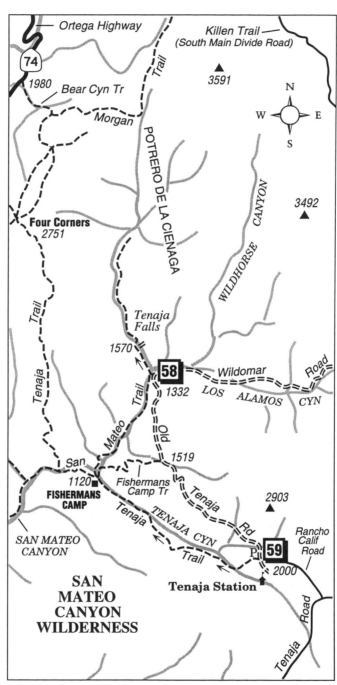

TENAJA FALLS & TENAJA CANYON

TRIP 59
Tenaja Canyon

Location	Santa Ana Mountains
Highlight	Riparian- and oak-woodland in a steep canyon
Distance	7.4 miles round trip (to Fishermans Camp)
Total Elevation Gain/Loss	1300'/1300'
Hiking Time	3½ hours (round trip)
Optional Map	USGS 7.5-min *Wildomar, Sitton Peak*
Best Times	November through May
Agency	CNF/TD
Difficulty	★★★

As the gloom of a late afternoon descends upon the deep-cut, linear furrow of Tenaja Canyon, dozens of orange-bellied newts waddle determinedly uphill and across the trail, oblivious to my footfalls. The cute faces and beady eyes of these little amphibians mirror a mindless desire I cannot fathom: Sex in a bower of leaf litter and ferns? A bellyful of succulent tree-dwelling insects, ripe for the taking?

With the recent completion of the Tenaja Trail in the Santa Ana Mountains, the newts of Tenaja Canyon have been getting cross traffic of the hiker and horse types. The trail, and a fancy new trailhead built to serve it, has opened parts of the San Mateo Canyon Wilderness area to ready access; no longer is it necessary to rattle down horrendous dirt roads to reach any sort of decent trail. The wilderness area itself stretches across 62 square miles of Cleveland National Forest lands. This is steep, rugged chaparral country to be sure, yet it is softened by narrow strips of oak woodland and riparian vegetation in the larger canyon bottoms.

To reach the Tenaja trailhead, exit Interstate 15 at Clinton Keith Road in the community of Murrieta. Proceed 6 miles south on Clinton Keith Road and 1.7 miles west on Tenaja Road to a marked intersection, where you must turn right to stay on Tenaja Road. Continue west on Tenaja Road for another 4.2 miles, then go right on

the one-lane, paved Rancho California Road. Proceed another mile to the trailhead parking area, which is just north of the Tenaja ranger station.

Sign in at the self-registration box, and head downhill on the trail going west. A few minutes descent takes you to the shady bowels of V-shaped Tenaja Canyon, where huge coast live oaks and pale-barked sycamores frame a limpid, rock-dimpled stream. Mostly the trail ahead meanders alongside the stream, but for the canyon's middle stretch it carves its way across the chaparral-blanketed south wall, 200–400 feet above the canyon bottom.

After 3.7 miles of general descent, you reach Fishermans Camp, a former drive-in campground once accessible by many miles of bad road. Today the site, distinguished by its parklike setting amid a live-oak grove, serves as a fine wilderness campsite for an overnight backpack trip (a wilderness permit is required for this). Its name hints of the fishing opportunities afforded by nearby San Mateo Creek during and after the rainy season.

At Fishermans Camp, three other trails diverge. Fishermans Camp Trail (the old road to the camp) travels east uphill to Old Tenaja Road. The San Mateo Trail, a narrow footpath, continues upstream to meet Old Tenaja Road and downstream many miles to the east boundary of Camp Pendleton.

TRIP 60
Santa Rosa Plateau
Ecological Reserve

Location	Near Temecula
Highlights	Green and golden hills, rare oaks, spring wildflowers, vernal pools
Distance	7.5 miles
Total Elevation Gain/Loss	650'/650'
Hiking Time	4 hours
Optional Map	USGS 7.5-min *Wildomar*
Best Times	November through June
Agency	SRPER
Difficulty	★★★

A circle, 100 miles in radius, centered on the Santa Rosa Plateau Ecological Reserve in the southwest corner of Riverside County, encompasses a megalopolis of some 20 million people. File this fact away in your mind, and then try to fathom its truth while walking amid the green and golden hills of this exquisitely beautiful reserve. Here is a classic California landscape of wind-rippled grasses, swaying poppies, statuesque oak trees, trickling streams, vernal pools, and a dazzling assortment of native plants (469 at last count) and animals. All who visit the reserve are struck by its timelessness and its insularity.

Starting with a nucleus of 3100 acres, purchased by The Nature Conservancy in 1984, the Santa Rosa Plateau reserve has expanded to enclose nearly 7000 acres—about 11 square miles—today. At present, the older (west) half of the reserve is laced with new hiking trails and well as old ranch roads.

The reserve can be reached in less than 90 minutes from either central Los Angeles or San Diego. Take Interstate 15 to the Clinton Keith exit in Murrieta, and head south for 6 miles to a sharp rightward bend in the road. Park along the side of the road and enter the reserve's main gate.

For a comprehensive look at the reserve, try the following half-day hike: From the main gate, start on the left branch of the Oak Tree Trail. It takes you through Engelmann oak woodland to the start of the Trans Preserve Trail. The Engelmann oak, with its distinctive gray-green leaves, is endemic to a narrow strip of coastal foothills stretching from Southern California into northern Baja California. Like other live oaks, the Engelmann oak retains its leaves throughout the year. Here in the preserve, you enjoy the finest examples to be found anywhere of this increasingly rare species.

The Trans Preserve Trail starts at the far end of the loop on the Oak Tree Trail. Follow it for 1.7 miles over rolling and sometimes wooded terrain to the Vernal Pool Trail atop Mesa de Colorado. Head left (east) past one of the largest vernal pools in California (39 acres at maximum capacity). The hard-pan surface underneath vernal pools is generally impervious to water, so once filled during winter storms, the pools dry only by evaporation. Unusual and sometimes unique species of flowering plants have evolved around the perimeter of many vernal pools, such as this one. As the pool's perimeter contracts during the steadily lengthening and warming days of spring, successive waves of annual wild-flowers bloom along the pool's moist margin. By July or August, there's nothing to be seen but a desiccated depression, its barren surface glaring in the hot sun.

Continue east on the Vernal Pool Trail, and descend from Mesa de Colorado toward the two adobe buildings of the former Santa Rosa Ranch. At around 150 years old, these are Riverside County's oldest buildings. If you are tired or hot, you can "bail out" here by making a bee line back to the main gate via the Lomas Trail.

Otherwise, continue on the 7.5-mile route by following the Punta Mesa Trail down across De Luz Creek and back uphill, heading north. Use the aptly named Vista Grande Trail to reach Tenaja Truck Trail, and return to the main gate on the latter.

Every Southern Californian should have at least one chance to see the Santa Rosa Plateau reserve at its stunning best—during March and April, following a wet winter. Make a note of it now in your calendar for the next spring season.

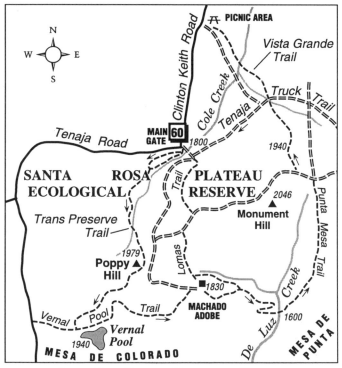

SANTA ROSA PLATEAU ECOLOGICAL RESERVE

TRIP 61
Agua Tibia Wilderness

Location	Near Temecula
Highlights	Spring wildflowers; valley and mountain views
Distance	1 to 9 miles round trip
Optional Map	USGS 7.5-min *Vail Lake*
Best Times	January through May
Agency	CNF/PD
Difficulty	★ to ★★★

The 18,000-acre Agua Tibia Wilderness lies northwest of Palomar Mountain, straddling the San Diego-Riverside county line in Cleveland National Forest. Agua Tibia Mountain, one of the three distinct mountain blocks of the Palomar range, is the centerpiece of the wilderness that bears its name. Forests of Coulter pine, bigcone Douglas-fir (a.k.a. bigcone spruce), incense-cedar, live oak, and black oak cover the highest elevations, while the lower slopes are scrub-covered and fluted by many steep canyons holding intermittent streams. The wilderness was named after one of these streams, Agua Tibia ("lukewarm water") Creek.

The Vail Fire of 1989 burned all of the lower and easily accessible parts of Agua Tibia Wilderness to a crisp, but heavy winter rains in the years that followed promptly produced a fresh new crop of chaparral vegetation. The more remote trails were quickly smothered by this new vegetation, and for a time were practically untraceable. Efforts are being made to reopen these trails. Meanwhile, the primary attraction of this area remains its fine displays of spring wildflowers. These are best seen along the lower, more accessible parts of the trail system.

Agua Tibia's only convenient entry point lies south of Highway 79, 10 miles east of Interstate 15 at Temecula. Turn south from Highway 79 at Dripping Springs Fire Station and continue 0.4 mile through Dripping Springs Campground to the road-end and trailhead. If the campground is closed, you can park outside the gate and walk in to reach the trailhead. You'll need a wilderness permit to cross the wilderness boundary just beyond the trailhead parking area. Permits are available at the nearby fire station (open approximately April through November). Better yet, call or visit the Palomar ranger district office, (619) 788-0250, well in advance of your visit to obtain the permit and to inquire about current trail conditions.

Just beyond the trailhead, ford Arroyo Seco Creek and begin a switchbacking ascent through sage scrub and chaparral vegetation, liberally sprinkled with annual wildflowers in March through May. The number and kind of flowers varies from season to season, especially because the recovering vegetation is still following a post-fire pattern of succession. After only 0.1 mile, there's a trail junction. Choose either way: the Wild Horse Trail, on the left, gains elevation relatively slowly. The Dripping Springs Trail, ahead, begins a steady and very crooked ascent of Agua Tibia Mountain's north flank. On either route (depending on the current state of maintenance), the farther you go, the more narrow and brushy the trail gets.

On the Wild Horse Trail, you quickly gain 400 feet of elevation to reach a level well above Arroyo Seco Creek, then contour for about 2 miles more, snaking around several small tributary canyons. Beyond these, the going is quite monotonous as the trail goes mostly upward another 4 miles to the Crosley Trail (an old dirt road descending from Agua Tibia's summit ridge).

As an alternative to following the Wild Horse Trail, you could try boulder-hopping or wading up Arroyo Seco Creek itself, starting back at the trailhead. Dry during much of the year, the creek comes alive with the sound of gurgling water in winter through spring. Sycamores, cottonwoods, alders and oaks, all recovering from the fire, line the bank. Encroaching vegetation may make travel slow and difficult. Watch out for poison oak too.

If you stick with the Dripping Springs Trail, your view to the north steadily improves, with Southern California's highest mountains—San Antonio, San Gorgonio and San Jacinto—coming into view after about 2 miles. On a clear winter day, these snow-covered summits standing bold against the blue sky are a memorable sight.

At about 3.5 miles (3100 feet elevation), the Dripping Springs Trail crosses the head of a small creek and continues upward amid new growths of manzanita and ribbonwood. At about 4 miles (3300 feet) you'll pass what little remains of the truly giant specimens of manzanita and ribbonwood that stood here until the 1989 fire. These century-old shrubs, up to 20 feet high, represented the equivalent of a "climax forest" consisting entirely of chaparral. The loss of this mature patch of vegetation was tragic, but it must be remembered that without the effect of fire-suppression measures enacted over the past century, the natural cycle of growth and incineration by natural causes (roughly every decade) would probably never have allowed so mature a stand of chaparral to develop.

At about 4.5 miles, the Dripping Springs Trail descends a little and crosses an area of poor soil. A view opens up to the southeast and south. The white dome of the Hale Telescope at Palomar Observatory gleams on a ridge about 9 miles southeast. You can now see the pine- and oak-fringed summit

ridge of Agua Tibia Mountain ahead. This point in the trail is about as far as most people would want to go on a one-day hike. The ridge ahead is fair game for backpackers, if the trail condition allows.

AGUA TIBIA WILDERNESS

TRIP 62
La Jolla Shores to
Torrey Pines Beach

Location	La Jolla
Highlights	Remote beach backed by sheer cliffs; body surfing
Distance	5.0 miles
Hiking Time	2½ hours
Optional Maps	USGS 7.5-min *La Jolla, Del Mar*
Best Times	All year
Agency	TPSR
Difficulty	★★

There are only a few places along the Southern California coastline where a person can hike for miles in a single direction and not catch sight of a highway, railroad tracks, powerlines, houses, or other signs of civilization. The Torrey Pines beaches are one such place. Here, for a space of about three miles, sharp cliffs front the shoreline and cut off the sights and sounds of the world beyond.

Plan to do this beach walk at low tide. High tides—especially in winter—could force you to walk on cobbles at the base of the cliffs or oblige you to wade in the surf. Beach sand is often carried away by the scouring action of the winter waves, but is usually replenished by currents as summer approaches.

A good place to start is Kellogg Park (La Jolla Shores Beach), where free parking is available when you can get it. If you're making this a one-way trip, leave a second car along North Torrey Pines Road, next to Torrey Pines State Beach, or in the adjacent Torrey Pines State Reserve—or have someone drop you off and later pick you up. Another option is to use local buses to get from the finish back to the start: At Torrey Pines Beach you can take a North County Transit bus south to UCSD, from where a

South of Torrey Pines State Reserve

transfer to a Route 34 San Diego city bus takes you to Kellogg Park.

Start your hike by walking north under Scripps Pier and on past the rocky tidepool area. Once beyond the last of the cobbles and wave-rounded boulders, you can slip off your shoes and enjoy the feel of the fine, clean sand underfoot.

Beyond the tide pools, you may notice that some people have doffed more than just shoes. You're now on Torrey Pines City Beach, also known as Black's Beach, San Diego's unofficial nude-bathing spot. The city rescinded a "clothing optional" policy for this beach in the late '70s, but old traditions have never died.

About a half mile past the tidepools, you'll see a paved road (closed to car traffic) going up through a small canyon. This is a good, safe way to reach (or exit from) the beach. There's a limited amount of 2-hour parking at the top along La Jolla Farms Road.

A bit farther ahead, where most Black's Beach users congregate, two precipitous trails ascend about 300 feet to the Glider Port, where hang gliders launch their craft. Look up to see antlike beachgoers lugging their gear up or down the zigzagging paths, and hang-gliders soaring overhead. The southern of the two trails, recently improved and widened, is the safer one. There's plenty of free, all-day parking at the top if you want to start or end your beach walk there.

Lifeguards patrol some areas of Black's Beach during busy periods, so you can feel fairly safe about jumping into the water, which may reach a temperature warmer than 70° in July through September. Elsewhere you swim at your own risk— watch out for rip currents.

At about 4 miles from Kellogg Park, you reach Flat Rock, where a protruding sandstone wall blocks easy passage. Follow the narrow path cut into the wall. From a low shelf on the far side, the Beach Trail begins its ascent to Torrey Pines State Reserve's visitor center.

In the fifth and last mile, the narrow beach is squeezed between sculpted sedimenta-

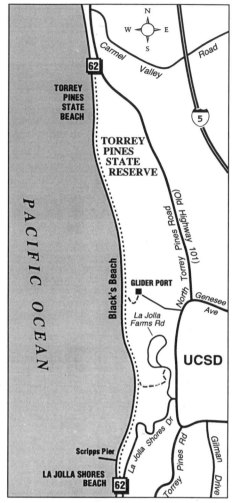

LA JOLLA SHORES TO TORREY PINES BEACH

ry cliffs on one side and crashing surf on the other. These are the tallest cliffs in western San Diego County. A close look at the faces reveals a slice of geologic history: the greenish siltstone on the bottom, called the Del Mar Formation, is older than the buff or rust-colored Torrey Sandstone above it. Higher still is a thin cap of reddish sandstone, not easily seen from the beach—the Linda Vista Formation.

In the end, the beach widens, the cliffs fall back, and you arrive at Torrey Pines State Reserve's entrance along North Torrey Pines Road.

TRIP 63
Torrey Pines State Reserve

Location	Del Mar
Highlights	Rare vegetation, wildflowers, ocean views
Distance	0.5- to 1-mile loops
Optional Map	USGS 7.5-min *Del Mar*
Best Times	All year
Agency	TPSR
Difficulty	★ to ★★

The rare and beautiful Torrey pines atop the coastal bluffs south of Del Mar are as much a symbol of the Golden State as are the famed Monterey cypress trees native to central California's coast. Torrey pines grow naturally in only two places on Earth: in and around Torrey Pines State Reserve and on Santa Rosa Island, off Santa Barbara. Of the estimated 10,000 native Torrey pines now living, about one-third grow within the reserve. A combination of drought and bark-beetle infestation killed about 15 percent of the reserve's Torrey pines during the late 1980s, but new seedlings planted in their place are thriving today.

Torrey Pines State Reserve would be botanically remarkable even without its pines. Three major plant communities can be found on the reserve's 1750 acres: the sage-scrub, chaparral, and salt-marsh plant communities. More than 330 plant species have been identified within the reserve so far. That number is approximately 20 percent of all the known plants native to San Diego County. This is especially noteworthy because San Diego County is widely regarded as being the most geographically and botanically diverse county in the continental United States.

If you're interested in identifying plants and wildflowers typical of coastal and inland Southern California, come here in the spring. Excellent interpretive facilities at the reserve's museum make plant identification an easy task. Besides the exhibits, you can

browse through several notebooks full of captioned photographs of common and rare plants within the reserve. You can also visit the native plant gardens surrounding the museum building and at the Parry Grove trailhead.

A network of trails over the eroded bluffs will take you nearly everywhere in the reserve, except into most canyon bottoms. It's important that you stick to these trails and eschew shortcuts and cross-country travel. The thin soils are easily eroded without the protection of healthy vegetation. As you'll plainly see, there are already enough instances of erosion here, due to both natural and human causes.

The entrance to the reserve is on North Torrey Pines Road (old coast Highway 101), about one mile south of Carmel Valley Road. Past the entrance a paved road goes up to a parking lot adjacent to the reserve office and museum. From there, you can walk to the beginning of any of the trails in 10 minutes or less. If that lot is full, you may be able to park in turnouts along the entrance road, in the beach parking lot at the reserve entrance, or along the shoulder of North Torrey Pines Road. The reserve has a finite carrying capacity. Access may be restricted on busy weekends, so get there early if you can.

After a stop at the museum for a bit of educational browsing, you might first explore nearby High Point, where your gaze encompasses a steep, off-limits section of the reserve known as East Grove. There, young Torrey pines are establishing a foothold on the bluffs and canyons in the aftermath of past wildfires.

Next, you might head south on the concrete roadbed of the "old" old coast highway (closed to car traffic) and pick up the Broken Hill Trail. The two east branches of this trail wind through thick chamise chaparral and connect with a spur trail leading to Broken Hill Overlook. You'll be able to step out (very carefully) onto a precipitous fin of sandstone and peer over to see what, except for a few Torrey pine trees here and there, looks like desert badlands. A third (west) branch of the Broken Hill Trail winds down a slope festooned with wildflowers and joins the Beach Trail at a point just above where the latter drops sharply to the beach.

The popular Beach Trail originates at the parking lot near the museum and intersects with trails to Yucca Point and Razor Point. Fenced viewpoints along both of these trails offer views straight down to the sandy beach and surf.

The Parry Grove and Guy Fleming loop trails wind among Torrey pine groves hit hard by the late '80s drought. The Guy Fleming Trail is mostly flat, while the Parry Grove Trail starts with a steep descent on stair steps. In spring, the sunny slopes along the Guy Fleming Trail come alive with phantasmagoric wildflower displays. Fluttering in the sea breeze, the flowers put on quite a show as several vivid shades of color dynamically intermix with the more muted tones of earth, sea and sky.

The Torrey Pines trails can be enjoyed the year round, but they're open only during daylight hours. Ranger-led walks are featured on weekends. You can't picnic in the reserve, but after you do your hiking, you can use the tables or the beach down near the entrance. Bring along binoculars: the soaring ravens and the red-tailed and sparrow hawks are interesting to watch, as are the hang-gliding humans you'll sometimes see.

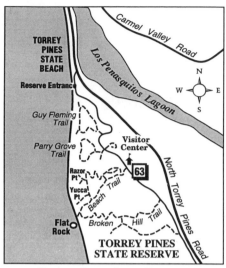

TORREY PINES STATE RESERVE

TRIP 64
Los Penasquitos Canyon

Location	Northern San Diego
Highlights	Oak-shaded coastal canyon; waterfall
Distance	6.2 miles round trip
Total Elevation Gain/Loss	300'/300'
Hiking Time	3 hours (round trip)
Optional Map	USGS 7.5-min *Del Mar*
Best Times	All year
Agency	LPCP
Difficulty	★★

Crickets sing, cicadas buzz, and bullfrogs groan. A sparrow hawk alights upon a sycamore limb, then launches with outstretched wings to catch a puff of sea breeze moving up the canyon. A cottontail rabbit bounds across the trail, and stops to take your measure with a sidelong stare. Los Penasquitos Creek slips silently through placid pools and darts noisily down multiple paths in the constriction known as "the falls."

Despite the noose of suburban development tightening around it, Los Penasquitos Canyon Preserve still retains its gentle, unselfconscious beauty. The preserve's 3000 acres of San Diego city- and county-owned open-space stretch for almost 7 miles between Interstates 5 and 15, encompassing much of Los Penasquitos Creek and one of its tributaries—Lopez Canyon.

Near the east end of the preserve, off Black Mountain Road, stands the refurbished, 1862 Johnson-Taylor adobe ranch house. Recent archaeological investigation has revealed its true antiquity: the house was build around an "ancient" (by West Coast standards) adobe cottage erected in 1824 by Captain Francisco Maria Ruiz, Commandant of the Presidio of San Diego. Tours of the ranch house, and guided nature hikes on the trails of the preserve, are offered year round; call (619) 484-3219 for recorded information.

Farther afield, hikers, joggers, and equestrians have the run of the preserve. Take along a picnic lunch and a blanket. There are many fine places—sunny meadows, oak-shaded flats, and the sycamore-fringed streamside—to stop for an hour's relaxation. For starters, you can try the following, nearly level hike to the falls and back.

Begin at the preserve's main parking lot west of Black Mountain Road and opposite Mercy Road. On foot (or on bike wheels—the route sometimes swarms with mountain bikers), head west on a dirt road. In the first

Pond below canyon falls

mile the road hugs Los Penasquitos Canyon's south wall, a steep, chaparral-covered hillside (*Penasquitos* means "little cliffs").

As you pass near the Johnson-Taylor ranch (screened from view by willows and dense vegetation along the creek), you'll notice several non-native plants—eucalyptus, fan palms, and fennel, for example—introduced into this area over the past century. Next you enter a long and beautiful canopy of intertwined live oaks, accompanied by a lush understory of mostly poison oak.

Mile posts along the roadside help you gauge your progress. At mile 2 the trail winds out of the dense cover of oaks and continues through grassland dotted with a few small elderberry trees. Wildflowers such as wild radish, mustard, California poppies, bush mallow, blue-eyed grass, and vio-

lets put on quite a show here in March and April. Look, too, for the fuchsia-flowered gooseberry, quite unmistakable when in bloom.

At the 3-mile marker the road starts winding up onto a chaparral slope in order to detour a narrow, rocky section of the canyon. At a wide spot in the road, where there are bike racks, take a path descending on the right toward a narrow, rocky constriction along the canyon bottom. During winter and early spring, water in decent quantity tumbles through here. Polished rock 10 feet up on either side and deep, circular potholes testify to its sometimes violent flow. The outcroppings of greenish-gray rock have been identified as Santiago Peak volcanics—the same hardened metavolcanic rock found farther north at Santiago Peak in the Santa Ana Mountains and farther south into Baja California.

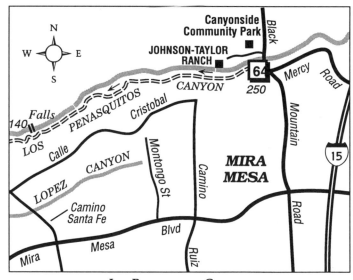

LOS PENASQUITOS CANYON

TRIP 65
Lake Hodges

Location	Escondido
Highlights	Wildflower-dotted hillsides; lake views
Distance	5.0 miles round trip
Total Elevation Gain/Loss	250'/250'
Hiking Time	2 hours (round trip)
Optional Map	USGS 7.5-min *Escondido*
Best Times	All year
Agency	SDRP
Difficulty	★★

Imagine a hiking, biking, and equestrian trail extending from the coast at Del Mar to the crest of the mountains in mid-San Diego County. Today, certain sections of this 55-mile-long route, known as the Coast to Crest Trail, are already open. These and other future sections of the trail will define the main axis of the San Dieguito River Park, now taking form along the watersheds of the San Dieguito River and its main tributary, Santa Ysabel Creek. Many pieces of the proposed park are in place today and open to the public, but fleshing out the entire 60,000 acres of parkland promises to involve much wrangling with landowners and long-term efforts by interested citizens and various local governments.

For a look at one of the more accessible and scenic segments of the Coast to Crest Trail, try this easy walk overlooking Lake Hodges, south of Escondido. Start hiking at the boat launch and fishing concession on the north shore of Lake Hodges (a reservoir), east of the quaint community of Del Dios. The parking lot there is usually open Wednesday, Saturday, and Sunday (dawn to dusk); if it is not open, you may have to park your car back near Del Dios and walk in along the access road.

From the boat-launch parking lot, head east on an old dirt road (now a wide trail), passing scattered oak and pepper trees, aromatic stands of buckwheat and sage, and clumps of laurel sumac. As the weather warms in spring, the hillside yuccas sprout flower stalks that look like exclamation points, and the patches of prickly pear cactus sprout yellow blossoms. The trail ascends easily as it follows the shore of the lake and wraps around the base of 1150-foot Bernardo Mountain on the left. Look for hawks and ravens patrolling the slopes above, and for snow-white egrets parasailing over the wind-rippled surface of the reservoir below.

After a rough, rutty, downhill section of trail, you cross a shallow creek where oaks and sycamores offer cool shade. Farther on, the trail sidles closer to the shoreline and approaches noisy Interstate 15. You've come about 2.5 miles, and this is a good point to turn around and head back.

A new section of the trail, opened in 1995, continues ahead, veering right to cross under I-15, just above the reservoir's high-water line. The new link curls north to join Sunset Drive just south of Via Rancho Parkway.

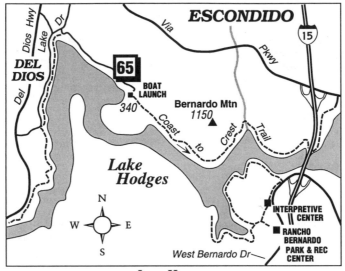

LAKE HODGES

TRIP 66
Cowles Mountain

Location	Eastern San Diego
Highlight	Best view of urban San Diego County
Distance	3.0 miles round trip
Total Elevation Gain/Loss	950'/950'
Hiking Time	2 hours (round trip)
Optional Map	USGS 7.5-min *La Mesa*
Best Times	October through June
Agency	MTRP
Difficulty	★★

Touted as one of the largest urban parks in the country, San Diego's Mission Trails Regional Park preserves some of the last remaining open space close to the heart of this sprawling city. Cowles Mountain, centerpiece of the regional park, stands 1591 feet above sea level, and is recognized as the highest point within San Diego's city limits. Hundreds of people walk the main south trail to its summit daily. Several newer trails have been laid out on the east and north slopes of the mountain in recent years, so now hikers can choose among several summit routes. We describe the ever-popular south route, which consistently offers vistas stretching from the Pacific Ocean to Mexico.

Parking is available at the trailhead, at Navajo Road and Golfcrest Drive in San Diego's San Carlos district. You ascend steadily, zigzagging almost constantly up through low-growing chaparral punctuated by outcrops of granitic rock. The trail was cut into decomposed granite, so it is quite susceptible to erosion. Don't shortcut the switchbacks, tempting as this may be, as this tramples plants and tends to destabilize the trail.

Nearly one mile up, a spur trail branches right toward a flat spot on the mountain's south shoulder. This, the site of ancient winter-solstice ceremonies by the ancestral Kumeyaay Indians, has become a popular place to visit at dawn on or near the solstice (December 21). If viewed from the right spot, the sun's disk, just peeping over the mountains to the east, gets momentarily split into two brilliant points of light by a large outcrop atop a distant ridge.

Just beyond the spur trail, another trail branches right and eventually descends the east slope. Stay left and continue up the slope on the series of long switchback segments leading to the rocky summit of the mountain. A blocky building bristling with microwave dishes obstructs the northward view somewhat, but otherwise the panorama is complete. With binoculars and a street map, you could spend a lot of time identifying features on the urban landscape. In the rift between the mesas to the west, there's a good view of Mission Valley and the tangle of freeways that pass over and through it. Southwest, the towers of downtown San Diego stand against Point Loma, Coronado, and sparkling San Diego Bay. Lake Murray shimmers to the south. The chain of Santee Lakes contrasts darkly with pale hills to the north. In all directions you look out over the abodes of the four million people now living in metropolitan San Diego and Tijuana.

On the clearest days, the higher peaks of San Diego County stand in bold relief against the sky. Southward into Baja, you should spot the flat-topped "Table

Mountain" behind Tijuana, and the Coronado Islands offshore. Try looking for the dusky profiles of Santa Catalina and San Clemente islands, to the northwest and west respectively.

Here's a suggestion for romantics and adventurers who don't mind descending the trail by flashlight: Catch the sunset from Cowles' summit when the moon is full. After the sun slides into the Pacific, turn around and enjoy the moonrise over the El Cajon valley!

COWLES MOUNTAIN

TRIP 67
Blue Sky Ecological Reserve

Location	Poway
Highlights	Riparian and oak woodland; spring wildflowers
Distance	2.5 miles round trip
Total Elevation Gain/Loss	100'/100'
Hiking Time	1½ hours (round trip)
Optional Map	USGS 7.5-min *Escondido*
Best Times	All year
Agency	BSER
Difficulty	★

Now that the California Department of Fish and Game has purchased the former Blue Sky Ranch near Poway, one of the finest examples of riparian woodland in Southern California will be fully preserved and protected. Never a ranch—just property held for investment—the 410 acres include typical sage-scrub/chaparral hillside vegetation and more than a mile's worth of lushly shaded canyon bottom.

After a wet winter, the whole place acquires an almost unbelievable sheen of green. Mosses, ferns, annual grasses, and fresh new shrub growth coats everything, even the rocks. Wildflowers appear in great numbers by about April, and start to fade by June, after the grasses have bleached to a straw-yellow color. More than 100 kinds of wildflowers have been identified here in a single year.

You'll find the reserve entrance on the east shoulder of Espola Road, about two miles east of Rancho Bernardo and 0.6 mile north of Lake Poway Road. At the kiosk there, you can find out about naturalist-led interpretive walks, held generally on Saturdays and Sundays.

On foot, follow the unpaved Green Valley Truck Trail along the south bank of a creek. Traffic noise disappears, and frogs entertain you with their guttural serenades. Live oaks spread their limbs overhead, casting pools of shade, while willows,

sycamores, and lush thickets of poison oak cluster along the creek itself. On the left, about one-quarter mile out, a wide side trail diverges toward the creek itself. There you can spot tadpoles, frogs, and perhaps other amphibious creatures. A narrower path takes you back to the truck trail.

At 1.0 mile, another side path on the right goes south and ties into the trail system of the Lake Poway Recreation Area. One-quarter mile farther, where powerlines pass overhead, the road splits three ways. The left branch (Green Valley Truck Trail) goes across the creek and starts climbing a sunny slope toward the Ramona Reservoir. This split in the road is the end of the line for casual hiking. If you want a lot more exercise, just keep walking up the left branch all the way to the Ramona Reservoir dam, 1.3 miles farther and several hundred feet higher.

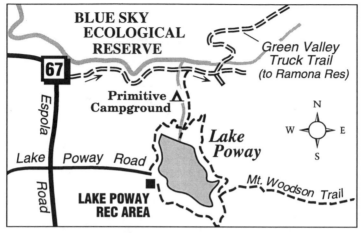

BLUE SKY ECOLOGICAL RESERVE

TRIP 68
Woodson Mountain

Location	Poway-Ramona
Highlights	Giant boulders; superb views
Distance	5.5 miles
Total Elevation Gain/Loss	1500'/1500'
Hiking Time	3 hours
Optional Map	USGS 7.5-min *San Pasqual*
Best Times	October through June
Agency	LPRA
Difficulty	★★

Indians called it "Mountain of Moonlit Rocks," an appropriate name for a landmark visible, even at night, over great distances. Early white settlers dubbed it "Cobbleback Peak," a name utterly descriptive of its rugged, boulder-strewn slopes. For the past 100 years, however, it has appeared on maps simply as "Woodson Mountain," in honor of a Dr. Woodson who homesteaded some property nearby well over a century ago.

The light-colored bedrock of Woodson Mountain and several of its neighboring peaks in the Poway/Ramona area is a type geologists call "Woodson Mountain granodiorite." When exposed at the surface, it weathers into huge spherical or ellipsoidal boulders with smooth surfaces. The largest boulders have a tendency to cleave apart along remarkably flat planes, forming "chimneys" from several inches to several feet wide. Sometimes, one half of a split boulder will roll away, leaving a vertical and almost seamless face behind. It's no wonder that Woodson Mountain (or "Mt. Woodson," as it is popularly called) is regarded as one of the finest places to practice the craft of bouldering in Southern California.

This looping route up and over Woodson's summit takes advantage of the new Fry-Koegel Trail along the mountain's bouldery north slope. Hikers have long had the opportunity of reaching the sum-

mit by either of two major routes, but there was never any easy way to avoid retracing steps.

Park on the wide shoulder of the east side of Highway 67, 3 miles north of Poway Road, opposite the entrance to the California Division of Forestry fire station. Carefully cross the four lanes of the highway (there's no crosswalk, though pedestrians scoot

Cleaved boulder, Woodson Mountain

across here frequently), and follow a well-beaten path south past the fire station to where it hooks up with a paved service road (closed to vehicular travel) curling up the mountain's east slope. The road underfoot is at times very steep, but offers good traction.

On most weekends, the sounds of nature along the road will be accompanied by the clink of aluminum hardware, plus the shouts of "On belay!" and other phrases in climbers' parlance. Even if you don't see climbers, chalk marks (from gymnast's chalk) on the larger boulders mark their favorite routes. Near the top of the mountain, the road passes narrowly between immense, egg-shaped boulders and split-boulder faces 20 to 30 feet high—some, perhaps, unclimbable by "ethical" means.

When you reach the top of the mountain, at 1.7 miles, you'll be amid a forest of radio antennae rising from the outsized boulders. Walk west, on dirt now, along the narrow summit ridge to reach a vantage point overlooking Poway, north San Diego County's coastal region, and the great blue expanse of the Pacific Ocean. Santa Catalina and San Clemente islands are visible on the clearest days. Nearby you'll spot an amazing cantilevered "potato-chip" flake of rock, the result of exfoliation and weathering. If you're weary, this is a good spot to turn back and return the way you came.

Otherwise, on ahead, you quickly pick up a rough trail which tilts downward, steeply at times, along Woodson's boulder-punctuated west ridge. After about 0.5 mile, there's a fork. Ignore the left branch, which descends toward the Mount Woodson Trail and Lake Poway, and continue down-ridge on the Fry-Koegel Trail.

After a few minutes, the trail switches back and starts an oblique dive down through wildly tangled, mature chaparral, bound for the Mount Woodson Estates subdivision at the north base of the mountain. Near the bottom, the trail meanders through spooky clusters of coast live oaks. Watch out for copious growths of poison oak through here.

Back in the open air again, the trail executes a rather annoying switchbacking detour around a block of new houses. Then it's a straight shot to Archie Moore Road, near Highway 67. A few minutes' walk along the highway shoulder from there takes you back to your car.

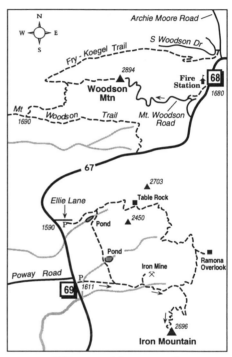

Woodson Mountain &
Iron Mountain

TRIP 69
Iron Mountain

Location	Near Poway
Highlights	Panoramic views
Distance	6.4 miles round trip
Total Elevation Gain/Loss	1200' /1200'
Hiking Time	3½ hours (round trip)
Optional Map	USGS 7.5-min *San Vicente Reservoir*
Best Times	October through June
Agency	LPRA
Difficulty	★★

North San Diego County's Iron Mountain thrusts its conical summit nearly 2700 feet above sea level, frequently well above the low-lying coastal haze. On many a crystalline winter day, the summit offers a sweeping, 360° panorama from glistening ocean to blue mountains and back to the ocean again. Access to the summit—by foot, horse, or mountain bike—is now afforded by a key link in the City of Poway's ever-expanding multi-use trails system.

The shortest way up the mountain (just over 3 miles one-way) takes you along signed pathways from the intersection of Poway Road and State Highway 67 to the summit. Thick stands of chaparral stood along these trails until 1995, when a wildfire swept east from Highway 67 and topped Iron Mountain's summit, burning to a crisp everything in its path. The summit trail remains in excellent shape, however, and the next several years will see the return of the vegetation and provide interesting lessons in fire ecology.

At 1.0 mile east of Highway 67, just before the trail dips to cross a ravine, a side trail goes north almost straight up a hill. If you care to make the short, strenuous side trip, you'll find a small pit where iron ore was once mined in small quantities. Dark, dense chunks of the ore lie strewn about—bring along a magnet to confirm their identity.

Once across the ravine, you commence a steeper ascent. At 1.5 miles you reach, in a saddle, a signed trail junction, where you turn right to head for Iron Mountain's summit. The summit lies only 1.7 miles away, despite the "2 miles" posted. On the trail's uppermost half-mile, numerous switchbacks take you back and forth across the ever-narrowing summit cone. In a mailbox on top, you'll discover a hikers' register—a notebook stuffed with hundreds of written comments. Also on the summit you'll find a massive, pier-mounted telescope (no coins required) thoughtfully provided for the purpose of scanning the near and far horizons.

You can return the easy way by simply reverse your steps, or opt for a more challenging traverse over hill and dale to the north. The northern loop, which passes Table Rock and two old cattle ponds, adds three additional miles to the round trip and involves several severe up and down pitches. The northern parts of this loop were untouched by the 1995 fire.

The Ellie Lane trailhead, a large equestrian staging area, offers an alternative starting point for the northern loop. It is typically underutilized and offers plenty of parking space in case there is no room for parking farther south.

TRIP 70
El Capitan Open Space Preserve

Location	Near Lakeside
Highlights	Frequent vistas of coastal lowlands and ocean
Distance	10.0 miles round trip
Total Elevation Gain/Loss	4000'/4000'
Hiking Time	5½ hours (round trip)
Optional Maps	USGS 7.5-min *San Vicente Reservoir, El Cajon Mtn.*
Best Times	November through April
Agency	SDCP
Difficulty	★★★★

As you walk along the granite-ribbed ridgeline, down the middle of the El Capitan Open Space Preserve, a binational panorama of ocean, islands, and innumerable mountain peaks lies in view. The broad San Diego River valley below curves beneath the sheer south face of El Cajon Mountain—the landmark informally known as "El Capitan."

The 2800-acre preserve was pieced together out of former BLM lands adjacent to the Cleveland National Forest. If you have the determination to tackle some really severe uphills and downhills, try following the main ridge-running trail—actually an old road bulldozed by miners years ago. It twists and turns over a scrubby, boulder-punctuated landscape that in

On the old mining road in El Capitan Preserve

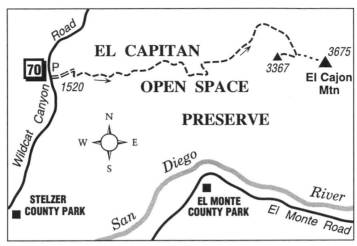

EL CAPITAN OPEN SPACE PRESERVE

spring comes alive with a blue frosting of ceanothus (wild lilac) blossoms.

If you follow the old road to its end, 5 miles out, you'll reach a 3367-foot peak subordinate only to the slightly higher summit of El Cajon Mountain nearby. This strenuous effort involves a surprising gain and loss of 4000 vertical feet (because of various ups and downs) over the entire round trip. Still, a nice vista of the surrounding mountains can be yours even if you hike less than a mile to reach the first of the five trailside rest stops along the way.

To reach the trailhead from Lakeside (northeast of San Diego), turn east on Mapleview Street where the freeway portion of Highway 67 ends. After 0.3 mile on Mapleview, turn left (north) on Wildcat Canyon Road and proceed 4.2 miles north to a signed parking lot for the El Capitan preserve on the right. (You can use the green mile markers by the roadside as your guide; slow down after mile marker 4.0.)

From the lot, walk east 0.4 mile on a graded dirt road, past some houses, to where the trail starts a steep, zigzag ascent up a cool, north-facing slope. You soon hook up with the old mining road, and the going gets easier for a while. Once you're past a small summit, the round top and sheer south brow of El Cajon Mountain become visible in the middle distance. Closer, on the left, rises

impressive Silverdome peak (in the Silverwood Wildlife Sanctuary), believed to be the largest granite monolith in San Diego County.

A very steep pitch, starting at 2.6 miles, will make you turn around and go back if you're not serious about this hike. A proposed trail will one day veer south from the 2.6-mile point and follow a south ridge down to El Monte Park, 1500 feet below.

At 4.0 miles, a rock-lined spring on the left, brimming with iron-rich water, serves horses (not people) that can make it this far. At 4.8 miles, the road arrives on a saddle between El Cajon Mountain's summit dome on the left and a smaller 3367-foot peak on the right (west). Turn right on the spur road going west to reach the latter summit, which offers a 270° view of distant horizons.

At the saddle, a sign indicates private property ahead (to the south). As an option on this hike, you can bag El Cajon Mountain's summit, which has a climber's register, by going due east about 0.4 mile through the chaparral. You'll pick up an informal trail, worn in by hikers, that goes through national forest land to the boulder-punctuated summit. The Forest Service is considering building a short connecting trail from the old road to the summit.

TRIP 71
Doane Valley

Location	Palomar Mountain State Park
Highlight	Verdant meadows, bubbling streams
Distance	2.5 miles
Total Elevation Gain/Loss	300'/300'
Hiking Time	1½ hours
Optional Map	USGS 7.5-min *Boucher Hill*
Best Times	All year
Agency	PSP
Difficulty	★★

This is a hike for inspiration. Here, at Palomar Mountain State Park, is some of Southern California's finest montane scenery, complete with trickling streams, mixed forests of pine, cedar and oak, and rolling meadows. The long, stomach-churning drive up Palomar's South Grade and East Grade roads is well worth the trouble once you get out of the car and start breathing in Palomar's sweet, tangy air.

You'll find the trailhead at the Doane Pond parking lot. Begin hiking on the Doane Valley Nature Trail, following Doane Creek downstream. Along the bank grow box elder trees, creek dogwood, wild strawberry, mountain currant, and Sierra gooseberry. You pass a massive incense-cedar towering 150 feet. If you weren't informed of its true identity, you might think it was a giant (sequoia) redwood.

After 0.3 mile, the nature trail curves and climbs around a hill to connect with Doane Valley Campground. At a trail junction here, bear left on the Lower Doane Trail, following Doane Creek through stately groves of white fir and incense-cedar. Walk all the way down to the weir at the end of the trail, and admire the stone-and-mortar structure above it. This small dam and gauging station were used in the late 1920s to test the hydroelectric potential of the stream. The tests proved there was not enough flow to justify construction of a

power plant. Today, the silted-in dam holds barely enough water to soak your feet in.

Some fishermen and hikers are familiar with the rugged and beautiful stretch of Pauma Creek below the weir. Currently, it's legal to scramble down the creek to the

Doane Valley Trail

park boundary, only 0.2 mile away. Beyond that point access is forbidden. The creek flows through the Pala Indian Reservation and eventually joins the San Luis Rey River in Pauma Valley. During high water, even the less-rugged stretch within the park can be quite treacherous. Several years ago, park rangers were surprised to discover banana slugs (like those in California's central and northern coast ranges) in this drainage.

From the weir, backtrack 0.2 mile and take the short connecting trail across Lower Doane Valley to the Lower French Valley Trail. Go left (north), passing into Lower French Valley. The setting is idyllic: rolling grasslands dotted with statuesque ponderosa pines, surrounded by hillsides clothed in oaks and tall conifers.

Several of the ponderosa pines are riddled with holes—some plugged with acorns. This is the handiwork of the acorn woodpecker, who uses the holes to store acorns filled with larvae. The birds retrieve these acorns and the grubs in leaner times. Listen for the repetitive, guttural call of this bird, and observe the distinctive red patch on its head and the white wing patch when in flight.

You can hike up as far as the bank of French Creek, then return along the same trail, staying left to finish the hike on Lower French Valley Trail.

The other trails of Palomar Mountain State Park are nearly as rewarding as the ones just described. Our map suggests additional loops you may be interested in making.

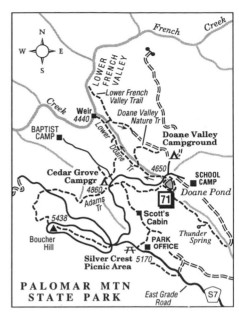

DOANE VALLEY

TRIP 72
Barker Valley

Location	Palomar Mountain, east side
Highlights	Remote valley; spectacular cascades
Distance	6.2 miles round trip (to foot of trail)
Total Elevation Gain/Loss	1000'/1000'
Hiking Time	4 hours (round trip)
Optional Map	USGS 7.5-min *Palomar Observatory*
Best Times	October through July
Agency	CNF/PD
Difficulty	★★★

Tucked into a dry and isolated corner of Cleveland National Forest, the oak-rimmed oasis of Barker Valley is a real surprise. The perennial west fork of the San Luis Rey River gurgles through the narrow valley floor, sustaining a growth of willows and sycamores along its banks. Centuries-old live oaks cast inviting pools of shade across grassy meadows that in late spring metamorphose from green to gold under the relentless rays of the sun.

Getting there requires some serious driving and hiking—first on an 8-mile stretch of bone-shaking truck trail that will surely loosen a nut or two on your vehicle, then on a gently descending, sun-exposed, 3-mile hiking trail. Get an early start if you're heading down for a picnic, so as to avoid some of the midday heat. (Check with the Forest Service to see if the road is open; storms can render it temporarily unusable.) Barker Valley is a popular destination for backpacking. No campfires are allowed, and you'll need a remote camping permit from the Forest Service for an overnight stay.

To reach the trailhead, turn west from Highway 79 onto Palomar Divide Road (Forest Road 9S07), 6.5 miles northwest of Warner Springs. Continue on the winding, unpaved road 7.8 miles to the Barker Valley Spur trailhead on the left side.

Park off the roadway and head down the trail (an old roadbed), which gradually descends along a chaparral-covered slope. The uneven growth is a consequence of various fires—some prescribed (to rid the hills of half-dead, mature shrubbery), others unintentional. For a while you pass through a grown-in section, unburned for perhaps several decades, choked with an attractive and colorful mix of manzanita, chamise, mountain mahogany, silk-tassel bush, ceanothus, and ribbonwood. The latter, almost the dominant shrub, spreads feathery plumes of light green foliage across the slopes. Notice its perpetually peeling, ribbonlike bark.

Keep an eye out for hawks and ravens soaring overhead. During the winter bald eagles are sometimes seen here, not far from where they roost on old snags near the shore of Lake Henshaw. Also keep a sharp eye on the ground for horned lizards. When not scurrying about, they're practically invisible against the decomposed granite soil.

After 1.7 miles of gradual descent, the old road bends sharply left. Continue around the U-curve, and within 0.1 mile veer to the right on a newer trail. You lazily zigzag down a dry slope and emerge on the floor of oak-rimmed Barker Valley. If you're looking for a campsite, they're abundant here. Just remember to select one at least 100 feet away from the nearest water—in this case, the West Fork San Luis Rey River.

Barker Valley is notorious for cold air drainage at night. I once had the interesting experience of sweating out an 85° July day, and awakening next morning to find frost along the stream.

By poking around the valley a bit, you may find evidence of former homesteads (various rusty pieces of metal and square nails), and evidence of early Indian use as well. Bedrock mortars (holes for grinding acorns) have been worn into some of the larger slab rocks. Keep in mind that all features are protected; there's no collecting allowed.

Many hikers come to Barker Valley in search of the rugged set of falls and pools a mile or so downstream from the foot of the Barker Spur Trail. These lie just below an old stone weir and gauging station. By following rough paths traversing the steep, brushy, north canyon wall, it's possible to reach hidden swimming holes worn in the water-polished rock. Wild trout can be found in the pools below the first falls (a license is needed for fishing). Don't attempt to explore this area unless you have the right footgear, and you're adept at scrambling across steep terrain and potentially slippery, water-polished rock. An ill-timed slip in a couple of places could result in a deadly, 50-foot plunge down a cascade.

When it's time to return, go back the same way, uphill this time. The consistently gradual trail is not at all challenging, but it may prove difficult after many hours of exposure to the warm sun.

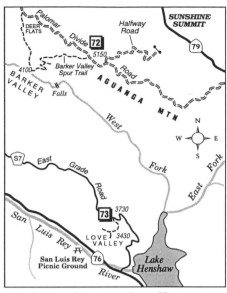

BARKER VALLEY & LOVE VALLEY

TRIP 73
Love Valley

Location	Palomar Mountain
Highlights	Secluded meadows and ponds
Distance	2.0 miles round trip
Total Elevation Gain/Loss	300'/300'
Hiking Time	1½ hours (round trip)
Optional Map	USGS 7.5-min *Palomar Observatory*
Best Times	November through June
Agency	CNF/PD
Difficulty	★

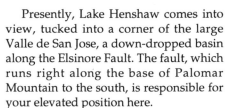

After a wet winter, shallow ponds in Love Valley hold the shimmering, upside-down image of a classic California landscape: a weathered barn nestled at the far end of an Ireland-colored meadow, rounded foothills studded with oaks, and white cumulus clouds billowing over the dark, conifer-draped Palomar crest. By May or June, the shallow ponds in the valley bottom shrink and disappear, leaving in their wake a brilliant display of yellow tidy tips and assorted other wildflowers.

This little-known, day-use destination near the foot of Palomar Mountain is great for a picnic of the sit-on-a-blanket type. The starting point is easy to find, a turnout on the south side of East Grade Road, 3.3 miles north of Highway 76. Using the mile markers on East Grade Road, the turnout is found between mile markers 3.0 and 3.5. From the turnout, walk around the locked vehicle gate, and follow a wide, dirt path over a low rise and then gently downhill.

As you descend, watch for three kinds of oak trees—black, coast, and Engelmann oaks. The Engelmann variety, characterized by gray-green leaves, is noted for its limited and shrinking habitat. The 3600-foot elevation here is a bit too low for the pines, cedars and firs that are so common a little higher on Palomar Mountain.

Presently, Lake Henshaw comes into view, tucked into a corner of the large Valle de San Jose, a down-dropped basin along the Elsinore Fault. The fault, which runs right along the base of Palomar Mountain to the south, is responsible for your elevated position here.

When you reach the edge of Love Valley at 0.8 mile, you can walk straight to the old barn (which, upon closer inspection, is made of unromantic and rusty corrugated metal), or you can veer left toward the two ephemeral ponds on the valley floor. Choose your picnic site so as to trample as little vegetation as possible. There are no trash barrels or other facilities in Love Valley, so remember to pack out whatever you pack in and do not consume.

Love Valley in spring

TRIP 74
Agua Caliente Creek

Location	Near Warner Springs
Highlights	Beautiful mountain stream
Distance	8.0 miles round trip
Total Elevation Gain/Loss	900'/900'
Hiking Time	4 hours (round trip)
Optional Maps	USGS 7.5-min *Warner Springs, Hot Springs Mtn.*
Best Times	November through May
Agency	CNF/PD
Difficulty	★★★

Until about 20 years ago, the middle reaches of Agua Caliente Creek seldom saw the intrusion of humans. After the Pacific Crest Trail was routed through, it became a favorite resting spot for hikers heading north or south. This is one of only four places in San Diego County where the PCT dips to cross a fairly dependable stream, and the only place where the trail closely follows water for a fair distance. The stream—if not perennial every year—is at least alive from the first rains of fall into early summer.

You begin hiking at the Agua Caliente Creek bridge at mile 36.6 on Highway 79, just outside Warner Springs. There's a turnout for parking just west (mile 36.7) and a dirt road slanting over to where the PCT crosses under the highway. Proceed upstream along the cottonwood-shaded creek, first on the left (north) bank, then on the right. In this first mile, the trail goes through Warner Ranch resort property on an easement. Near the Cleveland National Forest boundary, about one mile out, water flows or trickles from a canyon mouth (trail camping, with permit, is allowed on the lands beyond this point). The trail detours this canyon by swinging to the east and climbing moderately onto gentle, ribbonwood-clothed slopes. After almost 2 miles of somewhat tedious twisting and turning in the chaparral you join the creek again at the 3200-foot contour.

Now the gorgeous scenery begins. In the next mile the trail crosses the stream several times and passes a number of appealing small campsites well up on the bank. Live oaks, sycamores, willows, and alders line the creek. The canyon walls soar several hundred feet on either side—clad in dense chaparral on the southeast side, dotted with sage and yucca on the northwest.

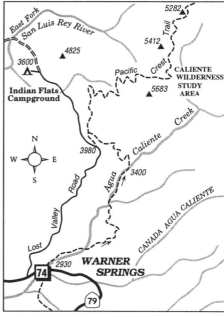

AGUA CALIENTE CREEK

After a final crossing of the creek, the trail doubles back and begins a switchbacking (and not too scenic) ascent northwest toward Lost Valley Road. This is a good place to turn around and return the same way.

If you are energetic and well supplied, nothing stops you from continuing north into the pristine Caliente Wilderness Study Area several miles ahead. Some day-hikers make the climb to Lost Valley Road, using a spur of the Pacific Crest Trail to reach the road. They then either jog down the road or hitch a ride back to the starting point.

If you want to explore farther upstream along Agua Caliente Creek from where the trail ascends out of the canyon, you can do it by boulder hopping and wading. Ahead, there's some serious scrambling around small waterfalls, and personal battles with the ever-present alder branches. Los Coyotes Indian Reservation property, requiring permission for entry, starts about a mile ahead.

Running the PCT along Agua Caliente Creek

TRIP 75
Hot Springs Mountain

Location	Near Warner Springs
Highlight	Summit is San Diego County's high point
Distance	5.5 miles round trip
Total Elevation Gain/Loss	1250'/1250'
Hiking Time	3½ hours (round trip)
Optional Map	USGS 7.5-min *Hot Springs Mtn.*
Best Times	March through November
Agency	LCIR
Difficulty	★★★

Some of the loftiest—and least visited—mountain country in San Diego County surrounds the resort community of Warner Springs. Hot Springs Mountain, on the Los Coyotes Indian Reservation to the east, is recognized as the county's highest point. At 6533 feet, it beats the better-known, 6512-foot Cuyamaca Peak to the south by a whisker.

Hikers and backpackers are in on a little secret when they discover the Los Coyotes Indian Reservation. This is the largest (25,000 acres) of the 18 reservations in San Diego County, yet one of the least populated. Visitors can make use of developed camping facilities there, as well as explore the undeveloped parts on a network of graded dirt roads, 4-wheel-drive roads, and trails. Motorcycles are prohibited on the reservation and the vehicle traffic is light on the roads, so you're quite likely to find this a pleasant place to go hiking. With its network of roads and trails that seem to go everywhere, the reservation has also become popular among mountain bikers.

To reach the Los Coyotes reservation, turn east on Camino San Ignacio from Highway 79 (mile 35.0) at Warner Springs. After 0.6 mile, bear right on Los Tules Road and continue 4.5 miles to the reservation gate. There you pay a fee for an entrance permit and pick up a sketch map of the roads and trails. The main camp-

ground (where water is available) lies another 2.7 miles onward via paved and dirt road. Los Coyotes is open year-round on the weekends and holidays, weather and road conditions permitting. Call or write first if you plan to visit on a weekday.

When road and weather conditions allow, it is possible to drive nearly all the way to the Hot Springs summit by way of the semi-maintained Lookout Road. Far more rewarding, from a hiker's point of view, is

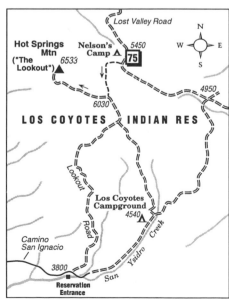

HOT SPRINGS MOUNTAIN

the moderately strenuous trek we describe here, starting from Nelson's Camp, which nestles beneath the mountain's cool north slope.

Drive up Los Coyotes' main road, past the developed campground, to an intersection in a valley 6.1 miles past the entrance gate. Turn left (west) and drive up the valley on a sandy road to reach a saddle above the valley, 2.2 miles farther. Just beyond this saddle, on the left (west) side of the road, you'll find Nelson's Camp amid a pleasant grove of live oak, pine and cedar trees.

Park and begin hiking southwest up along a small stream that flows north and west toward Agua Caliente Creek. You follow an old jeep trail up this drainage (still used occasionally by daring 4-wheel drivers who risk getting stuck), gaining more than 500 feet in just over a mile. At the top, you'll meet Lookout Road. Turn right (west) on this road and climb another 1.6 miles along the ridgeline to the tower.

You'll pass through dense forests of black oak, Coulter pine and white fir, and across sunny meadows dotted in late spring with wildflowers. In late October, the black oaks shimmer with yellow leaves, and gusts of wind unleash a pitter-patter of acorns.

The road leads to a dilapidated fire lookout tower, closed in 1976. The little "condo" atop the tower seems appealing to explore, but for safety reasons is not recommended as a vantage point for viewing the surrounding scenery. East of the old lookout tower, however, you can climb a little higher through chaparral and oaks to reach San Diego County's high point—a flat concrete platform atop a large boulder. A bit of hand-and-toe climbing is required to gain the last 20 feet of elevation. As seen from the platform, steep canyons yawn to the west and north, and the Salton Sea shimmers like a mirage on the eastern horizon.

Abandoned lookout, Hot Springs Mountain

TRIP 76
Cedar Creek Falls

Location	West of Julian
Highlights	Beautiful cascade and "punchbowl"
Distance	4.5 miles round trip
Total Elevation Gain/Loss	1200'/1200'
Hiking Time	2½ hours (round trip)
Optional Maps	USGS 7.5-min *Santa Ysabel, Tule Springs*
Best Times	November through June
Agency	CNF/PD
Difficulty	★★

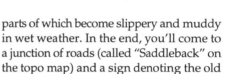

The San Diego River and its upper tributaries drain the pastoral valleys and forested hillsides around Julian, and the rugged western slopes of the Cuyamaca Mountains. The water flows generally southwest through V-shaped canyons, and eventually reaches El Capitan Reservoir, not far from San Diego's eastern suburbs. Quite frequently the water encounters resistant layers in the underlying igneous and metamorphic rocks. In several places it tumbles over cataracts up to a hundred feet high. The grinding of stones trapped in pockets below these falls has created deep pools, or "punchbowls." Cedar Creek Falls, along with its punchbowl, is one of the more attractive and accessible of these wonders.

Before the construction of El Capitan Dam in the early '30s, the falls were a popular destination for Sunday outings, and could be reached relatively easily on an auto road up the San Diego River valley from Lakeside. Now, the drive to the Cedar Creek Falls trailhead, which takes San Diegans nearly as far as Julian, is far more circuitous—but very scenic nonetheless.

At a point on Highway 78 one mile west of Julian, turn south on Pine Hills Road. After 1.5 miles, bear right on Eagle Peak Road. After 1.4 more miles, Eagle Peak Road veers right (Boulder Creek Road goes left). Now you and your vehicle face 8.2 miles of progressively poorer road,

parts of which become slippery and muddy in wet weather. In the end, you'll come to a junction of roads (called "Saddleback" on the topo map) and a sign denoting the old road ahead as the Cedar Creek Falls hiking and equestrian trail.

As you head downhill on foot, look up the canyon in the north to see Mildred Falls, arguably San Diego County's highest at more than 100 feet. Unfortunately, it's often little more than a dark stain on an orange-tinted cliff. In flood, however, it is truly an awesome sight.

The old road winds farther west, offering a splendid view of the upper San Diego River canyon, then turns south for a long descent to the river bed. At 1.4 miles, take

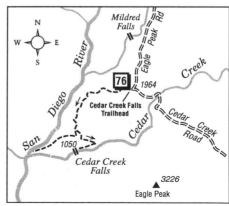

CEDAR CREEK FALLS

the spur road that goes left (southeast) over a low saddle into the Cedar Creek drainage. Descend to the bank of the creek and continue following the old road and trail down to the shallow, reflecting pool at the brink of the falls. Be extremely cautious here, as the rock is very slippery. Long-time San Diego hiker Uel Fisk remembers quite vividly watching one of his classmates fall to her death from this brink in 1926.

From a ridge on the right side, it's possible to admire the 90-foot-high cascade and the cottonwood-framed punchbowl at the bottom—some 50 feet across and 20 feet deep. After heavy rains, water thunders over the precipice, but by late summer the falls merely whisper. Many people obviously make the steep traverse down to the pool at the bottom, though the Forest Service advises against it.

There are other routes to the falls via the mouth of Cedar Creek canyon, but they necessitate crossing property owned by the Helix Water District (land below the 995-foot contour in the San Diego River drainage.) The Forest Service says that permission must be obtained from the landowner to cross this land.

When you've had your fill of the almost overwhelming natural beauty, return to your starting point the same way. If the spirit moves you, you can try this more adventurous, difficult route on the return: From the top of the falls, walk east along the north bank of Cedar Creek about 0.5 mile until the canyon walls close in. There you'll be forced into the creekbed. After about two hours (about 1.2 miles) of boulder-hopping, bushwhacking, and wading through a beautiful and isolated stretch of canyon, Cedar Creek Road will lie above you on the left. Climb north up the slope to that road and follow it a short distance up to your starting point.

Cedar Creek Falls

TRIP 77

Volcan Mountain

Location	Near Julian
Highlights	Pastoral mountain landscapes
Distance	3.0 miles
Total Elevation Gain/Loss	900'/900'
Hiking Time	2 hours (round trip)
Optional Map	USGS 7.5-min *Julian*
Best Times	October through June
Agency	SDCP
Difficulty	★★

Rising boldly above the apple orchards outside Julian, Volcan Mountain's oak- and pine-dotted slopes are swept by some of the freshest breezes found anywhere. Soughing through the trees like waves spending themselves against a sandy beach, these gusts bear the astringent dryness of the nearby desert as well as the volatile scents of pine needles and sun-baked grass.

Named by early Spanish or Mexican travelers for its dubious resemblance to a volcano, Volcan Mountain (called the "Volcan Mountains" on topographic maps) is really a fault-block mountain, like many others in the Peninsular Ranges. Two faults—the Elsinore and the Earthquake Valley faults— bracket the mountain on the southwest and northeast sides respectively.

Off-limits to public use for the past century, Volcan Mountain is gradually falling into the public domain today. As funding becomes available, privately owned land on the mountain is being purchased piece-meal by San Diego County and by the San Dieguito River Park joint powers authority. One such parcel has already become an unsung crown jewel in the county parks system—Volcan Mountain Wilderness Preserve.

An obscure wooden sign, just north of Wynola Road along Farmer Road (about 2 ½ miles north of Julian), announces the preserve. Park alongside Farmer Road and walk east on a dirt access road. After 0.2 mile, you come upon a carved entry structure and stonework designed by noted Julian artist James Hubbell. There's also a small, open-air *kiva* with a compass rose imbedded in the floor, used during interpretive programs. The Elsinore Fault, a major splinter of the San Andreas, passes almost directly under this spot.

Just beyond this formal entrance, your wide path leads sharply up a hill over-looking an apple orchard. You soon swing sharply right and continue climbing in earnest along a rounded ridgeline leading toward the Volcan Mountain crest. Along the ridge, wind-rippled expanses of grassland alternate with dense copses of live oak and black oak. The rust-red bark of the many manzanita shrubs along the way perpetually peels, revealing a green undercoat. Look for the *manzanitas* ("little apples" in Spanish)—the ripe, reddish brown berries that look and taste a bit like the apples hanging from the trees down in the valley below. As you climb higher, the view expands to include parts of Julian, the dusky Cuyamaca Mountains to the south, and—on the clearest days—the blue arc of the Pacific Ocean in the west and south-west.

A locked gate at 1.5 miles (and 900 feet higher than where you started) blocks further progress up the dirt road. At some

future date, when the property above opens
to the public, you will be able to continue
walking toward Volcan peak (elevation
5353 feet) on the summit ridge.

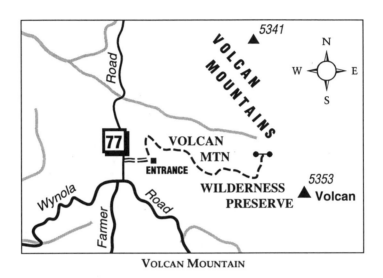

VOLCAN MOUNTAIN

TRIP 78
Kelly Ditch Trail

Location	Cuyamaca Rancho State Park
Highlights	Beautiful coniferous/deciduous forest; historic interest
Distance	5.5 miles
Total Elevation Gain/Loss	1000'/1600'
Hiking Time	4 hours
Optional Maps	USGS 7.5-min *Julian, Cuyamaca Peak*
Best Times	All year
Agency	CRSP
Difficulty	★★★

The Kelly Ditch Trail, completed in 1985, is perhaps the most beautiful pathway yet built in the Cuyamaca-Julian area. This hiking/horse trail is routed partly along a century-old diversion ditch. You'll also tread over dim traces of "skid roads" where freshly cut logs were slid down off the mountain ridges to serve as lumber and fuel for the mines and boom towns of Julian's late-1800s gold rush period.

On the Kelly Ditch Trail

Hiking the trail is rewarding in any season, but it's hard to beat the fall-color season, which reaches its peak around late October. By then the black oaks exhibit full crowns of crispy, golden leaves, and fat, glossy acorns litter the ground. Crimson squaw bush and poison oak leaves show their stuff amid the glades of russet-colored bracken fern.

The Kelly Ditch Trail is best hiked one-way, with the aid of a car shuttle or a drop-off-and-pick-up arrangement. The easier (mostly downhill) direction is south to north—Cuyamaca Reservoir to William Heise County Park. The starting point is on Highway 79, 8.3 miles south of Julian, near the intersection of Engineers Road and Highway 79. The trail ends at a parking lot just inside William Heise County Park. Heise Park can be reached by turning south from Highway 78 on Pine Hills Road (just west of Julian) and following well-placed directional signs to the park.

You first pick up the trail west of Engineers Road and just north of where Highway 79 crosses the low dam impounding the waters of Cuyamaca Reservoir. In the first mile you'll travel in, or on the rim of, the remnant Kelly Ditch, constructed by pick-and-shovel labor more than a century ago. Its purpose was to divert runoff from the south slope of North Peak into the then-new reservoir. Poison oak grows alongside the trail—take care to avoid contact with it.

After a mile the trail climbs abruptly out of the ditch, veers north through a sun-struck patch of chaparral, and then crosses paved Engineers Road. You pass a spring-fed horse trough, and continue a short distance to join a disused dirt road. Turn right and follow the road's gentle uphill course around the west slope of North Peak. You'll stroll past a couple of ancient sugar pines, and enter a delightful, parklike meadow, dotted with black oaks and carpeted by bracken ferns. On the clearest days, blue sky meets the blue Pacific horizon more than a hundred miles to the west.

At the next fork (about 2.5 miles from the start), you're directed left across a sunny bowl, and then up to a low ridge shaded by live oaks, black oaks, Coulter pines, incense-cedars, and white firs. From this point, the highest elevation of the hike, a long series of switchbacks leads you steadily downward (and north) to a small stream—a fork of Cedar Creek—fringed with ferns and wild berries.

On past the creek, the trail goes up a steep ravine evidently cut deeply by some agent other than running water. This is the remnant of one of the skid roads. After a 130-foot gain, the trail tops a saddle and joins a dirt road. You descend to a second creek (the main fork of Cedar Creek), cross a meadow beyond, and pick up the last link of trail leading to the Heise Park entrance.

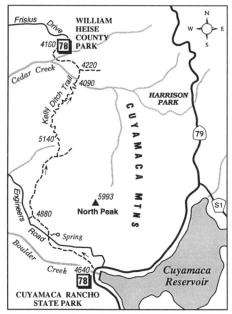

Kelly Ditch Trail

TRIP 79
Azalea Glen Trail

Location	Cuyamaca Rancho State Park
Highlights	Verdant meadows and forest; botanical interest
Distance	3.0 miles
Total Elevation Gain/Loss	550′/550′
Hiking Time	1½ hours
Optional Map	USGS 7.5-min *Cuyamaca Peak*
Best Times	All year
Agency	CRSP
Difficulty	★★

Cuyamaca Rancho State Park, the favorite mountain park of San Diegans, sprawls across more than 25,000 acres of chaparral, pine forest, gentle meadows, and gurgling, sycamore-lined streams. Of all the trails in the park, the Azalea Glen loop trail is surely the best for leisurely walking and for showing off a great variety of attractive natural features. On it you explore dense forests, a sunny meadow, a trickling brook, Indian *morteros*, and a refreshing spring—all in a span of only 3 miles.

You begin at Paso Picacho campground/picnic area, located at the high point along Highway 79, 10 miles south of Julian and 12 miles north of Interstate 8 near Descanso. The trail begins across from

the picnic area, not far from the restrooms at the entrance. First follow the trail 0.2 mile west to a split. Take the right fork to hike the trail counterclockwise—the way I'll describe it.

Contour through a mixed forest of oaks, pines, firs, and cedars, crossing three small ravines. At 0.6 mile from the split, you emerge from the shade into a cheerful, bracken-fringed meadow. It's hard to miss the fine collection of morteros on the nearby granite slabs. Leaving the meadow, you plunge into the dark forest again, and descend to the bank of a small brook, informally called Azalea Creek. Here, western azalea, thimbleberry, and other moisture- and shade-loving plants form a delicate understory of greenery under dense stands of white fir and incense-cedar. Come in May or June to see the azaleas in bloom. The Azalea Glen route joins the California Riding and Hiking Trail and turns steeply uphill through white fir forest, then through thickets of manzanita and other brush forms. After about 0.5 mile, the trail tops out, joining Azalea Spring Fire Road in a clearing.

Western azalea

Azalea Spring is nearby, serving as a popular resting place and water stop for hikers and horses. A giant pine, with a trunk perhaps 6 feet in diameter, stands on the slope just south of the spring.

From Azalea Spring, it's back into the forest again as you descend moderately on the last leg of the Azalea Glen Trail. Let gravity pay its debt, but don't rush through: watch and listen for gray squirrels, chipmunks, chickadees, acorn woodpeckers, and the ubiquitous Steller's jays.

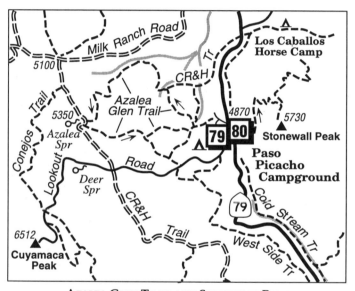

AZALEA GLEN TRAIL AND STONEWALL PEAK

TRIP 80
Stonewall Peak

Location	Cuyamaca Rancho State Park
Highlights	Outstanding views from summit block
Distance	4.5 miles round trip
Total Elevation Gain/Loss	850′/850′
Hiking Time	2½ hours (round trip)
Optional Map	USGS 7.5-min *Cuyamaca Peak*
Best Times	All year
Agency	CRSP
Difficulty	★★

Stonewall Peak's angular summit of white granite is a conspicuous landmark throughout Cuyamaca Rancho State Park. Although Stonewall stands some 800 feet lower than nearby Cuyamaca Peak, it's unique position and steep, south exposure provides a more inclusive view of the park area itself.

Beginning across the highway from the entrance to Paso Picacho Campground (see driving directions in Trip 79 above), the trail climbs steadily and moderately on a set of well-engineered switchbacks up the west slope of Stonewall Peak. Thick groves of live and black oaks keep you in semi-shade most of the way.

About halfway up the trail, a view opens to the north and east. Cuyamaca Reservoir lies to the north, its level and its extent varying according to the season and the year's precipitation. When it is full, its surface covers nearly 1000 acres.

When you reach the top of the switchbacks, turn right (south) toward the summit of the peak. (The trail to the left descends sharply to Los Caballos Camp; if you prefer, this can be used as an alternate, but substantially longer, return route.) Follow the trail through chaparral and scattered trees to the base of the exposed granite cap. A series of steps hewn in the rock and a guardrail are provided in the last hundred

feet or so. Small children would certainly need assistance here.

On top, you won't see any ocean views (the main Cuyamaca massif stands tall in the west), but the foreground panorama of the park's rolling topography is impressive enough. Patches of meadow along the streamcourses and the bald grassland areas below change color with the seasons: green in spring, yellow in summer, brown or gray in fall, and occasionally white with fallen snow in winter. The forested slopes appear as a tapestry of color, the light green or yellow-tinted black oaks playing counterpoint to the rather dark hues of the conifers and live oaks. Direction-finders atop Stonewall's summit block assist in the identification of major peaks in the middle and far distance.

Swallows or swifts practically rake the summit during their high-speed maneuvers, and larger birds—ravens, hawks, and even bald eagles may cruise by. Eagles, along with egrets, herons, and ospreys, are sometimes attracted to the shoreline of nearby Cuyamaca Reservoir, especially in winter.

TRIP 81
Sweetwater River

Location	Cuyamaca Rancho State Park
Highlight	Riparian and oak woodland; sparkling mountain stream
Distance	3.8 miles round trip
Total Elevation Gain/Loss	400'/400'
Hiking Time	1½ hours (round trip)
Optional Maps	USGS 7.5-min *Descanso, Cuyamaca Peak*
Best Times	October through June
Agency	CRSP
Difficulty	★★

Fed by countless ravines and rivulets on the slopes of the Cuyamaca Mountains, the Sweetwater River eventually becomes a watercourse worthy of the name "river"— at least in the rain or snow season. In the south end of Cuyamaca Rancho State Park, the sweet, bubbling liquid slides placidly down a pleasant little gorge lined by alders, willows, and live oaks. The Merigan Fire Road—a wide, oak-shaded path for hikers, horses and mountain bikers—clings to the high bank of the river for more than a mile, offering the self-propelled traveler vistas of cool, sparkling water tumbling over a gravelly canyon floor. For years there were sporadic attempts to introduce beavers along this stretch of the river, so look for evidence in the form of dams made of willow saplings and mud.

View north from Stonewall Peak

As the river begins to slacken in March or April, the chaparral-covered hills above the path brighten from a dull to a bright shade of green. Millions of urn-shaped, white and pink blossoms pop out on the manzanitas, attracting frantic hordes of bees. Blue-flowering ceanothus kicks in by early April, spreading waves of color and an ineffable fragrance across the sun-warmed slopes. Mountain mahogany becomes conspicuous in late summer, sporting thousands of hairy seed tufts that resemble twisted pipe cleaners.

To reach the starting point from Interstate 8 near Descanso, drive north 2.7 miles on Highway 79 and turn left (north) toward Cuyamaca Rancho State Park, staying on 79. After another 0.2 mile, turn left on Viejas Boulevard. Continue 1.1 miles to an obscurely marked trailhead parking lot next to a ranger residence on the right.

From the lot, walk past a vehicle gate. The Merigan road beyond takes you across a sunny meadow, then up onto a brushy slope toward a saddle. In springtime, the air rising along the slopes bears both the tangy fragrance of new growth in the chaparral and the humid scent of the stream-hugging willows just ahead.

Just beyond the saddle, the first of two short spur trails branches left and downward toward the river and its accompanying strip of riparian vegetation. The second spur trail, 0.4 mile farther, leads to an artificial waterfall—a silted-in diversion dam.

After some further mild climbing, the road enters a magnificent grove of live oak trees and sidles up against the high banks of the river. At 1.9 miles, the fire road turns east toward Highway 79, while two other trails continue north toward Green Valley Falls and Green Valley Campground. Hikers and equestrians may continue on the narrow trails ahead; they connect to the more than 100 miles of footpaths and fire roads in the central part of the park. Mountain bikers must stick to the fire road.

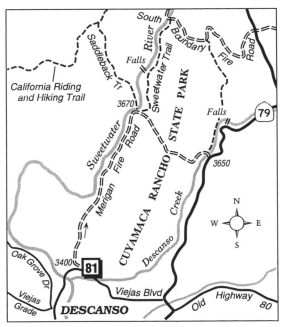

SWEETWATER RIVER

TRIP 82
Horsethief Canyon

Location	Pine Creek Wilderness
Highlights	Cascades and shallow pools
Distance	3.2 miles round trip (to Pine Valley Creek)
Total Elevation Gain/Loss	500'/500'
Hiking Time	2 hours (round trip)
Optional Maps	USGS 7.5-min *Barrett Lake, Viejas Mountain*
Best Times	November through June
Agency	CNF/DD
Difficulty	★★

The croak of a soaring raven cracks the stillness as my companions and I saunter down the green-fringed path. A groggy dragonfly flits through a beam of morning sunlight. Cool air, slinking down the night-chilled slopes, caresses our faces and sets aflutter the papery sycamore leaves overhead. Approaching the pools and cascades of Pine Valley Creek, we smell the moist exudations of mule-fat and willow. We cup the clear, cold water in our palms and dash it across our heads.

If you want this kind of escape from the city—and you want it relatively quickly—Pine Creek Wilderness, east of San Diego, is one great place to find it. The 13,000-acre wilderness, part of Cleveland National Forest, was created by an act of Congress in 1984, and now includes about 25 miles of hiking trails within its borders. Dayhiking the wilderness requires no permit, though you must obtain a wilderness permit for overnight backpacking.

Average or better winter rains followed by spring sunshine transform the place into a foothill garden, with water dancing down the larger ravines and careening off boulders in Pine Valley Creek—the large drainage bisecting the wilderness. The tough chaparral vegetation coating the slopes gets to looking temporarily soft, the green of emerging annual grasses turns positively lurid, and the live oaks, sycamores,

and cottonwoods send out new leaves and branches in a burst of growth.

The quickest and most impressive route into the wilderness is by way of Horsethief Canyon. The trailhead, at mile 16.4 on Lyons Valley Road, is similarly quick and easy for San Diegans to reach. From Interstate 8 at Alpine, follow Tavern Road 2.7 miles south, Japatul Road 5.8 miles east, and Lyons Valley Road 1.5 miles south to the trailhead. From Jamul, in south San Diego County, drive east and north, using Skyline Truck Trail and Lyons Valley Road, to get to the same point.

From the trailhead parking lot, a sign directs you north along a gated dirt road for about 300 yards. You then veer right down a ravine on the signed Espinosa Trail. After a fast 400-foot elevation loss, the path bends right (east) to follow oak- and sycamore-lined Horsethief Canyon. True to its name, this corral-like canyon was used in the late 1800s by horse thieves to stash stolen horses in preparation for their passage across the international border. The canyon bottom is dry most of the year, but agreeably shaded throughout. After another mile and not much more descent, you reach Pine Valley Creek, which in winter and early spring brims with runoff from the creek's headwaters in the Laguna Mountains.

Upstream from the pool, you can make your way alongside or over a jumble of car-sized boulders and past several small cascades. Tangled willows and mule-fat (a willow look-alike) impede your progress. Watch your step on slippery slabs of rock, and be aware of poison-oak thickets, possible rattlesnakes, and fast water if your visit comes immediately on the heels of a big storm. You can continue in this manner—straight up the canyon bottom—for 3 picturesque miles or more.

If you're hooked on loop hikes, you can try the following, less-scenic return route: Proceed downstream from Horsethief Canyon along the west bank of Pine Valley Creek for 0.7 mile. At a point opposite the Espinosa Creek confluence, turn right (west) on an old roadbed paralleling a ravine. Follow its steep course upward through chaparral and over a summit to the trailhead parking lot.

Note: As of 1996, Operation Gatekeeper, the federal government's attempt to stave off illegal immigration from Mexico into the United States, is resulting in an eastward shift in migration patterns (from Tijuana/San Ysidro to points well east of there) and a dramatic increase in migrant foot traffic northward through the canyons of Pine Creek Wilderness. It is not known whether this will be a temporary or a long-term problem. Since safety issues may be a concern, you should contact Cleveland National Forest (Descanso Ranger District) for the latest update.

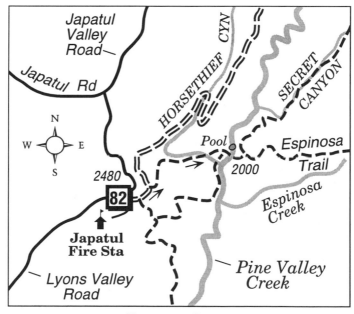

HORSETHIEF CANYON

Corte Madera Mountain

Location	South of Pine Valley
Highlights	Panoramic views
Distance	6.5 miles round trip
Total Elevation Gain/Loss	1750'/1750'
Hiking Time	4 hours (round trip)
Optional Maps	USGS 7.5-min *Morena Reservoir, Descanso*
Best Times	November through May
Agency	CNF/DD
Difficulty	★★★

On a clear day atop Corte Madera Mountain, you can see forever—or at least as far as Santa Catalina and San Clemente islands to the west, and the mile-high Sierra Juarez plateau in Baja California to the south. From many parts of San Diego, Corte Madera Mountain's sheer south face appears as an abrupt drop in the profile of the eastern horizon. On the summit, you stand near the edge of that 300-foot-high precipice.

To reach the hike's starting point, exit Interstate 8 at Buckman Springs Road and proceed 3 miles south to Corral Canyon Road. Turn right (west), and proceed 4.8 miles on narrow pavement to a sharp hairpin turn. Unsigned, gated Kernan Road goes northwest from the hairpin. Park nearby off the road.

First, squeeze around the gate and walk 0.5 mile uphill on Kernan Road. Where the road bends right in a horseshoe curve, go left on the Espinosa Trail and continue northwest. After one more mile of climbing, you top a saddle and intersect Los Pinos Road. Turn right and continue 0.3 mile to another saddle, this one a half mile southeast of boulder-studded, Coulter-pine-dotted peak 4588. Leave the road there and find and follow a path that works its way up past peak 4588 and across another saddle just northwest of the peak.

Continue following the path northwest, then finally southwest along a crest to the summit plateau of Corte Madera Mountain. The view north includes a fabulous vista, available nowhere else on public land, of privately owned Corte Madera Valley. A beautiful lake and oak-studded meadows fill the valley. The name Corte Madera ("woodyard") apparently refers to the use of this area as a source of timber during the building of the San Diego area missions.

Corte Madera Mountain's summit plateau is covered by large sheets of granitic rock supporting patches of chaparral. From the southernmost point on the plateau you can peer over the abrupt face into the canyon drained by Espinosa Creek. To the southeast is Los Pinos Mountain, topped by a fire lookout, one of the few remaining in Southern California that are used on a regular basis.

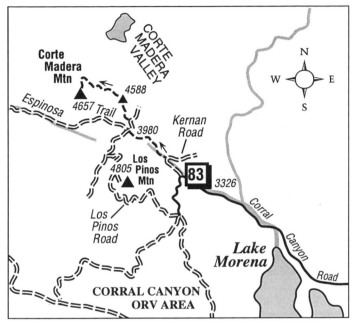

CORTE MADERA MOUNTAIN

TRIP 84
Cottonwood Creek Falls

Location	Laguna Mountains
Highlights	Cascades and shallow pools
Distance	1.8 miles round trip
Total Elevation Gain/Loss	500'/500'
Hiking Time	1 hour (round trip)
Optional Map	USGS 7.5-min *Mount Laguna*
Best Times	December through June
Agency	CNF/DD
Difficulty	★★

Hidden in the apex of a narrow valley in the Laguna Mountains near the town of Pine Valley, a small stream has worn its way down to metamorphic bedrock. Engorged on occasion by spates of heavy rain or melting snow, the stream comes alive, alternately dancing over ledges or inclined slabs, and pausing in placid pools. This is no Yosemite Falls, to be sure, but merely one of many secret beauty spots tucked away in the Southern California's mountainous folds. Known as Cottonwood Creek Falls, it remains attractive through spring and early summer. By July or August, summer's heat sucks it dry.

Access to the falls (over a route through Cleveland National Forest lands) is by way of a brushy draw leading down from Sunrise Highway at a point 2 miles north of Interstate 8. Park anywhere in either of the two large turnouts north of mile marker 15.0, and walk over to the start of the unmarked trail, directly beneath a small powerline. In the late spring white-blossoming ceanothus, beard tongue, and woolly blue curls brighten the trailside.

As you approach Cottonwood Creek, 0.7 mile down, turn sharply left and go upstream past some large oaks toward the cascades. After a bit of rock scrambling, and two easy crossings of the stream, you'll reach the uppermost fall, where the stream drops 10 feet into a crystalline pool at least head-high deep. By May or June, the water warms to a temperature suitable for comfortable bathing, though by that time the flow in the creek may be sluggish and the water unappealingly tainted by algae.

Cottonwood Creek Falls

The broad banks of the creek just below the falls area provide some nice camping space—if you don't mind packing overnight gear and hauling it on such a short journey.

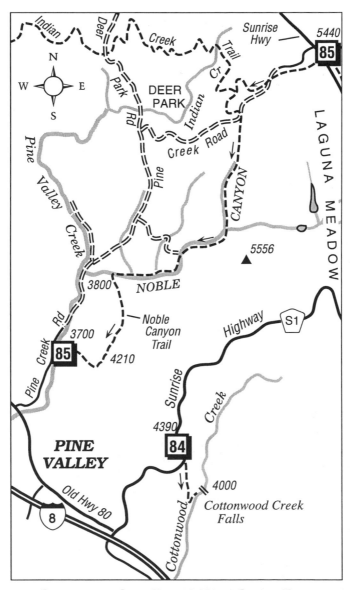

COTTONWOOD CREEK FALLS & NOBLE CANYON TRAIL

TRIP 85
Noble Canyon Trail

Location	Laguna Mountains
Highlights	Sparkling mountain stream; wildflowers
Distance	10.0 miles
Total Elevation Gain/Loss	650'/2400'
Hiking Time	5 hours
Optional Maps	USGS 7.5-min *Monument Peak, Mount Laguna, Descanso*
Best Times	October through June
Agency	CNF/DD
Difficulty	★★★

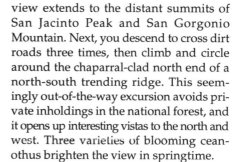

The Noble Canyon National Recreation Trail is an extension and reworking of an older trail built across the Laguna Mountains in the 1930s by the Civilian Conservation Corps. Since its completion in 1982, the trail has proven very popular among hikers, equestrians, and more recently mountain bikers.

With transportation arrangements set up in advance, you can travel one-way along this trail in the relatively easy downhill direction. You'll find the top end of the trail at the Penny Pines trailhead, mile 27.3 on Sunrise Highway, where parking space is plentiful along the highway shoulder. The bottom end is the Noble Canyon trailhead on Pine Creek Road near Pine Valley. Potable water is not available at either trailhead.

Good campsites are fairly abundant along the trail, particularly on shady terraces along the mid-portion of Noble Canyon (remember to establish your camp no less than 100 feet from water). Water flows in the canyon bottom year-round, though it slows to a trickle before the first rains of autumn. Purification is necessary if you intend to rely on it for your drinking or cooking.

From the starting point, head west along the marked Noble Canyon Trail. After passing through a parklike setting of Jeffrey pines, you rise a bit along the north slope of a steep hill. From there, the tree-framed

view extends to the distant summits of San Jacinto Peak and San Gorgonio Mountain. Next, you descend to cross dirt roads three times, then climb and circle around the chaparral-clad north end of a north-south trending ridge. This seemingly out-of-the-way excursion avoids private inholdings in the national forest, and it opens up interesting vistas to the north and west. Three varieties of blooming ceanothus brighten the view in springtime.

Next, you descend into the upper reaches of Noble Canyon, where the grassy hillsides show off springtime blooms of blue-purple beard tongue, scarlet bugler, woolly blue curls, yellow monkey flower, Indian paintbrush, wallflower, white forget-me-not, wild hyacinth, yellow violet, phacelia, golden yarrow, checker, lupine, and blue flax.

The trail sidles up to the creek at about 3.0 miles, and stays beside it for the next 4 miles. Past a canopy of live oaks, black oaks, and Jeffrey pines, you emerge into an steep, sunlit section of canyon. The trail cuts through thick brush on the east wall, while on the west wall only a few hardy, drought-tolerant plants cling to outcrops of schist rock.

Back in the shade of oaks again, you soon cross a major tributary creek from the east. This drains the Laguna lakes and Laguna Meadow above. Pause for a while in this shady glen, where the water flows over somber, grayish granitic rock and gathers in languid pools bedecked by sword and bracken fern. Look for nodding yellow Humboldt lilies in the late spring or early summer.

You continue within a riparian area for some distance downstream. Mixed in with the oaks, you'll discover dozens of fine California bay trees and a few scattered incense-cedars. The creek lies mostly hidden by willows and sycamores—and dense thickets of poison oak, squaw bush, wild rose, wild strawberries, and other types of water-loving vegetation. The line of trees shading the trail is narrow enough that light from the sky is freely admitted. Greens and browns—and in fall, yellows and reds—glow intensely.

You'll pass some mining debris—the remains of a flume and the stones of a disassembled arrastra (a horse- or mule-drawn machine for crushing ore). This dates from gold-mining activity in the late 1800s. Next, you'll come upon the foundations of two cabins, then two more cabins in disrepair. Someone long ago planted what is now a huge cypress tree in front of the larger cabin.

Crossing to the west side of the creek, you break out of the trees and into an open area with sage scrub and chaparral vegetation. The trail contours to a point about 100 feet above the creek, then maintains this course as it bends around several small tributaries. Midday temperatures, even in spring, can be uncomfortably warm along this stretch. Yucca, prickly-pear cactus, and even hedgehog cactus—normally a denizen of the desert—make appearances here. There are also excellent vernal displays of beard tongue, scarlet bugler, paintbrush, peony, wild pea, milkweed, wild onion, chia, and larkspur.

At about 7 miles, the trail switches back, crosses the Noble Canyon creek for the last time, and veers up a tributary canyon to the south. The trail joins the bed of an old jeep road, reaches a saddle after about 2 miles from Noble Canyon, then diverges from the road, going right (west) over another saddle. It then descends directly to the Noble Canyon trailhead near Pine Creek Road.

Ceanothus in bloom, Noble Canyon Trail

TRIP 86
Oasis Spring

Location	Laguna Mountains
Highlight	Hidden, shady spot with a spring, overlooking the desert
Distance	2.0 miles round trip
Total Elevation Gain/Loss	300'/300'
Hiking Time	1 hour (round trip)
Optional Map	USGS 7.5-min *Monument Peak*
Best Times	All year
Agency	CNF/DD
Difficulty	★

A more restful place could scarcely be imagined. A warm breeze from the desert below wafts up the shady canyon, bringing with it the scent of sage and California bay. A lone bigleaf maple tree shimmers in the sunlight. A sparkling stream gushes out of the ground and begins a headlong rush toward the dry desert sands a half mile below. "Oasis" is a perfectly apt name for this idyllic spot.

Oasis Spring lies only 200 yards from Sunrise Highway, near its summit in the Laguna Mountains, and about 300 feet lower in elevation. The best way to reach the spring is by way of a gradually descending dirt road from the south. This gated road intersects Sunrise Highway at mile 26.7, but parking is very limited here. An east-side turnout at mile 26.5 offers more room. Just below this turnout, you can pick up the Pacific Crest Trail and follow it north. After about 300 yards, the PCT dips into a shallow ravine and briefly joins the road to Oasis Spring. Stay on the road and continue descending through an elfin forest of mostly mountain mahogany.

Curving left, the road leaves the ravine and briefly traverses the abrupt face of the Laguna escarpment. From the lip of the road there's a dramatic view of distant alluvial fans and barren peaks in the desert far below. The road soon ends, but from

there a trail descends on tight switchbacks through a thick growth of live oak and bay to reach an old pumphouse. Nearby is the aforementioned bigleaf maple tree. This particular specimen was evidently planted here. The natural range of the bigleaf maple within the Pacific coast states extends no farther south than the Santa Ana and San Bernardino mountains.

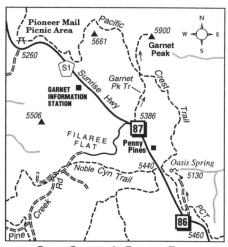

Oasis Spring & Garnet Peak

TRIP 87
Garnet Peak

Location	Laguna Mountains
Highlights	Outstanding desert views
Distance	2.4 miles round trip
Total Elevation Gain/Loss	500'/500'
Hiking Time	1½ hours (round trip)
Optional Map	USGS 7.5-min *Monument Peak*
Best Times	All year
Agency	CNF/DD
Difficulty	★★

Although Garnet Peak isn't the highest peaklet along the Laguna Mountain rim, its exposed position makes it a good place to view both the pine-clad Laguna plateau and the raw desert below. Especially rewarding is a predawn pilgrimage to observe the sunrise from its summit. Around the time of the winter solstice, the sun's flattened disk peeps up over the desert wastes of northwestern Sonora, Mexico, some 150 miles away. On the clearest mornings at that time of year, you might witness the famed "green flash," an event occasionally seen on the horizon at sunset on the coast, but seldom seen at sunrise anywhere.

Park on the shoulder (but off the pavement) of Sunrise Highway near mile 27.8.

Take the signed Garnet Peak Trail 0.5 mile north through Jeffrey pine forest to where it crosses the Pacific Crest Trail. Continue north, out in the open chaparral now, on the rocky path that slants up along the shoulder of the peak. Lord's candle yucca stalks, heavy with white flowers in the spring and early summer, poke through the ceanothus and manzanita brush along the trail.

The summit is crowned by a jagged cluster of layered, tan-colored metasedimentary rock, the type seen along much of the Laguna escarpment. The peak falls away abruptly to the east and south, revealing a vertiginous panorama of Storm Canyon and its distant alluvial fan. Along the horizon lie the Salton Sea and Baja's Laguna Salada, both desert sinks. To the south and west, the Laguna crest, dusky with oak and pine forests and patches of chaparral, seems to roll like a frozen wave to the edge of the escarpment.

Summer Milky Way over Garnet Peak Trail

TRIP 88
Sunset Trail

Location	Laguna Mountains
Highlight	Colorful spring and autumn vegetation, views
Distance	7.2 miles
Total Elevation Gain/Loss	700'/700'
Hiking Time	4 hours
Optional Map	USGS 7.5-min *Monument Peak, Mount Laguna*
Best Times	September through June
Agency	CNF/DD
Difficulty	★★★

The newly completed Sunset Trail permits easy access by foot along the west rim of the high Laguna Mountain plateau. Like its analog a few miles east—the sunrise-facing Pacific Crest Trail—the Sunset Trail offers fine panoramas, but on the sunset side of the mountain. Early mornings are by far best (certainly during the warm summer season) to take advantage of cool temperatures and clear, tangy air. In the hour or two after sunrise, you can often look down upon a white and frothy ocean of stratus clouds hugging a hundred-mile strip of coastline.

Park along Sunrise Highway at the Meadows Information Station, mile 19.1, about 5 miles uphill from Interstate 8 at Pine Valley. Walk a little way up the highway shoulder to reach the trailhead, marked by a large wooden sign. The gradual climb up the trail takes you toward a gently undulating ridge crest dotted with vanilla-scented Jeffrey pines and black oaks. After nearly a mile, the trail suddenly veers left to circle a rocky outcrop. There, a view opens of velvet-smooth Crouch Valley, some 500 feet below, and much of coastal San Diego County whenever clear air pre-

On the Big Laguna Trail

vails at lower altitudes. The view is worth the trivial effort invested so far.

Thereafter, the trail loses about 300 feet of elevation and crosses a tributary of Noble Canyon that drains Laguna Meadow. (A short side path on the right, just before the crossing, goes up to the lowermost lake, known as "Water of the Woods," in Laguna Meadow.) The water tumbling or trickling down this steep and densely overgrown ravine eventually reaches Pine Valley Creek, Barrett Reservoir, Rio Tijuana in Mexico, and finally the Tijuana River Estuary just north of the border. Much of the Laguna Mountains sheds water which, if not intercepted by aqueducts, flows through Mexico 20 or more miles to the south—a little-known fact.

After the ravine crossing, you climb back up to the crest again, with more opportunities to view the broad western horizon. Farther north, you pass over a hilltop and descend to the northernmost arm of Laguna Meadow. Turning east, the trail meets, at 3.9 miles, the Big Laguna Trail. If the ground is soggy, you may want to turn around here and return the same way. Otherwise, you can loop back across Laguna Meadow as follows:

Turn right on the Big Laguna Trail and follow it south about 1.5 miles to Big Laguna Lake, the biggest of several shallow, ephemeral lakes in the meadow. In an average rainy season, these lakes begin to fill with water or snow by December or January. By April or May, as the meadow dries, carpets of wildflowers—tidy tips, buttercups, goldfields, dandelions, wild onions, and western irises—begin to appear. Summer heat causes water levels in the lakes to decline rapidly.

Just past Big Laguna Lake the trail turns decidedly east. You can leave it at this point and head straight across the broad meadow, almost due south, toward a brown house at Laguna Ranch. During the rainy season, walking across the lower parts of the meadow may be akin to wading. Later in the year you may have to thread your way through cattle in the meadow. The ranch and

the meadow are now on public land, but ranchers retain grazing rights. As you get closer to the ranch, veer right so you can get through a gate in a barbed-wire fence some 300 yards west of the ranch house. Continue bearing southwest until you intersect the Sunset Trail near the point where you began your hike.

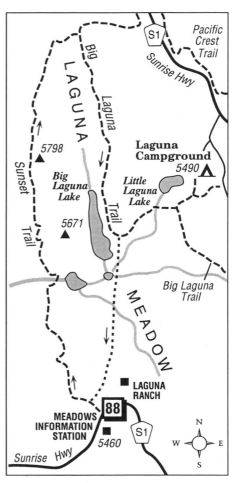

SUNSET TRAIL

TRIP 89
Culp Valley

Location	Northern Anza-Borrego Desert State Park
Highlights	Secluded, oasislike spring; desert views
Distance	1.7 miles
Total Elevation Gain/Loss	300'/300'
Hiking Time	1 hour
Optional Map	USGS 7.5-min *Tubb Canyon*
Best Times	September through June
Agency	ABDSP
Difficulty	★

While the low desert swelters, the temperature hovers in a more moderate register at Culp Valley, 3000 feet higher. This is the only designated camping area in the Anza-Borrego Desert where the heat on the cooler days of May, June or September is quite bearable. July and August daytime temperatures there are probably too warm for most people's tastes—typically the 90s and 100s.

Stark, gray boulders are piled up all around the floor of Culp Valley, thrusting upward into an azure sky. The west wind blows capriciously, often whistling eerily through the rocks. Nearby, out of sight from the valley, is a hillside spring surrounded by an oasis of green grass and small trees. It's this kind of contrast that makes hiking here especially rewarding.

To reach the starting point, drive to mile 9.2 on Montezuma Highway (2.8 miles east of the highway summit near Ranchita; 9.4 miles west of Borrego Springs) and turn north on the unpaved entrance road to Culp Valley Primitive Camp. The campground is truly no frills—just a few nooks and crannies where you can park your car overnight. Our little hike can start from the end of the road that forks west toward Pena Spring.

From the roadend, walk downhill on the remnants of a jeep road that used to lead to Pena Spring, quickly passing the much narrower California Riding and Hiking Trail. After 0.3 mile, you'll reach a thicket of large sugarbush shrubs. Go west through shoulder-high yerba santa and other shrubby vegetation to the spring, which lies amid a soggy hillside meadow. Yerba mansa flowers poke up through the grass blades where the ground is saturated. Rabbits, coyotes, and other animals partake of the clear, cold water, which emerges from a small, raised pipe. Nearby, you can look for a large, flat boulder pocked with several deep morteros, or Indian grinding holes.

After visiting the spring, backtrack up the road 0.2 mile to the intersection of the California Riding and Hiking Trail, marked by a small wooden post. Go east on this trail, climbing up, then along, a rather flat-topped ridge that offers good views of shallow Culp Valley on the right, and tantalizing glimpses of the deep gorge on the left—Hellhole Canyon. Along the ridge you find high-desert vegetation intermixed with common chaparral: juniper, catclaw, desert apricot, various cacti, buckwheat, Mojave and Lord's candle yucca, and white sage.

After 0.5 mile on the California Riding and Hiking Trail, you come to an unmarked trail junction in a saddle; Culp Valley Campground lies 0.3 mile south. Just north of the saddle are rock outcrops offering a great view of the Hellhole Canyon gorge, Borrego Valley, and the great wall of mountains beyond the valley. The pinyon-fringed, flattish summit of Rabbit Peak is conspicuous as the highest point visible on the long crest of the Santa Rosa Mountains in the northeast.

Ahead 0.2 mile on the California Riding and Hiking Trail is a vista point ("Lookout" on some maps), offering a more panoramic but somewhat less spectacular view than you saw earlier. Northwest down the slope from the Lookout point is a huge, weathered boulder split cleanly down the middle; it's fun to squeeze through the slot, or to "chimney" up to the top.

Back at the junction, take the trail south toward the campground and follow dirt roads from there over to your parked car.

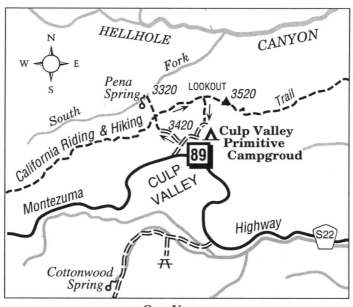

CULP VALLEY

TRIP 90
Hellhole Canyon

Location	Northern Anza-Borrego Desert State Park
Highlight	Hidden waterfall in desert canyon
Distance	5.0 miles round trip
Total Elevation Gain/Loss	900' /900'
Hiking Time	3½ hours (round trip)
Optional Map	USGS 7.5-min *Tubb Canyon*
Best Times	December through May
Agency	ABDSP
Difficulty	★★★

In the midst of what is regarded as one of America's hottest and driest deserts, it seems a bit surprising to find a place where mosses, ferns, sycamores, and cottonwoods flourish around a sparkling waterfall. Maidenhair Falls is such a place, and it lies not far from Borrego Springs and the popular Anza-Borrego Desert State Park visitor center.

You start hiking at the large parking area on the west side of Montezuma Highway, 0.7 mile south of Palm Canyon Drive in Borrego Springs. From the west side of the lot, head west on a wide trail (an old roadbed) straight across and up an alluvial fan toward the gaping mouth of Hellhole Canyon. The sandy surface of the fan supports a variety of vegetation, stratified according to elevation. Indigo bush, chuparosa, cheesebush, burroweed, creosote bush, desert lavender, and buckhorn cholla are the common plant species of the lower fan. They're largely replaced by jojoba, brittlebush, ocotillo, and teddy-bear cholla on the upper fan. Everywhere, jackrabbits flit among the bushes, startled by your approach.

As you approach the canyon mouth, a mile from the trailhead, you may hear (in a wet year, at least), the sound of flowing water. Usually the water doesn't get very far on the surface; it quickly sinks into porous sand as it spreads out and slows on the fan below. As the canyon walls pinch in, you soon find yourself threading a path near the flowing water. Generally, you'll want to stay away from the boulder-filled and vegetation-choked canyon bottom. Sooner or later you'll get involved in difficult scrambles over large boulders and fallen trees, and perhaps have unpleasant encounters with catclaw thorns. The remnants of trees that litter the canyon are a result of past wildfires. Fan palms—the signature tree of the Anza-Borrego Desert—begin to appear.

About 200 yards past a dense cluster of palms, the canyon walls pinch in really tight. Tucked away in a corner of the canyon bottom—hard to find—you'll discover the grotto containing Maidenhair Falls. The falls plunge about 25 feet into a shallow pool. Tiers of maidenhair fern adorn the grotto, and sopping wet mosses cover the places the ferns don't.

Further travel up-canyon from Maidenhair Falls involves much battle with the underbrush—slow going on a day hike, and slower if you're backpacking. Ambitious hikers can explore the remote higher reaches of the canyon. Some have traveled up the canyon's South Fork tributary, which leads to Pena Spring near Culp Valley.

Maidenhair Falls

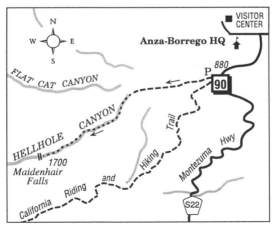

HELLHOLE CANYON

TRIP 91
Borrego Palm Canyon

Location	Northern Anza-Borrego Desert State Park
Highlights	Most dramatic display of native palms in California; spring wildflowers
Distance	3.0 miles round trip
Total Elevation Gain/Loss	450'/450'
Hiking Time	1½ hours (round trip)
Optional Map	USGS 7.5-min Borrego Palm Canyon
Best Times	October through May
Agency	ABDSP
Difficulty	★

In the first mile, there's nothing but sun-blasted vegetation, either thorny or low and prostrate. As you round a bend, you suddenly catch sight of a patch of iridescent green cradled in the yawning mouth of the canyon ahead. Hundreds of noble palms stand there, each holding high a crown of feathery, fan-shaped fronds. Water splashes over boulders and gathers in pools, delighting all the senses. It's enough to make anyone as yet unimpressed with the desert an instant convert to the ranks of "desert rats"!

You can learn more about the California desert flora on this trail than anywhere else around Anza-Borrego. Be sure to pick up the interpretive leaflet for the Borrego Palm Canyon Nature Trail at the Anza-Borrego visitor center, or upon entering Borrego Palm Canyon Campground, where the hike begins.

Park at the far end of the campground, in the trailhead parking area. A pond holding transplanted desert pupfish is nearby. Interpretive markers and plaques line the trail in the first mile. The trail soon crosses the seasonal stream on a wooden bridge, and starts winding up the rocky alluvial fan toward the canyon's mouth. You'll see and identify various cacti, mesquite and catclaw (with the parasitic desert mistletoe), indigo bush, desert lavender, creosote bush, brittlebush, ocotillo, desert-

willow, chuparosa, and sage. Much of this vegetation looks drab most of the year, but really lights up in a rainbow of colors by March in a wet year. Recently, the native bighorn sheep that frequent the canyon have become quite accustomed to passing hikers. If passersby are quiet and make no sudden motions, the sheep may graze contentedly only a stone's throw from the trail.

Soon after the palms first become visible, the trail enters the portals of the canyon. Desert-varnished rock walls soar 3000 feet up on both sides. After a second stream

BORREGO PALM CANYON

crossing, the trail goes up a series of steps hewn in the rock, passes a gauging station and a waterfall, crosses the stream once again, and enters the shade of the so-called first grove of palms.

The palms are of one variety, *Washingtonia filifera*, the only palm indigenous to California. Although they are generally well-adapted to wildfire, some headless or fallen trunks in this grove show that not all can survive the trauma of fire. A few alders and sycamores struggle for light among the massive, straight trunks of the palms.

The trail terminates at a point just below a small waterfall and pool at the upper end of the palm grove, 1.5 miles from the trailhead. On the return leg, you can try a somewhat longer alternate trail that winds along the upper edge of the alluvial fan. Here you can study how plants are stratified according to habitat. Higher on the slope, less water is absorbed by the soil, so the drought-tolerant ocotillo dominates.

The first grove is only the starting point for boulder-hopping journeys of various lengths into the remote recesses of upper Borrego Palm Canyon. Sturdy footwear and long pants are recommended for any such forays, as you'll be brushing past poison oak and spiny vegetation, and scrambling over potentially ankle-busting terrain. This challenge is most rewarding after winter storms, when the stream flows vigorously and gathers in crystalline pools. Too much rain in the mountains to the west, however, can trigger floods large enough to make these extended canyon treks dangerous.

Fan palms in Borrego Palm Canyon

TRIP 92
Cougar Canyon

Location	Northern Anza-Borrego Desert State Park
Highlights	Riparian vegetation, waterfalls, pools, wildflowers
Distance	10.0 miles round trip
Total Elevation Gain/Loss	1500'/1500'
Hiking Time	6 hours (round trip)
Recommended Map	USGS 7.5-min *Borrego Palm Canyon*
Best Times	November through April
Agency	ABDSP
Difficulty	★★★★

Cougar Canyon is a place where new worlds open up at every turn. There are more beautiful sights to see along a half-mile of this canyon than in a full day's hiking in many other parts of Anza-Borrego.

Cahuilla Indians were using seasonal camps in the area around the mouth of the canyon as recently as about 160 years ago, and the evidence left behind in the form of bedrock morteros and ceremonial caves gives another interesting dimension to a hike here.

If you plan to stay overnight, the flat, open areas just below the mouth of the canyon make spacious and convenient campsites for backpackers. A few marginal camping areas do exist in the canyon proper, but these have been overused and are really too close to the canyon stream to be considered appropriate places to set up camp.

In recent years, the approach by road to Cougar Canyon and its neighbor to the north, Sheep Canyon, has been getting less and less "friendly." A rough, steep section of the Coyote Canyon road leading in has become ever-more eroded and rocky, so that even the toughest of high-clearance, 4-wheel-drive vehicles are having trouble negotiating it. This means, for the purpose of this description, that we will park our vehicle and begin hiking below Lower Willows in Coyote Canyon, just shy of

where the awful stretch of road begins. To reach this "trailhead," drive north from the end of the paved DiGiorgio Road in Borrego Springs onto the unpaved, 4-wheel-drive road up along the east side of Coyote Canyon. After 5.6 miles and three (possibly four, depending on the season) wet crossings of Coyote Creek, you reach a point, below Lower Willows, where the road turns sharply left to climb a steep ravine. Parking space is fairly abundant just below the steep grade.

Following the road on foot now, you gain about 200 feet of elevation in 0.3 mile, then begin to level off as you approach a saddle. Once over the top you admire spacious Collins Valley and the boulder-heaped San Ysidro Mountains ahead, which spread before you as if in a panoramic photo. Continue generally west on dirt roads, always bearing left, following signs toward Sheep Canyon Primitive Camp. As you approach the campground, 3.6 miles from the start, take the spur road south along the base of the mountains toward Cougar Canyon. Follow a trail for 0.7 mile past the end of the spur road (meanwhile crossing the Cougar Canyon stream three times) and arrive at a point a little beyond the mouth of Cougar Canyon. Find the informal path that veers right (west) up Cougar's alluvial fan. A little northwest of this point, on a bench overlooking the stream, is a rock cave reputed to have been used as an Indian *temescal*, or sweat-house.

Follow the path west and cross the stream once more. Now on the north bank, the path climbs to about 50 feet above the stream as the canyon walls close in rather tightly. Another rock cave yawns from the hillside.

As you stay on the path well above the stream, it seems almost a shame to miss the beautiful scenery down below along the sycamore-shaded creek. But soon, steep walls of granite and gneiss force you to descend anyway. Go up the cobbled bed of the stream to the beginning of a palm grove, then climb up to a sandy, shaded bench on the left bank. On a rock facing the bench is a huge psychedelic "eye"—rock art, circa 1970. Just beyond the eye, upstream, is a deep, shaded pool fed by a silvery waterfall.

The path, now obscure, continues up the south wall of the canyon to avoid a narrow section just beyond the eye. After climbing over a series of rock buttresses, you'll come to a point overlooking a feathery cascade of water flowing down a slab of banded rock in the canyon bottom. Just beyond this

you can descend to the streambed again, and work your way up-canyon to a large cottonwood tree nestled beside a sculpted granite wall. Using the limbs of this tree to hoist yourself up and over, you'll come upon the most beautiful spot of all—a clear, deep pool surrounded by sheer, polished granite walls, fed by a 20-foot waterfall.

This pool and waterfall, 5 miles out from where you started, mark the end of progress in Cougar Canyon proper without resorting to technical climbing aids. For those who are interested, a long detour up along the canyon's brushy south wall to the ridgeline above is necessary to bypass the next 0.6 mile of canyon bottom. On the ridgeline, there are bird's eye views of palm groves hidden in the deep cleft of Cougar Canyon to the north and in two canyons to the south.

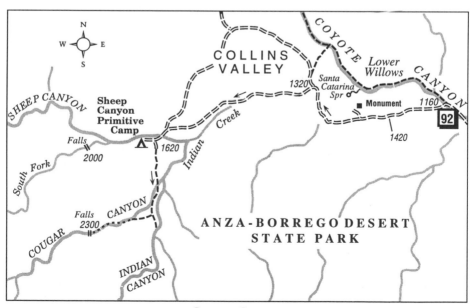

COUGAR CANYON

TRIP 93
Villager Peak

Location	Santa Rosa Mountains (northern Anza-Borrego)
Highlights	Ever-present dramatic views
Distance	13.0 miles round trip
Total Elevation Gain/Loss	5000'/5000'
Hiking Time	11 hours (round trip)
Recommended Maps	USGS 7.5-min *Fonts Point, Rabbit Peak*
Best Times	October through May
Agency	ABDSP
Difficulty	★★★★

Despite its remoteness, Villager Peak is one of the more popular destinations for "serious" Southern California peak baggers. More than a hundred people every year succeed in reaching the summit, and the box containing the peak register is often overflowing with business cards and other mementos. Many people backpack the route, but others, who must start at or before sunrise, manage to complete the round trip as a day hike. The importance of taking plenty of water on this wholly water-less route cannot be overemphasized.

The approach to Villager Peak is straight-forwardly up, using a single north-trend-ing ridge. One or more paralleling trails follow this ridge—the result of recent use by hikers, prehistoric use by desert-dwelling Indians, and more or less continual use by bighorn sheep. On the way down, how-ever, navigational difficulties may be encountered where watershed divides split and go their separate ways. Bighorn sheep don't necessarily stick to the main route, and their trails may lure you off the main ridge onto some steeply plunging side ridge.

Park in the northside turnout at mile 31.8 on Borrego-Salton Seaway (County Highway S-22), 13 miles northeast of Borrego Springs. On foot, proceed north toward the east end of a long, sandy ridge 0.5 mile away. The north face of this ridge is a huge scarp along the San Jacinto Fault—said to be one of the largest fault scarps in uncon-solidated earth material in North America. North of this ridge, flash-floods exiting from Rattlesnake Canyon have cut a series of braided washes in a swath about 0.6 mile wide. A faint path marked by "ducks" (small piles of stones) takes you over this dis-sected terrain to the base of the long, ram-plike ridge leading to Villager Peak.

The initial climb is very steep, but the route soon levels off to a rather steady gradient averaging about 1000 feet per mile. Stay on the highest part of the ridge to remain on route. Creosote bush, ocotil-lo, and glistening specimens of barrel cac-tus, hedgehog cactus, and silver, golden, and teddy-bear cholla cactus grace the slopes below 3000 feet. Dense thickets of wicked-looking agave at 3000 to 4000 feet will slow you down. At times, you feel as if you were threading a spiny gauntlet.

Along the lower part of the ridge you'll come upon several Indian "sleeping circles," which may have been used as windbreaks or to anchor shelters made from local veg-etation. At about the 3000-foot level (3.0 miles) a green patch marking Rattlesnake Spring comes into view in a tributary canyon of Rattlesnake Canyon about 1.5 miles east.

At 4100 feet (4.3 miles), you'll pass along the edge of a spectacular dropoff overlooking Clark Valley. The white band of rock prominently displayed along the face of this escarpment is marble—metamorphosed limestone. Thought to be some of the oldest rock exposed in San Diego County, it originated from ocean-floor sediments deposited about half a billion years ago. Just beyond the 4800-foot contour (5.0 miles), the ridge descends a little to a small, exposed campsite with airy views both east and west.

In the next mile the ridgeline becomes quite jagged. Pinyon, juniper, and nolina (a relative of the yucca) now dominate. At 6.5 miles, you reach the rounded, 5756-foot summit of Villager Peak, offering good campsites amid a sparse forest of weather-beaten pinyon pines. The views are pseudo-aerial all around the compass. A clear, calm, moonless night spent here is an unforgettable experience. Despite the horizon glows of cities from Los Angeles to Mexicali, the stars above shine fiercely in a charcoal sky. At dawn, the silvery surface of the Salton Sea mirrors the red glow spreading across the east horizon.

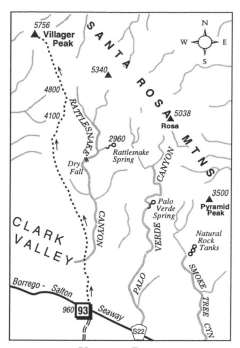

VILLAGER PEAK

View east into Coachella Valley from Villager Peak

TRIP 94
Calcite Mine

Location	Northern Anza-Borrego Desert State Park
Highlights	Eroded, slotlike gorges; historic interest
Distance	4.2 miles
Total Elevation Gain/Loss	800'/800'
Hiking Time	2 hours
Optional Map	USGS 7.5-min *Seventeen Palms*
Best Times	November through April
Agency	ABDSP
Difficulty	★★

Thousands of years of cutting and polishing by water and wind erosion have produced the chaotic rock formations and slotlike ravines you'll discover in the Calcite Mine area. The highlight of this hike is, of course, the mine itself. During World War II, this was an important site—indeed the only site in the United States—for the extraction of optical-grade calcite crystals for use in gunsights. Trench-mining operations throughout the area have left deep scars upon the earth, seemingly as fresh today as when they were made.

Park in the roadside turnout at mile 38.0 along Borrego-Salton Seaway (County Highway S-22); then walk 0.1 mile east to the Calcite jeep road intersection. An interpretive panel here gives some details about the history of the mine. Follow the jeep road as it dips into and out of South Fork Palm Wash, and continues northwest toward the southern spurs of the Santa Rosa Mountains. Ahead you will see an intricately honeycombed whitish slab of sandstone, called Locomotive Rock, which lies behind (northeast of) the mine area.

About 1.4 miles from S-22, the road dips sharply to cross a deep ravine. Poke into the upper (north) end of this ravine and you'll discover one of the best slot canyons in Anza-Borrego. (Skilled climbers can squeeze through the slot and go up a break

on the right side to reach a point above and northwest of the mine area.)

At road's end You may find bits of calcite crystals strewn about on the ground, glittering in the sunlight. You could spend a lot of time exploring the mining trenches and the pocked slabs of sandstone nearby. Palm Wash, a frightening gash in the earth, precludes travel to the east.

On the return, try this alternate route: Backtrack 0.5 mile to the aforementioned deep ravine. Proceed downstream along its bottom. As you pass through deeper and deeper layers of sandstone strata, the ravine narrows until it allows the passage of only one person at a time. When you reach the jumbled blocks of sandstone in Palm Wash at the bottom of the ravine, turn right, walk 0.3 mile downstream, and exit the canyon via a short link of jeep trail that leads back to the Calcite road.

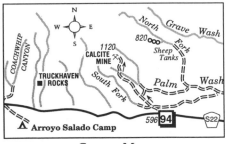

CALCITE MINE

TRIP 95
Oriflamme Canyon

Location	Southern Anza-Borrego Desert State Park
Highlight	Hidden waterfall
Distance	2.6 miles round trip (to waterfall)
Total Elevation Gain/Loss	500′/500′
Hiking Time	2½ hours (round trip)
Optional Maps	USGS 7.5-min *Earthquake Valley, Julian*
Best Times	November through April
Agency	ABDSP
Difficulty	★★★

Oriflamme Canyon's gurgling waters are borne to the open air at a spring high on the east slope of the Laguna Mountains. For 5 miles or so they trickle over polished granite and schist bedrock, tumble over small waterfalls, and nourish a line of oaks, sycamores, willows and cottonwoods. At Mason Valley, down on the Anza-Borrego Desert floor, they finally sink into porous sand.

As soon as the late-fall or winter rains come, the flow of water down Oriflamme Canyon is copious. At one point the water cascades impressively over a 15-foot precipice within a hidden grotto of rock and riparian vegetation. This is the destination of the short but semi-rough hike described here. Wear long pants, or you'll be subjected to intolerable levels of flagellation meted out by the low-growing catclaw, prickly pear, and cholla cactus. Also be aware that this is prime rattlesnake habitat, so be especially alert and cautious during warm weather.

From mile 26.8 on County Highway S-2 (1 mile south of Box Canyon Historic Site in central Anza-Borrego Desert State Park), turn west on the dirt road signed ORIFLAMME CANYON (4-wheel-drive recommended). In a high-clearance vehicle, you can drive the 3 mostly rough miles in; otherwise you may have to walk this stretch. Drive on the unpaved road for 2 miles, stay left as the road forks at Rodriguez

Canyon, and continue for another 0.8 mile to a rough side road on the left, leading down to a Depression-era road camp. Park off this road somewhere, and find and follow an old, partly overgrown cattle trail that follows, in the upstream direction on the right bank, a sloping bench overlooking the canyon bottom. After 0.5 mile the trail dips and then crosses the stream for the first time. In the narrower canyon bottom ahead, you walk back and forth across the bubbling stream and over orange and brown leaf litter. Look for Indian morteros (grinding holes) worn into some of the streamside boulders.

After 1.3 miles, a major tributary comes in from the right (west). Proceed another 0.1 mile south and you'll come upon the sublime, almost hidden 15-foot cascade and a shallow pool, framed by the twisted trunks of sycamores. Watch out for poison oak growing along the stream hereabouts.

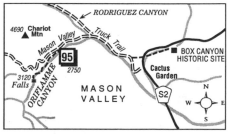

ORIFLAMME CANYON

TRIP 96
Ghost Mountain

Location	Southern Anza-Borrego Desert State Park
Highlight	Historic interest
Distance	2.0 miles round trip
Total Elevation Gain/Loss	400'/400'
Hiking Time	1½ hours (round trip)
Optional Map	USGS 7.5-min *Earthquake Valley*
Best Times	October through May
Agency	ABDSP
Difficulty	★★

The California desert has been home to many an eccentric person, but possibly none so audacious as Marshal South. From 1931 until the mid-'40s. Marshal and his poetess wife, Tanya, lived atop what was then a very remote mountaintop in the arid Anza-Borrego Desert, depending in large part on local resources for food, water, and shelter. Here, they built an adobe cabin, "Yaquitepec"; fashioned an ingenious rainwater collection system; raised three children; and tried to emulate, as completely as possible, the life of the pre-historic Indians.

The ruins of Yaquitepec are today one of Anza-Borrego's noted attractions—and quite easy to reach. At mile 22.9 on Highway S-2 (between Highway 78 and Box Canyon), turn east into Blair Valley. Follow the dirt road around the east edge of Blair Valley for 2.7 miles, then turn right (southwest) toward the foot of Ghost Mountain, site of the cabin. From the road-end parking area a trail climbs in switchbacks up the rocky slope, and turns east along the ridge to the Yaquitepec site. Little remains of the dwelling except some of the walls and the water cistern, but the view from the site is impressive.

When not consumed with the business of survival, Marshal South wrote magazine articles detailing the family's experiences on what was then an extremely remote mountaintop. His writings appeared frequently in *Desert Magazine* during the 1940s. These articles are well worth looking up in the library.

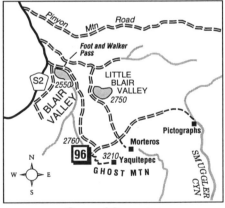

GHOST MOUNTAIN

TRIP 97
Whale Peak

Location	Southern Anza-Borrego Desert State Park
Highlights	Dwarf pinyon-juniper forest; huge boulders; panoramic desert views
Distance	4.5 miles round trip
Total Elevation Gain/Loss	1500'/1500'
Hiking Time	3½ hours (round trip)
Recommended Map	USGS 7.5-min *Whale Peak*
Best Times	October through May
Agency	ABDSP
Difficulty	★★★

Whale Peak is probably the most visited major summit in Anza-Borrego Desert State Park. Hundreds of people every year day-hike or backpack into this serene, wooded island in the desert sky. Whale Peak yields to approaches from nearly every direction. The area around it, however, can prove distressing from a navigational point of view. The peak lies within a complex of similar-looking hogback ridges and gentle valleys, and the peak itself remains hidden from view until you are almost upon it. Count on no sources of water along the way—even storm runoff sinks immediately into the porous, decomposed granite soil.

We describe here Whale Peak's north-approach route, which is the shortest and involves the least elevation gain. A long drive on a primitive dirt road is required this way, however. At mile 21.4 on Highway S-2 (4 miles south of Highway 78), turn east on signed Pinyon Mountain Road. High clearance is recommended for this road, and 4-wheel drive helps. Stay right (east) at the fork in 0.1 mile, and continue up the alluvial fan toward the Vallecito Mountains and their domelike crown, Whale Peak. The road is never steep, but there are patches of soft sand and occasional protruding rocks. After 5.7 miles the road tops a watershed divide at 3980 feet in the middle of a saddle called Pinyon Mountain Valley. Find a place to park in one of the turnouts or spur roads nearby. In his *Anza-Borrego Desert Guide Book*, Horace Parker describes Pinyon Mountain Valley as being "caressed by some of the most invigorating air found anywhere in the world . . . it has the tang and coolness of the high mountains and the warmth and dryness of the deserts."

Head directly up the small canyon to the south. A little hand-and foot climbing is required to negotiate some large boulders. The canyon soon widens into a sandy flat just below 4400 feet. You can now pick up an informal trail trending southeast over and around several rocky summits. This route is fairly well marked with ducks (small piles of stones), but it is easy to lose it in several spots. You might want to keep track of your position by map and compass techniques. Flat areas for trail camping are quite abundant along the way.

The mature pinyon pine, juniper, scrub oak, manzanita, yucca, and nolina on the north slopes of Whale Peak are characteristic of the pinyon-juniper woodland plant community. Similar habitats lie on the rim of the Mojave Desert and on the Sierra Juarez plateau just below the Mexican border—some 30-60 miles south.

Eventually, you'll come to a small valley west-northwest of Whale Peak. From this point you scramble south and upward to the peak's west ridge, and then follow the ridge upward to the flattish 5349-foot summit. A climbers' register is normally found tucked amid Whale Peak's summit boulders. On a clear day, the panorama is superb: the Salton Sea in the east, Baja's mesalike Sierra Juarez in the south, and the impressive wall of the Laguna Mountains to the west.

Weathered boulder near Whale Peak

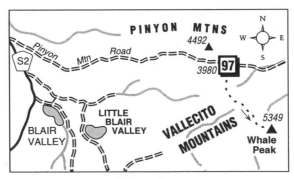

WHALE PEAK

TRIP 98
Arroyo Tapiado-Arroyo Diablo Loop

Location	Southern Anza-Borrego Desert State Park
Highlights	Geological features; mud caves
Distance	16.5 miles
Total Elevation Gain/Loss	600'/600'
Hiking Time	8 hours
Optional Map	USGS 7.5-min *Arroyo Tapiado*
Best Times	November through April
Agency	ABDSP
Difficulty	★★★★

Much of Anza-Borrego Desert State Park is laced with low-elevation, hot, intricately dissected terrain known as badlands. In the south half of the park, the extensive Carrizo Badlands feature spectacular examples of erosion in soft claystones, mudstones, and sandstones. There you'll find abundant instances of clay hills, mud caves, small arches and windows, receding cliffs, sinuous washes, and deep-cut ravines. This loop tour, long on length but rich in sights and possible side trips, explores the heart of this area. Except for any side trips, you'll be following rough or sandy roads suitable for 4-wheel-drive vehicles.

This is one of the longest hikes described in this book, but one of the flattest and most relaxing— relaxing, that is, if you pick the right day or days. Avoid holiday weekends; otherwise you'll share these badland arroyos with too many motor vehicles. As a self-propelled alternative to hiking the entire loop, consider taking along one mountain bike for every two hikers in your party. Biking the entire route is tedious because of the soft sand here and there, while hiking can get tedious as well. By taking turns, however, you never get tired of either type of exercise. If you're backpacking the route, secluded campsites well off the roads can be found in the upper reaches of both Arroyo Tapiado and Arroyo Seco del Diablo.

The highlight of the trip comes early: the Arroyo Tapiado cave formations. Some of the caves are pitch dark; bring two flashlights (per person) and a hard hat or a rock-climbing helmet if you intend to explore them.

To reach the starting point for hiking, find the signed Palm Spring turnoff near mile marker 43.0 on County Highway S-2. Drive east down the broad Vallecito Wash, staying in the main (unsigned) wash when the spur road to Palm Spring forks left. At 4.5 miles from S-2, a small sign on the left marks Arroyo Tapiado, a broad, shallow, and uninteresting drainage at this point. This is as good a spot as any to begin hiking the loop.

On foot, proceed north along Arroyo Tapiado (meaning "mudwall wash"). After 2.0 miles you reach the beginning of a deep, twisting gorge. The next 2 miles will take you through what geologists call pseudokarst topography. Like the karst topography found in many parts of the world, pseudokarst contains caves, subterranean drainage systems, sinkholes, and blind valleys that end in swallow holes. Unlike karst, which results from the dissolution of limestone or similar material by water, this topography is the result of an unusual process: First, flood waters gouge out slotlike tributaries in the soft claystone walls of the main arroyo (Arroyo Tapiado).

Second, landslides fill in the slots. Third, flood waters dig tunnels through the bottom levels of the landslide debris.

Some of the caves (subterranean stream channels) in the area are over 1000 feet long, with rooms up to 80 feet high and 30 feet wide. Others are tall and narrow, much like a meandering slot canyon with a roof overhead. Some have multiple levels, and one contains a 45-foot subterranean "dry fall." Sinkholes (skylights) illuminate the interiors of some caves. Most cave passages eventually lead upstream through a swallow hole to a "blind" valley.

The bigger and more mature caves are quite stable, having ages on the order of thousands of years. Except during an earthquake or flood, the hard-packed floors of these caves should offer safe passage. It is very dangerous, however, to wander around topside in the pseudokarst valleys (those with sinkholes) and blind valleys (those ending in swallow holes). There would be no exit if one were to fall into some of these holes—or incipient holes. (This may explain the reported disappearance of travelers who tried various shortcuts across the Carrizo Badlands in the early days. It was said that these hapless individuals "went in, and didn't come out.")

A small grove of mesquite on the left at 2.7 miles is the clue to finding the entrance to one of the longer caves. Halfway through this cave is a tiny skylight, perhaps 50 feet up. Another cave entrance on the left at 2.9 miles offers an easy passage of several hundred feet to a wide swallow hole. This cave also features a large sinkhole in the roof of its midsection, and a curious oxbow, or alternate passage.

On the right at 3.1 miles you'll find the entrance to the "Big Mud Cave," the collapsed remnants of a former cave passage. It's an easy and worthwhile side trip, and you don't need a flashlight: Walk through the punctured cavern at the front and continue up the narrow wash bridged by many arches. After about 0.4 mile, on the left, you can climb out of the wash for a look at the mazelike terrain above. Stay on the ridge-line, don't wander through the valleys, and keep track of your footprints—you must reenter the same wash to get back safely!

Don't miss the slotlike passage just south of the Big Mud Cave entrance, on the same canyon wall. After squeezing through, let your eyes adjust to the dark and behold an amazing sight.

Other passage entrances penetrate the walls of Arroyo Tapiado and some of its tributaries. So do "pipes," or upper-level conduits, which spew forth waterfalls during rare flash floods.

Arroyo Tapiado widens after 4.0 miles and sets a straighter course northwest. The canyon divides at 6.3 miles; take the right fork, following the sign indicating "Arroyo Diablo." At 6.7 miles, the road goes up the slope to the right and meanders southeast to join Arroyo Seco del Diablo at 9.0 miles. (In case you were thinking about taking your car on the loop, note that last mile of this road is extremely sandy and soft—a sure trap for non-4-wheel-drive vehicles.)

Shallow at first, Arroyo Diablo deepens steadily between golden-colored walls of sandstone—quite unlike the gray-green claystone walls you saw in Arroyo Tapiado.

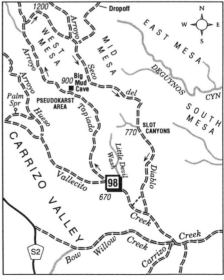

Arroyo Tapiado-Arroyo Diablo Loop

Sandstone concretions, most shaped like balls or bullets, lie half-imbedded in the water-polished walls. Others have completely weathered out and lie on the ground. Between 11.0 and 13.0 miles, there are many interesting tributaries to explore if you have time. The one at 12.3 miles, on the west side, divides into a maze of narrow slot canyons chock-full of concretions, each one a unique sculpture. (Leave 'em as they lie—even rocks are protected in the state park.)

Down near the mouth of Arroyo Diablo are some mesquite groves, and a small seep in the floor of the canyon. When you emerge onto flat land just beyond the mouth, save some time and distance by leaving the wheel tracks and turning west and hiking cross-country to pick up the sandy road in Vallecito Creek wash.

Big Mud Cave in Arroyo Tapiado

TRIP 99
Moonlight Trail

Location	Agua Caliente County Park
	(Southern Anza-Borrego)
Highlights	Desert views; geologic interest
Distance	1.5 miles
Total Elevation Gain/Loss	350'/350'
Hiking Time	1 hour
Optional Map	USGS 7.5-min *Agua Caliente Springs*
Best Times	October through May
Agency	SDCP
Difficulty	★

Take in a deep breath of clean, dry air. Bask in the larger-than-life brilliance of the desert sun. Sink into the womblike comfort of warm spring water. At Agua Caliente Springs you can have your cake and eat it too—hike first, then enjoy a relaxing soak in the hot springs.

A San Diego County park has been established here in the midst of state park lands on the edge of the Tierra Blanca Mountains. You'll find it along County Highway S-2, 27 miles northwest of Interstate 8 at Ocotillo, and 22 miles southeast of Highway 78. In recent years, the park has been closed during the summer months.

A splinter of the Elsinore Fault is responsible for the upwelling of 98°F, mineral-rich water. The Elsinore Fault passes through the Lake Elsinore area and Warner Springs, where hot springs are also found. There are two options for hot-water soaking at Agua Caliente Springs: a large indoor jacuzzi (open 9-3), where the water temperature is boosted to more than 100°; and a shallow, outdoor pool (open daylight hours) at a temperature averaging about 95°.

As for the hiking part, the Moonlight Trail—one of several short trails in the area—is a good one to start on. This well-marked but somewhat steep and rugged trail climbs over a rock-strewn saddle, drops into a small wash mysteriously named Moonlight

Canyon, descends past some seeps and a little oasis of willows in the wash bottom, and finally circles back to Agua Caliente Springs. You'll find the trailhead near the shuffleboard court at the south end of the campground. Although moonlight treks on this trail are possible, a good flashlight wouldn't hurt after dark.

True to their name, the Tierra Blanca ("white earth") Mountains are composed of light-colored granitic rock that tends not to develop desert varnish. The rock fractures easily, and its component mineral crystals break down into coarse sand.

From the high point on the Moonlight Trail, 300 feet above the campground, you can climb off-trail an additional 250 feet to reach Peak 1882, offering a superb view of Carrizo Valley and the Vallecito Mountains, including Whale Peak. Another, longer side trip, again cross-country, can be made up-canyon (south) in Moonlight Canyon to a point overlooking the Inner Pasture, an isolated valley ringed by the boulder-punctuated Tierra Blanca and Sawtooth mountains.

MOONLIGHT TRAIL

Pygmy Palms, Mountain Palm Springs

TRIP 100
Mountain Palm Springs

Location	Southern Anza-Borrego Desert State Park
Highlights	Groves of native palms
Distance	2.5 miles
Total Elevation Gain/Loss	350'/350'
Hiking Time	1½ hours
Optional Map	USGS 7.5-min *Sweeney Pass*
Best Times	October through May
Agency	ABDSP
Difficulty	★

If you like the contrast between mini-oases of palm trees and a raw landscape of sand and eroded rock, you'll love Mountain Palm Springs. The palms here are gregarious, growing in dense clusters, often with pools of water at their feet. Many have never been burned: they still hold full skirts of dead fronds around their trunks, the better to serve the local population of rodents and snakes. In late fall and early winter, the sticky, sweet fruit of the palms hangs in great swaying clusters, sought after by birds and the sleek coyotes that prowl up and down the washes.

The palm groves are distributed along several small washes that drain roughly a square-mile area on the east side of the Tierra Blanca Mountains near the south end of Anza-Borrego Desert State Park. A primitive camping area sits on the alluvial fan just below the point where the washes join together. A short dirt road leads to this campground from mile 47.1 on Highway S-2.

Consider the loop hike described here as a fairly complete tour of the area; but do be enticed to extend your explorations in the form of side trips or extended loop trips if the spirit moves you.

Begin by walking up the small canyon southwest of the camping area. Past some small seeps you'll come upon the first groups of palms—Pygmy Grove. Some of

these small but statuesque palms grow out of nothing more than rock piles.

A long pause is in order ahead at Southwest Grove, a restful retreat shaded by a vaulted canopy of shimmering fronds. A rock-lined catch basin fashioned for the benefit of the local wildlife mirrors the silhouettes of the palms. A couple of elephant trees cling to the slopes just above the grove, but for a better look at these curious plants, you can climb a spur trail to Torote Bowl, where a bigger group of elephant trees will be found.

From Southwest Grove, pick up the well-worn but obscure trail that leads north over a rock-strewn ridge to Surprise Canyon Grove in Surprise Canyon. Up-canyon from this small grove lies Palm Bowl, filled

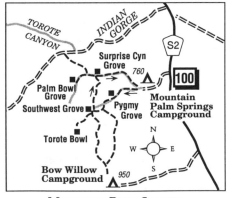

Mountain Palm Springs

with tangled patches of mesquite and fringed on its western edge by more than a hundred palms. On warm winter days, the molasseslike odor of ripe palm fruit wafts upon the breeze, and phainopepla hoot and flit among the palm crowns, their white wing patches flashing.

North of Palm Bowl Grove, an old Indian pathway leads over a low pass to Indian Gorge and Torote Canyon, where many more elephant trees thrive—another possible diversion. To conclude the loop hike, however, you return to Surprise Canyon Grove and continue down-canyon to the campground. On the way, you pass North Grove, hidden in a side drainage on the left.

Spring at Southwest Grove

TRIP 101
Mortero Palms to Goat Canyon

Location	Southern Anza-Borrego Desert State Park
Highlights	Rugged, palm-filled canyon; view of historic railroad
Distance	5.0 miles round trip (to view of trestle)
Total Elevation Gain/Loss	2500'/2500'
Hiking Time	5 hours (round trip)
Recommended Map	USGS 7.5-min *Jacumba*
Best Times	November through April
Agency	ABDSP
Difficulty	★★★

The 200-foot-high, 600-foot-long trestle over Goat Canyon on the San Diego & Arizona Eastern rail line is revered among railroad buffs everywhere. It has been called the longest curved railroad trestle and one of the highest wooden trestles in the world.

Dubbed the "impossible railroad," the San Diego & Arizona Eastern tracks were laid through southern Anza-Borrego's Carrizo Gorge in the second decade of the 20th Century. Starting in 1919, the railroad carried freight, and for a time passengers, between San Diego and the Imperial Valley. The gorge section features 11 miles of twisting track, 17 tunnels, and numerous trestles. The current Goat Canyon trestle, built over a tributary of Carrizo Gorge, was completed in 1933 as part of a realignment of the original route. In 1976, a Mexican *chubasco* called Hurricane Kathleen spun out of the Gulf of California, moved north into Anza-Borrego, and severely mangled the gorge section of the railroad, rendering it impassable for almost five years. After reopening in 1981, the line was quickly severed again, this time by a fire that burned several trestles. The Carrizo Gorge section has remained out of service ever since.

Goat Canyon Trestle

In recent years, there has been much talk of restoring the railroad for freight hauling, for hauling San Diego's garbage out to some future Imperial Valley landfill, and for sightseeing excursions. If, on the other hand, the right-of-way is ultimately abandoned, it would likely be converted into a state-park multiuse trail. The railroad is privately owned today, and walking along the tracks is expressly forbidden. The following direct but moderately difficult hike allows you to reach a point overlooking the remote Goat Canyon trestle.

Start hiking at the Mortero Palms trailhead, rather close to the rock outcrop known as Dos Cabezos ("two heads"). To get there from Interstate 8 at Ocotillo, proceed north and west on Highway S-2 four miles to an unsigned dirt road on the left (from this point on, high clearance or 4-wheel drive may be needed). Go south on this road and swing right after 1.1 miles. Continue west for another 4.6 miles, and turn left across the disused San Diego & Arizona Eastern railroad tracks on a paved crossover. Go right, continue another 0.1 mile, then veer left, away from the tracks. Go another 1.6 miles, staying left at the next two junctions, and then go right to the end of the road. A wide wash lies below; the Mortero Palms are in the canyon to the west (not the narrower canyon to the south).

A path follows the south side of the canyon for a while, avoiding the vegetation-choked streambed. Soon you begin climbing over granitic boulders. Look for a half-dozen *morteros* (Indian mortars), namesakes of the palm grove, in the center of the drainage 100 yards below the beginning of the palms. A path also threads the north canyon wall—but you miss the morteros if you follow it.

The dense growth of palms arises from seeps amid a jumble of huge boulders; the latter reminiscent of the rock piles at Joshua Tree National Park. On warm days this is a seductively cool spot, and it takes some will power to get moving again to tackle the short but steep stretch of canyon ahead.

Traverse left or right, or climb the water-polished rocks directly if you're a real daredevil.

At the 2440-foot contour it's easier to leave the canyon bottom temporarily and go up on the slope to the north through stands of teddy-bear cholla. Drop back in at about 2750 feet, but leave the canyon again at the 2840-foot contour. Proceed west and southwest across a small saddle and continue west over a divide into the Goat Canyon drainage.

Descend to a delightful, juniper-dotted bowl at about 3200 feet, a nice spot to spend the night if you are backpacking. Goat Canyon descends steeply farther west of here. Down at about 2700 feet in the canyon, there's an excellent, though somewhat distant view of the curved trestle, framed by the steep walls of the canyon.

Further exploration in the area might include a visit to 4512-foot Jacumba peak, the high point of the Jacumba Mountains, which lies some 2 miles south.

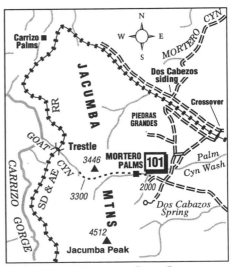

MORTERO PALMS TO GOAT CANYON

Summary of Hikes

Hike	Difficulty*	Terrain	Principal Attractions
1	★★★	Coastal foothill and canyon	Views, botanical interest
2	★★★	Coastal peak	Views, geological formations
3	★★	Coastal canyon	Geological formations
4	★	Coastal foothills	Views, wildflowers
5	★★★★	Coastal canyon	Stream and cascades, views
6	★★	Beach	Intertidal exploration, views
7	★	Coastal canyon	Sheltering oak groves
8	★★	Coastal foothill and canyon	Views, botanical interest
9	★	Coastal foothills	Views
10	★★	Inland foothills	Botanical interest
11	★★	Inland foothills	Views, historical interest
12	★★★	Inland foothill and canyon	Streams, geologic formations
13	★★	Inland foothill canyon	Waterfall, historical interest
14	★★★	Inland foothills	Views
15	★★	Mountain canyon	Waterfall
16	★★★★	Mountain peak and canyon	Views
17	★★★	Mountain canyon	Stream and cascades
18	★★	Mountain peak	Views
19	★★★	Mountain canyon	Stream, historical interest
20	★★★	Mountain slope	Views, historical interest
21	★★	Inland foothill canyon	Waterfall
22	★★★	Mountain canyon and slope	Streams, historical interest
23	★★	Mountain peak	Views
24	★★	Mountain canyon	Waterfall
25	★★★	Mountain slope	Views
26	★	Desert canyon	Geological formations
27	★★★	Mountain peaks	Views
28	★	Mountain slope	Botanical interest
29	★	Mountain canyon	Waterfalls
30	★★★	Mountain peak	Views
31	★★★★	Mountain canyon	Cascading stream
32	★★	Inland foothill ravine	Oak and riparian woodland
33	★★★	Inland foothills and ravines	Oak and riparian woodland, views
34	★★★	Mountain peak	Views

Hike	Difficulty*	Terrain	Principal Attractions
35	★★★★	Mountain peak	Cascading stream, views
36	★★	Mountain slope	Botanical interest, views
37	★★★★	Mountain slope and peaks	Streams, views
38	★★★★	Mountain slope	Streams, alpine lake
39	★	Mountain canyon	Waterfall
40	★★★★	Mountain peak	Streams, views
41	★	Desert oasis	Streams, birding and wildlife
42	★★★★	Desert canyons	Geological interest
43	★★	Desert peak	Views
44	★★★	Mountain peak	Views
45	★★★★★	Desert to mountain peak	Views, botanical interest
46	★★★	Mountain peak	Views
47	★★	Mountain peak	Views
48	★★	Island peak	Views, botanical interest
49	★★	Inland foothill ravine	Oaks and riparian vegetation
50	★	Inland foothill	Stream, oaks
51	★★	Coastal canyon	Oaks and riparian vegetation
52	★★	Inland foothill ravine	Oak woods, geological formations
53	★★★	Mountain peak	Views
54	★★★	Mountain canyon and ridge	Wildflowers, views
55	★★	Inland foothill and canyon	Geologic and botanical interest
56	★	Mountain canyon	Waterfall and pool
57	★★★	Mountain peak	Views
58	★	Mountain canyon	Waterfall
59	★★★	Mountain canyon	Cascading stream, oaks
60	★★★	Inland foothills	Wildflowers, vernal pools
61	up to ★★★	Mountain slope	Wildflowers, views
62	★★	Beach	Unspoiled coastline
63	up to ★★	Coastal hills	Unique pines, wildflowers, views
64	★★	Coastal canyon	Oaks, waterfall
65	★★	Inland foothills	Wildflowers, views
66	★★	Inland foothill peak	Views
67	★	Inland foothill canyon	Wildflowers, riparian vegetation
68	★★	Inland foothill peak	Geological formations, views
69	★★	Inland foothill peak	Views
70	★★★★	Foothill slopes and peak	Views

Hike	Difficulty*	Terrain	Principal Attractions
71	★★	Mountain meadow	Streams, botanical interest
72	★★★	Mountain slope and canyon	Waterfalls
73	★	Mountain meadow	Wildflowers
74	★★★	Mountain canyon	Cascading stream
75	★★★	Mountain peak	Views
76	★★	Mountain slope	Waterfall
77	★★	Mountain ridge	Views
78	★★★	Mountain slope and ravine	Botanical and historical interest
79	★★	Mountain meadow and ravine	Botanical interest
80	★★	Mountain peak	Views
81	★★	Mountain canyon	Oak woodland, canyon stream
82	★★	Mountain canyon	Cascades and pools
83	★★★	Mountain peak	Views
84	★★	Mountain canyon	Cascades and pools
85	★★★	Mountain canyon	Wildflowers, cascading stream
86	★	Mountain ravine	Hidden spring, views
87	★★	Mountain peak	Views
88	★★★	Mountain slope and meadow	Views, botanical interest
89	★	Desert slope	Views, hidden spring
90	★★★	Desert canyon	Waterfall
91	★	Desert canyon	Cascading stream, native palms
92	★★★★	Desert flat and canyon	Wildflowers, waterfalls
93	★★★★	Desert ridge and peak	Views, botanical interest
94	★★	Desert slope	Geologic historical interest
95	★★★	Desert canyon	Waterfall
96	★★	Desert slope	Historical interest
97	★★★	Desert peak	Botanical interest, views
98	★★★★	Desert badlands	Geological features
99	★	Desert slope	Geological interest, views
100	★	Desert slope and ravine	Botanical interest
101	★★★	Desert canyon and slope	Botanical and historical interest

* Difficulty ratings are as follows:

★	Easy
★★	Moderate
★★★	Moderately strenuous
★★★★	Strenuous
★★★★★	Very strenuous

Recommended Reading

Bakker, Elna, *An Island Called California*, 2nd edition, University of California Press, 1984.

Belzer, Thomas J., Roadside *Plants of Southern California*, Mountain Press Publishing Company, 1984.

California Coastal Commission, *California Coastal Access Guide*, 4th edition, University of California Press, 1991.

Clarke, Herbert, *An Introduction to Southern California Birds*, Mountain Press Publishing Company, 1989.

Dale, Nancy, *Flowering Plants, The Santa Monica Mountains, Coastal & Chaparral Regions of Southern California*, Capra Press, 1986.

Furbush, Patty A., *On Foot in Joshua Tree National Park*, 4th edition, M.I. Adventure Publications, 1995.

Gagnon, Dennis R., *Hike Los Angeles*, Volumes 1 and 2, Western Tanager Press, 1985.

Jaeger, Edmond C. and Smith, Arthur C., *Introduction to the Natural History of Southern California*, University of California Press, 1971.

Lindsay, Diana and Lowell, *The Anza-Borrego Desert Region*, 3rd edition, Wilderness Press, 1991.

McAuley, Milt, *Hiking Trails of the Santa Monica Mountains*, Canyon Publishing Company, 1987.

Moser, David and Schad, Jerry (eds.), *Wilderness Basics, The Complete Handbook for Hikers and Backpackers*, The Mountaineers, 1992.

Munz, Philip A., *California Spring Wildflowers*, University of California Press, 1961.

Munz, Philip A., *California Desert Wildflowers*, University of California Press, 1962. ·

Munz, Philip A., *California Mountain Wildflowers*, University of California Press, 1963.

Peterson, P. Victor, *Native Trees of Southern California*, University of California Press, 1966.

Raven, Peter H., *Native Shrubs of Southern California*, University of California Press, 1966.

Robinson, John W., *Trails of the Angeles*, 6th edition, Wilderness Press, 1990.

Robinson, John W., *San Bernardino Mountain Trails*, 4th edition, Wilderness Press, 1986.

Schad, Jerry, *Afoot and Afield in Los Angeles County*, Wilderness Press, 1991.

Schad, Jerry, *Afoot and Afield in Orange County,* 2nd edition, Wilderness Press, 1996.

Schad, Jerry, *Afoot and Afield in San Diego County,* 2nd edition, Wilderness Press, 1992.

Schaffer, Jeffrey P., et al. *The Pacific Crest Trail,* Volume 1: California, 5th edition, Wilderness Press, 1995.

Schoenherr, Allan A., *A Natural History of California,* University of California Press, 1992.

Sharp, Robert P. and Glazner, Allen F., *Geology Underfoot in Southern California,* Mountain Press Publishing Company, 1993.

Information Sources

Angeles National Forest,
Arroyo Seco District (ANF/ASD)
Oak Grove Park
Flintridge, CA 91011
(818) 790-1151

Angeles National Forest,
Mt. Baldy District (ANF/MBD)
110 N. Wabash Ave.
Glendora, CA 91740
(818) 335-1251

Angeles National Forest,
Tujunga District (ANF/TD)
12371 N. Little Tujunga Canyon Rd
San Fernando, CA 91342
(818) 899-1900

Angeles National Forest,
Valyermo District (ANF/VD)
29835 Valyermo Road
Valyermo, CA 93563
(805) 944-2187

Anza-Borrego Desert State Park
(ABDSP)
P.O. Box 299
Borrego Springs, CA 92004
(619) 767-4684 (recording)
(619) 767-4205 (visitor center)
(619) 767-5311 (administration)

Big Morongo Canyon Preserve (BMCP)
(619) 363-7190

Blue Sky Ecological Reserve (BSER)
(619) 486-7238

Bureau of Land Management,
Palm Springs (BLM/PS)
(619) 251-4800

Caspers Wilderness Park (CWP)
(714) 728-0235

Charmlee Natural Area (CNA)
(310) 457-7247

Chatsworth Park (CP)
(818) 341-6595

Chino Hills State Park (CHSP)
(909) 780-6222

Cleveland National Forest
Descanso District (CNF/DD)
3348 Alpine Blvd.
Alpine, CA 91901
(619) 445-6235

Cleveland National Forest
Palomar District (CNF/PD)
1634 Black Canyon Road
Ramona, CA 92065
(619) 788-0250

Cleveland National Forest
Trabuco District (CNF/TD)
1147 E. 6th St.
Corona, CA 91720
(909) 736-1811

Crystal Cove State Park (CCSP)
(714) 494-3539

Cuyamaca Rancho State Park (CRSP)
(619) 765-0755

Devil's Punchbowl Natural Area
(DPNA)
(805) 944-2743

Eaton Canyon County Park (ECCP)
(818) 398-5420

Joshua Tree National Park (JTNP)
74485 National Monument Drive
Twentynine Palms, CA 92277
(619) 367-7511

Lake Poway Recreation Area (LPRA)
(619) 679-4393

Los Angeles County Dept. of Parks
and Recreation (LADPR)
(213) 738-2961

Los Coyotes Indian Reservation (LCIR)
P.O. Box 248
Warner Springs, CA 92086
(619) 782-3269

Los Padres National Forest
Ojai District (LPNF/OD)
1190 E. Ojai Ave.
Ojai, CA 93023
(805) 646-4348

Los Penasquitos Canyon Preserve
(LPCP)
(619) 685-1365

Mission Trails Regional Park (MTRP)
(619) 668-3275

Mount San Jacinto State Wilderness
(MSJSW)
(909) 659-2607

Palomar Mountain State Park (PSP)
(619) 742-3462

Placerita Canyon Natural Area (PCNA)
(805) 259-7721

Point Mugu State Park (PMSP)
(805) 488-5223 or (805) 986-8591

San Bernardino National Forest
Big Bear District (SBNF/BBD)
North Shore Drive, Highway 38
Fawnskin, CA 92333
(909) 866-3437

San Bernardino National Forest
San Gorgonio District (SBNF/SGD)
34701 Mill Creek Rd.
Mentone, CA 92359
(909) 794-1123

San Bernardino National Forest
San Jacinto District (SBNF/SJD)
54270 Pinecrest
Idyllwild, CA 92549
(909) 659-2117

San Diego County Parks and
Recreation Department (SDCP)
(619) 694-3049

San Dieguito Regional Park (SDRP)
(619) 235-5445

Santa Catalina Island hiking information
(SCI)
(310) 510-2800

Santa Monica Mountains
National Recreation Area (SMMNRA)
30401 Agoura Road, Suite 100
Agoura Hills, CA 91301
(818) 597-9192

Santa Rosa Plateau Ecological Reserve
(SRPER)
(909) 677-6951

Santiago Oaks Regional Park (SORP)
(714) 538-4400

Solstice Canyon Park (SCP)
(310) 456-7154

Torrey Pines State Reserve (TPSR)
(619) 755-2063

Whiting Ranch Wilderness Park
(WRWP)
(714) 589-4729

Will Rogers State Historic Park
(WRSHP)
(310) 454-8212

Index

Explore Southern California

If you enjoyed *101 Hikes in Southern California*, and want to do more exploring in the area, be sure to look for these Wilderness Press books:

Afoot and Afield in San Diego County by Jerry Schad. San Diego County contains a wealth of areas to explore and discover, including unspoiled coastal canyons, pine-crested mountains, and spectacular desert landscapes. The 192 hikes in this book cover every hiking possibility.

Afoot and Afield in Orange County by Jerry Schad. Surrounding Orange County's densely populated areas are 150,000 acres of parks and public lands that contain a vast range of natural landscapes from intertidal zones to oak woodlands.

Afoot and Afield in Los Angeles County by Jerry Schad. This book covers 175 trips in this wide-ranging county—from the coast to the mountains, from sea level to 10,000 feet.

The Anza-Borrego Desert Region by Lowell and Diana Lindsay. This is a comprehensive guide to Southern California's most popular desert park. The park, much of it still wilderness, covers one-third of San Diego County and parts of Riverside and Imperial counties.

Desert Hiking by Dave Ganci. Hiking in the desert can be an exhilirating experience with the proper planning and knowledge. This desert manual contains all the information an explorer needs to sojourn into the lands of little water.

50 Best Short Hikes in California Deserts by John Krist. This guide covers the best day hikes in and around Death Valley National Park, Joshua Tree National Park, and Mojave National Preserve. Discover the richness of the desert landscape by spending a few hours on a trail.

If you like to adventure in the great outdoors, we publish over 100 books that will help you find new places to explore. Check your local bookstore or outdoor equipment dealer for our titles, or write for our complete catalog:

Wilderness Press
2440 Bancroft Way
Berkeley, CA 94704
(800) 443-7227

READ THIS

Hiking in the backcountry entails unavoidable risk that every hiker assumes and must be aware of and respect. The fact that a trail is described in this book is not a representation that it will be safe for you. Trails vary greatly in difficulty and in the degree of conditioning and agility one needs to enjoy them safely. On some hikes routes may have changed or conditions may have deteriorated since the descriptions were written. Also, trail conditions can change even from day to day, owing to weather and other factors. A trail that is safe on a dry day or for a highly conditioned, agile, properly equipped hiker may be completely unsafe for someone else or unsafe under adverse weather conditions.

You can minimize your risks on the trail by being knowledgeable, prepared and alert. There is not space in this book for a general treatise on safety in the mountains, but there are a number of good books and public courses on the subject and you should take advantage of them to increase your knowledge. Just as important, you should always be aware of your own limitations and of conditions existing when and where you are hiking. If conditions are dangerous, or if you are not prepared to deal with them safely, choose a different hike! It's better to have wasted a drive than to be the subject of a mountain rescue.

These warnings are not intended to scare you off the trails. Millions of people have safe and enjoyable hikes every year. However, one element of the beauty, freedom and excitement of the wilderness is the presence of risks that do not confront us at home. When you hike you assume those risks. They can be met safely, but only if you exercise your own independent judgment and common sense.